Songs for Young Singers

An Annotated List for Developing Voices

J. Arden Hopkin

The Scarecrow Press, Inc.
Lanham, Maryland, and London
2002

SCARECROW PRESS, INC.

Published in the United States of America
by Scarecrow Press, Inc.
4720 Boston Way, Lanham, Maryland 20706
www.scarecrowpress.com

4 Pleydell Gardens, Folkestone
Kent CT20 2DN, England

British Library Cataloguing-in-Publication Information Available

Library of Congress Cataloging-in-Publication Data

Hopkin, J. Arden, 1947–
    Songs for young singers : an annotated list for developing voices / J. Arden Hopkin.
      p. cm.
    Includes bibliographical references and index.
    ISBN 0-8108-4077-4 (cloth : alk. paper)
      1. Songs—Bibliography—Graded lists. 2. Sacred songs—Bibliography—Graded
lists. 3. Songs—Indexes. I. Title.

ML132.S6H72002
016.78242'0263—dc21   2001040624

Acknowledgments

The project would not have been possible without the dedicated assistance of the following research associates and computer specialists. Research assistants changed as the years went by, beginning with Kim Stambaugh, who compiled all of the material from the various state music education agencies. Teresa Pesci and Tara Smith compiled the main body of analysis found in this work, later assisted by Rachel Beck. My computer wizard has been Greg Thomas.

The project received initial impetus and continued encouragement from my friend Susan Conkling, formerly a colleague with me at Brigham Young University, and currently on the faculty at the Eastman School of Music.

Contents

Contents

Foreword

History

What began as a modest project with limited scope grew over time into a significant challenge. A 1993 meeting with the music education faculty at the university where I teach revealed several negative perceptions concerning voice instruction at the university. First, music education students received different treatment than performance majors. Rarely did music education students study with professors; rather, they shuttled from one part-time teacher to another, more to balance faculty loads than to meet the educational needs of the students. Second, and more critically, no clearly defined curriculum had been established for music education students. Intuitively, the students sensed the need to become role models for their future choral students, yet in voice lessons and juried exams, they were encouraged away from that paradigm and toward a more vigorous vocal model. Too often their training encouraged overproduction instead of healthy singing. They studied, and were judged on, the same advanced songs and arias and the same vocal techniques used by opera majors.

As these students graduated and entered the public school arena, they taught what they had learned—the same advanced literature and over-production they had learned in college. High school Solo and Ensemble Festivals highlighted the problem as young voices attempted to sing material too advanced for their beginning skill levels. Students who followed the aggressive approach received the high ratings and won the scholarships. The message was clear to students and teachers alike, so few dared to follow a more moderate approach to vocal development, not-withstanding the widely held feeling that the course being followed was destructive to long-term vocal health.

The scenario I describe applied to Brigham Young University and the State of Utah in particular, but it could fit many other states and regions of the United States as well.

In an effort to remedy the difficulties outlined above, I met with Susan Conkling, Vocal Music Education specialist (now on the faculty at the Eastman School of Music), and Rosemary Matthews, a part-time vocal instructor with whom many music education majors studied (now a public school choir director herself). Our discussions led to the beginning of this project. The project goals were clear:

Develop a course of study for vocal music education majors that would equip them for success in their teaching roles, namely, to
- be a good model of healthy vocal production and
- know the song literature appropriate for developing voices.
- Establish song literature guidelines for young, developing voices to be used at the State Solo and Ensemble Auditions.

MEA Survey

In an effort to see the practices of other states, each state Music Education Association received a questionnaire about their Solo and Ensemble repertoire requirements. Some states had recommended repertoire lists and clear guidelines, but most did not. In fact, only seventeen of the fifty states had any established guidelines. In the absence of such guidelines, choral directors and voice teachers were left to their own discretion. Some agencies referred their members to the song lists from the established state agencies, especially New York, Pennsylvania, and Texas.

The song lists from the seventeen state agencies were entered into a database to see which songs appeared most frequently. Interestingly, only 150 songs appeared on at least five lists. 300 songs appeared on at least three lists. These 300 songs became the foundation of this study.

Gathering these songs together for study revealed an interesting fact about publishers. Most song literature is no longer available in sheet music. Instead, publishers have, for some time, marketed song collections. An-thologies may contain several well-known songs to attract buyers together with less-well-known pieces to flesh out the anthology. To collect the 300 songs required the purchase of at least two dozen anthologies.

The Pennsylvania Music Education Association, understanding this phenomenon, published a list of commonly-used anthologies. The current study began with the thirteen most often recurring anthologies on the PMEA list (in some cases, several songbooks belonged to the same series, so the actual number of songbooks was closer to twenty-four). To that point, the study remained selective.

However, events conspired to turn the study away from selectivity toward comprehensiveness. Several prominent anthologies were missing from the most popular twenty-four, and I decided to include them. More significantly, the beginning of this study coincided with the beginning of a resurgence of art song publication, spearheaded by Alfred and Hal Leonard publishing houses. Although the new anthology titles had not had the time to establish their popularity, I decided to include them. Indeed, completing the project before the next new publication became a race I was destined to lose time and again. The final list includes seventy anthologies.

To make these anthologies truly useful, all of the songs contained therein, not just the popular ones, were analyzed. That decision increased the size, and scope—and value—of the study. In its current design, the study reviews over two thousand songs appropriate for the beginning and intermediate level singer. These songs might well serve as high school contest repertoire. They might also form the foundation of the college-level repertoire study for future high school choir directors and voice teachers.

The Analysis Protocol

Not all songs are created equal. Choosing the right song for the right student and occasion becomes almost an art in itself. As an aid for voice teachers and choir directors of beginning and intermediate singers, this study includes an analysis of each of the songs in order to determine its level of difficulty. The analysis protocol takes into consideration seven values: **melodic contour, phrasing, language, rhythm, accompaniment, harmonic language, and dynamics.** Each of these values receives a numeric score, as described below. The sum of the scores places the song in one of three categories: elementary, intermediate, and advanced.

Melodic Contour

The melodic contour may be the most significant indicator of a song's difficulty. Narrow ranges make fewer vocal demands than do wide ranges. High tessitura challenges the student's ability to sing a unified scale. Wide or frequent leaps, or other awkward melodic contours further stretch basic vocal skills. These observations inform the melodic values thus:

- For a song with a small range (an octave or less)   1
- For a song with a moderate range (an octave and a half or less)   2
- For a song with a wide range (more than one and a half octave)   3
- For high tessitura   add 1 point

Phrasing

Phrasing places demands on another basic vocal skill: breath management. Most young singers have no difficulty singing four to six second phrases. They experience moderate difficulty in singing phrases of six to ten seconds in length, and only the more advanced singers can manage the breath demands of phrases lasting ten seconds or longer. Some fast songs leave little time to breathe, thereby adding value to this element.

- For a song with short phrases (6 seconds or less)   1
- For a song with moderate phrases (10 seconds or less)   2
- For a song with long phrases (more than 10 seconds)   3
- For a song which leaves little time for breathing   add 1 point

Rhythm

More than metronomic markings or tempo indications, the rapidity of melodic articulation marks one of the vocal complexities of a song. Melodies of moderate speed, with little or no demands placed upon articulation present no difficulties to a young singer, while melodies requiring either fast or sustained articulation present more challenge, the melodies demanding very fast (including coloratura) or very slow articulation of notes being the most difficult. Changing meters, cross rhythms, hemeolas, and other rhythmic devices add to the overall rhythmic complexity of a song.

- Moderate motion   1
- Rapid or slow motion   2

- Very fast or very slow motion (including coloratura)   3
- Rhythmic complexities (syncopation, cross meters, etc.) add 1 point

Text

Foreign language texts add a level of complexity to the singer's task, particularly if the singer takes seriously the desire to communicate the text's meaning, while texts in the native language do not divide the singer's concentration. More commonly, failure to absorb the meaning of a foreign text leads to rote memorization of meaningless tone syllables and uninspired performances.

- For native language texts   1
- For foreign language texts   2

Accompaniment

Accompaniment patterns generally fall into three categories: mirror, supportive, and independent. Accompaniments which mirror the melody, either exactly or approximately, simplify the task of singing the melody for the young singer. Patterns which support the melodic line without mirroring the melody presume greater musical autonomy of the young singer. Independent—even antagonistic—accompaniments demand the singer's musical self-reliance.

- Mirror accompaniments   1
- Supportive accompaniments   2
- Independent accompaniments   3

Harmonic language

The harmonic language of a song—diatonic, chromatic, or atonal—plays an important role in the ability of a young singer to successfully perform a given song. The more complex the harmonic language, the more developed must be the young singer's musicianship.

- For traditional, diatonic harmonies   1
- For chromatic harmonies   2

Dynamics

If the singer is to perform as the composer intended, then dynamics must play a part of the equation. Dynamics become increasingly difficult to manage the more extreme their contrast becomes.

Level of Difficulty

A song's difficulty grows out of the combination of its several elements. Most critical for the young singer are the vocal demands of a song, its melodic contour, range and tessitura, the length of its phrases, the rapidity of it articulations, and its dynamic contrasts. Musical elements also play a significant role. Foreign or obscure texts, rhythmic complexities, harmonic language, and the accompaniment patterns all influence the overall difficulty of a song.

The analysis protocol reviews basic elements in a quick and simple way and might be applied to any song or aria in order to determine its appropriateness for a singer's level of development. The combination of the seven values will indicate a song's level of difficulty.

Elementary level	Scores between 7-11.
Intermediate level	Scores between 12-16.
Advanced level	Scores above 17.

A song can be simplified by reducing the difficulty of its elements (i.e., by singing shorter phrases, translating foreign texts, disregarding dynamic values, and, in some cases, singing alternate high or low notes to shrink the range or tessitura). The degree to which one departs from the desires of the composer must be resolved by each singer and teacher and may differ for songs studied and songs performed in public. In this study—and in most auditions and competitions—the composers' wishes will be honored.

Teachers and singers should not choose a song primarily because of its level of difficulty. A simple song sung well outshines a difficult song sung poorly. Rather, songs should be chosen to match the development of the singer. As musical and vocal skills improve, more difficult literature may be sung successfully. Discouragement attends those whose techniques fall short of the demands of a selection, while confidence grows with each success.

Organization of the Material

Tables

This section includes the Table of Abbreviations used and the Table of Anthologies reviewed in this book

In the Table of Anthologies, the column on the right briefly summarizes the difficulty of the songs therein printed. For example, the anthology listed below contains songs on all three levels of difficulty, but emphasizes the 3rd level.

Anthology Title	*Total Ranking Available*
20th Century Art Songs	1, 2, **3**

This section provides useful information when shopping for music. *20th Century Art Songs* contains something for everyone, but advanced singers will find it most useful. A beginner might wish to buy something more accessible for the time being. While simple, this concept encourages a sensible approach to building a vocal music library.

Section 1: Songs by Title

The next section of the reference work organizes the songs by title and gives the anthologies in which they are found, together with the song's level of difficulty as published in that particular anthology. In most cases, the level of difficulty will remain the same for all listings, but in some cases, particularly in reference to songs from the seventeenth and eighteenth centuries, where editorial suggestions for ornamentation may make greater demands than the original version, the numbers may vary between listings.

Too often, songs go unsung for want of finding them. This section will aid singers and the teachers alike to locate a particular song.

Section 2: Songs by Composer

Teachers and singers can find all of the songs in the study by a particular composer in this section, together with the anthologies in which the songs may be found. This section will help in planning studio or solo recitals.

Sections 3, 4, and 5: Songs by Level of Difficulty

For the singer or teacher with limited knowledge of song literature, this next section provides a valuable service by listing song titles by their level of difficulty. All elementary songs are listed together alphabetically, as are the songs of each of the other levels. The searcher can choose from among the selections in the desired difficulty level before turning to other sections to locate it and review the values of its seven elements.

High school choir directors, beset by students preparing for solo festivals, can quickly find songs appropriate to the students' level of development. The students themselves can search out their own selections under the guidance of the director. The seasoned voice teacher may find pleasure in looking beyond the limits of his or her customary repertoire to find good songs for curious and eager elementary, intermediate, and advanced students.

Section 6: Individual Anthology Listings

The heart of the study, this section contains an entry for each anthology, listing each song it contains alphabetically followed by the composer's name. Near the top of the listing, publication information is given, the name of the compiler or editor, and whether the volume is available in more than one vocal range. The main body of the page presents important information about each song in the volume.

Each song is listed alphabetically, followed by nine columns. In these columns, the seven elements—**melodic contour, phrasing, rhythmic complexity, dynamic contrast, text, accompaniment**, and **harmonic** language—receive a numeric value. The eighth column lists the sum of these seven values, and the last column indicates the song's level of difficulty. By studying the values of each element, together with its level of difficulty, an intermediate level singer, for example, who still struggles with breath management will be able to steer clear of (or search out) those songs with high values for phrasing.

Intended Audience

This reference work has been compiled with the needs of the high school age singer—and those that teach them—in mind. It provides lists of songs by level of difficulty; elsewhere, it tells the reader where the songs can be found, and in that location, it explains in quick and easy terms what challenges the song presents to the singer.

For those interested in building a song library, this reference presents a reasonably thorough review of the anthologies commonly available for young singers. Much of the material included is in English. Most of the songs in other languages have singable English translations.

Anthologies specializing in operatic arias and song collections of specific composers have not, for the most part, been included in this reference work. The merits of such songs and arias, collectively, do not recommend them to the developing singers, who should, rather, find pleasure in singing songs equal their vocal skills and grow gradually into more advanced literature. By so doing, it is hoped, they will develop their powers of expression as they simultaneously develop their vocal prowess.

This reference work might also provide meaningful focus for vocal music education majors in college. While the vocal prowess of such students will doubtlessly progress beyond the developmental stage of younger voices, nevertheless, future teachers tend to teach what they have been taught, and without exposure to this foundational repertoire, they may inadvertently fail to include it in their future library. For those whose formal vocal training begins with college, this study could serve as a primary resource for the study of song literature. For those who enter college with years of formal study behind them, this study may serve as a reminder of songs studied at earlier stages of development.

Tables

Abbreviations

Tables

SC	Songs Through the Centuries
SunS	Sunday Songbook
SVR-1	Standard Vocal Repertoire Book One
SVR-2	Standard Vocal Repertoire Book Two
WS	Weekday Songbook
YS-B	Young Singer, The, Book One, Baritone(Bass)
YS-M	Young Singer, The, Book One, Contralto(Mezzo-soprano)
YS-S	Young Singer, The, Book One, Soprano
YS-T	Young Singer, The, Book One, Tenor

Anthologies

(Rankings marked in bold are most prominent in the anthology)

Anthology Title	*Song Ranking Available*
15 American Art Songs	1, **2**, 3
20th Century Art Songs	1, **2**, 3
26 Italian Songs and Arias	1, **2**
28 Italian Songs and Arias	1, **2**
50 Art Songs from the Modern Repertoire	1, **2**, 3
55 Art Songs	**1**, 2, 3
56 Songs You Like To Sing	1, **2**, 3
Anthology of Songs for the Solo Voice	1, **2**, 3
Art Songs for School and Studio, First Year	1, **2**, 3
Art Songs for School and Studio, Second Year	1, **2**
Basics of Singing Third Edition	**1**, 2
Broadway Repertoire, for Bass-Baritone	1, **2**
Broadway Repertoire, for Mezzo-Soprano	1, **2**
Broadway Repertoire, for Soprano	1, **2**, 3
Broadway Repertoire, for Tenor	1, **2**
Classic Italian Songs for School and Studio, Vol. I	1, **2**, 3
Classic Italian Songs for School and Studio, Vol. II	1, **2**
Classic Italian Songs for School and Studio, Vol. III	1, **2**
Classical Contest Solos—Baritone/Bass	**1**, 2
Classical Contest Solos—Mezzo-Soprano	**1**, 2
Classical Contest Solos—Soprano	1, **2**

Tables

Tables

Songs by Title

Song Title	Composer	Anthology
Absence	Berlioz, H.	GAS
Ach Lieb, ich muss nun scheiden	Strauss, R.	FS
Across the Western Ocean	Dougherty, C., arr.	20CAS
		FBBS
Adela	Rodrigo, J.	CCS-B
		CCS-T
Adelaide	Beethoven, L.	NIE-T
Adieu	Fauré, G.	FBTS-2
	Mozart, W. A.	NIE-C
Adieu pour jamais	Loeffler, C. M.	50ASMR
After a Dream (Après un rêve)	Fauré, G.	ES-2
Ah! mio cor	Handel, G. F.	ASSV
		FBMS-2
Ah! quanto è vero	Cesti, M. A.	CIS-2
Ah! Willow	Wilson, H. L., arr.	SBBS
Ah, Love of Mine (Caro mio ben)	Giordani, G.	55AS
Ah, May the Red Rose Live Always	Foster, S. C.	ES
Ah, No Stormy Wind	Russian	PS-4
Ah, Poor Heart (Ah! mio cor from "Alcina")	Handel, G. F.	ES-2
Ahi, troppo è duro	Monteverde, C.	CIS
Ain't Misbehavin'	Waller & Brooks	FS
Air (Care Selve)	Handel, G. F.	PS-3
Air from Comus	Arne, T.	STC
		SVR-1
All Day on the Prairie	Guion, D. W.	FBTS
All in the April Evening	Roberton, H. S.	20CAS
All My Trials	Schram, R. E., arr.	FSSS-2
All Soul's Day (Allerseelen)	Strauss, R.	56S
		ES-2
All the Pretty Little Horses	American	BS
All the Things You Are	Kern, J.	FBBS-S
All Through the Night	Christy, V. A., arr.	ES-1

Song Title	Composer	Anthology
All Through the Night	Old Welsh	CCS-B
		FBTS
	Schram, R. E., arr.	FSSS-2
All Your Shades	Lully, J. B.	NIE-Bs
Alleluia!	Old English	SBTS
Allerseelen	Strauss, R.	50SS
		ASSV
Alma del core	Caldara, A.	26ISAA
		28ISAA
		CIS-2
		CCS-B
Almost Like Being in Love	Loewe, F.	BS
Aloha oe	Liliuokalani, Queen	56S
Alone in the Fields (Wäldeinsamkeit)	Brahms, J.	55AS
Alone in the Forest	Strauss, R.	NIE-M
Amarilli	Caccini, G.	CIS
		PS-3
Amarilli, mia bella		26ISAA
		28ISAA
		STC
Amarylis		NIE-T
Amazing Grace	Althouse, J., arr.	FSSS
		SSS
America the Beautiful	Ward, S. A.	FS
American Lullaby	Rich, G.	15AAS
		FBMS
Amor dormiglione	Strozzi, B.	CIS-3
An die Geliebte	Beethoven, L.	CCS-T
		FBTS-2
An die Leier	Schubert, F.	GAS
An die Musik		CCS-M
		FS
		SBMS
		STC

Song Title	Composer	Anthology
An die Nachtigall	Brahms, J.	SBMS
An Immorality	Hoiby, L.	CAS
And All That Jazz	Kander, J.	BR-MS
And This Is My Beloved	Wright, R.	FBBS-S
Andenken	Beethoven, L.	FBSS-2
Angels through the Night	Kern, P.. arr.	FSSS
Angels, Ever Bright and Fair	Handel, G. F.	NIE-M
Animal Crackers	Hageman, R.	FBSS-2
Annie Laurie	Scott, Lady John	SBBS
Anyone Can Whistle	Sondheim, S.	BR-MS
		FS
Après un rêve	Fauré, G.	50ASMR
		55AS
		ASSV
		BS
April Weather	Archer, V.	SS-6
Arise Ye Subterranean Winds	Purcell, H.	NIE-Bs
		SBBS
Arm, Arm, Ye Brave	Handel, G. F.	SBBS
Arrival of the Royal Barge, The	Purcell, H.	SVR-1
Art Is Calling For Me	Herbert, V.	SBSS
Art Thou Troubled?	Handel, G. F.	SS-6
As a Sunbeam at Morn	Caldara, A.	NIE-C
As Ever I Saw	Warlock, P.	NIE-T
As From the Sun A Ray (Come raggio di sole)	Caldara, A.	PS-4
As I Walked Forth	Foss, H.	SS-6
As I Went A-Roaming	Brahe, M. H.	FBMS-2
As Long as He Needs Me	Bart, L.	FBBS-M
Asra, The (Der Asra)	Rubinstein, A.	55AS
Asturiana	de Falla, M.	ES
At Last	Brahms, J.	NIE-S

Song Title	Composer	Anthology
At Sea	Ives, C. E.	ES
At the Ball	Tchaikovsky, P.	50ASMR
		55AS
		FBTS
At the Cry of the First Bird	Guion, D. W.	20CAS
At the River	Lowry, R. R.	FS
At the Well	Hageman, R.	50ASMR
Au bord de l'eau	Fauré, G.	SBMS
Auf dem grünen Balcon	Wolf, H.	50SS
		GAS
Auf dem Kirchhofe	Brahms, J.	50SS
Auf dem Meere	Franz, R.	FBMS-2
Auf geheimem Waldespfade	Griffes, C. T.	50ASMR
Aufträge	Schumann, R.	50SS
		GAS
Auld Lang Syne	Ward, S. A.	FS
Aupres de ma Blonde	Paton, J. G., arr.	FS
Aurore	Fauré, G.	50ASMR
		GAS
Author of All My Joys	Gluck, C. W. von	NIE-C
Autumn Evening	Quilter, R.	SBTS
Ave Maria	Abt, F.	FBSS-2
	Saint-Saëns, C.	FBTS-2
	Schubert, F.	56S
		AS-2
		STC
Ave Verum	Mozart, W. A.	FBMS-2
Away Over Yandro	Christy, V. A., arr.	ES-1
Bacchus, God of Mirth and Wine	Arne, T.	NIE-Bs
Bald wehen uns des Frühlings Lüfte	Haydn, J.	FS
Bali Ha'I	Rodgers, R.	BR-MS
		FBBS-M
Barcarolle	Offenbach, J.	56S

Song Title	Composer	Anthology
Baruch and Hamakom	Glick, S. I.	SS-5
Be Thou Faithful Unto Death	Mendelssohn, F.	SBTS
Beatitudes, The	Malotte, A. H.	FBSS
Beau Soir	Debussy, C.	56S
		ASSV
		ES
Beautiful	Duncan, C.	SS-4
Beautiful Dreamer	Foster, S. C.	CCS-B
		SR-1
Beautiful Savior	Christy, V. A., arr.	ES-1
Because	D'Hardelot, G.	SVR-1
Begli occhi, io non mi pento	Perti, J. A.	CIS-3
Begone Dull Care	Christy, V. A., arr.	ES-1
Bei Dir!	Schubert, F.	GAS
Bel nume	Cimador, G. B.	ES
Bel Piacere	Handel, G. F.	FBSS
Bella porta di rubini	Falconieri, A.	CIS-3
Bella vittoria	Bononcini, G.	ES
Bells of Aberdovey, The	MacMillan, E., arr.	SS-2
Bells of Clermont Town, The	Goodhart, A. M.	FBBS
Bells, The (Les Cloches)	Debussy, C.	PS-4
Beloved Strand (Spiagge Amate)	Gluck, C. W. von	PS-3
Below in the Valley (Da unten im Tale)	Brahms, J.	PS-2
Belshazzar	Schumann, R.	NIE-Br
Beneath a Weeping Willow's Shade	Hopkinson, F.	55AS
		BS
		FBMS-2
Benedictus	Schubert, F.	ASSV
Bescheidene Liebe	Wolf, H.	50SS
		SBSS
Bewitched	Rodgers, R.	BR-S
Bid me To Live	Lawes, H.	55AS

Song Title	Composer	Anthology
Bird and the Rose, The	Horrocks, A. E.	SR-1
Birds in the High Hall-garden	Somervell, A.	NIE-Br
Birthday of a King, The	Neidlinger, W. H.	FBTS-2
Bist du bei mir	Bach, J. S.	FBMS-2
		STC
Bitten	Beethoven, L.	FS
Black Dress, The	Niles, J. J.	FBTS
Black is the Color of My True Love's Hair	American	BS
	Niles, J. J.	FBTS
Black Roses	Sibelius, J.	SVR-1
Black Roses (Svarta rosor)		SVR-2
Black Swan, The from "The Medium"	Menotti, G. C.	20CAS
Blacksmith's Song, A	Schumann, R.	SS-1
Blacksmith, The	Brahms, J.	NIE-M
Blessed Redeemer (Liebster Herr Jesu)	Bach, J. S.	PS-4
Blessing, A	Telfer, N.	SS-6
Blind Ploughman, The	Clarke, R. C.	FBBS
Blow High, Blow Low	Dibdin, C.	55AS
		FBBS
Blow, Blow, Thou Winter Wind	Arne, T.	55AS
		ASSV
		ES
		FBBS-2
	Quilter, R.	FBBS
Blow, Ye Winds	Dougherty, C., arr.	FBBS-2
Blue are Her Eyes	Watts, W.	AS-2
Blue Bird	Crist, B.	SR-1
Blue-Bell, The	MacDowell, E.	CCS-M
		FBMS-2
Boat Song (Im Kahne)	Grieg, E.	55AS

Song Title	Composer	Anthology
Bois épais	Lully, J. B.	ASSV
		ES
		FBBS-2
		SVR-2
Bonjour Suzon	Delibes, L.	YS-S
Bonjour, Suzon!		FBTS-2
Bonne Nuit	Massenet, J.	FBSS
Bonnie Earl of Murray, The	Gurney, I.	NIE-Br
Botschaft	Brahms, J.	50SS
		GAS
Boy's Song, A	Beaulieu, J.	SS-3
Bread of Angels (Panis Angelicus)	Franck, C.	ES-1
Bride's Song, The	Schumann, R.	NIE-M
Bright Is the Ring of Words	V. Williams, R.	BS
		FBBS-2
Bring Him Home	Schönberg, C. M.	FBBS-T
Broadway Baby	Sondheim, S.	FS
Brooklet, The	Loder, E. J.	NIE-T
Brother Will, Brother John	Sacco, J.	20CAS
		FBTS
Brush Up Your Shakespeare	Porter, C.	FS
Buckle, The	Bliss, A.	20CAS
Build Thee More Stately Mansions	Andrews, M.	FBBS-2
Butterflies (Les papillons)	Smith, L.	SS-Int
By Mendip Side	Coates, E.	FBTS
By the Brook	Grieg, E.	50ASMR
By the Grave	Rachmaninoff, S.	NIE-Bs
By the Light of The Moon (Au clair de la lune)	Lully, J. B.	PS-2
C'est l'extase langoureuse	Debussy, C.	50ASMR
C'est Mon Ami	Crist, B., arr.	FBMS-2
Cabin	Bowles, P.	15AAS
		20CAS

Song Title	Composer	Anthology
Cäcilie	Strauss, R.	50ASMR
		50SS
Call Me Irresponsible	Van Heusen, J.	BS
Call, The	V. Williams, R.	SBTS
Calm as the Night (Still wie die Nacht)	Bohm, C.	56S
Calm at Sea (Meeresstille)	Schubert, F.	PS-2
Camptown Races	Althouse, J., arr.	FSSS-2
Can't Help Lovin' Dat Man	Kern, J.	BR-S
		FBBS-S
Canción del niño por nacer	Gonzalez, L. J.	ES
Candle on the Water	Kasha, A.	BS
Cantique de Noël	Adam, A.	STC
Captive, The (L'Esclave)	Lalo, É.	ES-2
Cara e dolce	Scarlatti, A.	BS
Care Selve	Handel, G. F.	NIE-S
		STC
		SVR-2
		YS-S
		YS-T
Carmeña	Wilson, H. L.	FBMS-2
Caro mio ben	Giordani, G.	26ISAA
		28ISAA
		CIS
		CCS-T
Carol of the Birds, The	Niles, J. J.	FBMS-2
Carry me back to old Virginny	Bland, J. A.	56S
Cease, Oh Maiden	Scarlatti, A.	NIE-Br
Chanson d'Amour	Fauré, G.	ES
Chanson espagnole	Ravel, M.	50ASMR
Charmant Papillon	Campra, A.	FBSS-2
Che fiero costume	Legrenzi, G.	26ISAA
		28ISAA

Song Title	Composer	Anthology
Che fiero costume	Legrenzi, G.	CIS-2
Chère Nuit	Bachelet, A.	GAS
Cherry Ripe	Horn, C. E.	SR-1
Cherry Tree, The	Gibbs, C. A.	FBMS
Chestnut, The	Schumann, R.	NIE-S
Chi vuol la zingarella	Paisiello, G.	ES
		FBMS
Chi vuole innomorarsi	Scarlatti, A.	CIS-3
Child of The Flowing Tide	Shaw, M.	SBBS
Children of the Lord	Sleeth, N.	SunS
Children's Bedtime	Schumann, R.	SS-Int
Christkind	Cornelius, P.	SBTS
Christmas at the Cloisters	Corigliano, J.	CAS
Christmas Carol, A	Rorem, N.	FS
Christopher Robin is Saying His Prayers	Fraser-Simson, H.	FBMS
Cicerenella	Italian	PS-4
Cindy	Althouse, J., arr.	FSSS-2
	Boardman, R., arr	SVR-2
Circus Clown, The	Kurth, B.	SS-Int
Clair de lune	Debussy, C.	GAS
Climb Ev'ry Mountain	Rodgers, R.	BR-S
		FBBS-S
Climbin' Up the Mountain	Simms, P. F., arr.	SSS
Cloths of Heaven, The	Dunhill, T.	FBTS-2
Cloud-Shadows	Rogers, J. H.	FBMS
Clouds	Charles, E.	FBMS-2
Cock-Eyed Optimist, A	Rodgers, R.	FBBS-M
		FS
Cockles and Mussels	Christy, V. A., arr.	FS
	Irish	SVR-1
Col mio sangue comprerei	Stradella, A.	CIS-2

Song Title	Composer	Anthology
Colours	Brook, H.	SS-Int
Come Again, Sweet Love	Dowland, J.	55AS
		BS
		CCS-T
		FBTS
		NIE-Br
Come and Trip It	Handel, G. F.	FBSS-2
Come Follow!	Hilton, J., arr.	FS
Come Let's be Merry	Old English	YS-B
Come raggio di sol	Caldara, A.	26ISAA
		28ISAA
		CIS-2
Come Saturday Morning	Karlin, F.	BS
Come Sweet Repose	Bach, J. S.	SR-2
Come to the Fair	Martin, E.	FBSS-2
Come Unto These Yellow Sands	Purcell, H.	55AS
		ES-2
		SS-6
Come Where My Love Lies Dreaming	Foster, S. C.	STC
Come Ye Blessed	Gaul, A.	FBMS-2
	Scott, J. P.	SBBS
Come, Let Us All This Day	Schemelli, G. C.	SS-5
Come, Sweet Death (Komm, Süsser Tod)	Bach, J. S.	PS-3
Comedy Tonight	Sondheim, S.	FBBS-B
Con amores, la mi madre	Obradors, F. J.	BS
Con Rauco Mormorio	Handel, G. F.	SBMS
Consecration	Manney, C. F.	AS-2
Corals	Treharne, B.	50ASMR
Corner Of The Sky	Schwartz, S.	BR-T
Cosi, amor, mi fai languir!	Stradella, A.	CIS-3
Could I (Vorrei)	Tosti, F. P.	SR-2

Song Title	Composer	Anthology
Country of the Camisards, The	Homer, S.	FS
Crabbed Age and Youth	White, M. V.	FBMS
Cradle Carol (Berceuse)	Ouchterlony, D.	SS-4
Cradle Song	Flies, J. B.	SS-Int
	Mendelssohn, F.	NIE-C
	Mozart, W. A.	PS-1
	Schubert, F.	NIE-M
Cradle Song (Wiegenlied)	Brahms, J.	AS-1
		PS-2
	Schubert, F.	PS-3
Cradle-song (Wiegenlied)	Brahms, J.	56S
Cradles, The (Les Berceaux)	Fauré, G.	ES-2
		PS-2
Cradlesong of the Poor	Moussorgsky, M. P.	55AS
Create in Me a Clean Heart, O God	Mueller, C. F.	FBBS
Crépuscule	Massenet, J.	FBMS-2
Cross the Wide Missouri	Besig, D., arr.	FSSS
Crucifixion	Payne, J., arr.	FBMS
Crucifixion, The	Barber, S.	15AAS
		FBSS
Crying of Water, The	Campbell-Tipton, L.	FBSS-2
Cuckoo, The	Lehmann, L.	SVR-1
		YS-C
		YS-S
Curliest Thing, The	Dunhill, T.	SS-1
D'Anne jouant de l'espinette	Ravel, M.	50ASMR
D'Une Prison	Hahn, R.	GAS
Da unten im Tale	Brahms, J.	ES
Daisies, The	Barber, S.	15AAS
		FBTS
Dance Song	Czech	PS-1
Dance, Maiden, Dance (Danza, danza Fanciulla)	Durante, F.	PS-3

Song Title	Composer	Anthology
Dank sei Dir, Herr	Handel, G. F.	GAS
Danny Boy	Irish	FBMS-2
	Knowles, J., arr.	FSSS
Dans les Ruines d'une Abbaye	Fauré, G.	GAS
Danza, danza, fanciulla gentile	Durante, F.	26ISAA
		28ISAA
		CIS-2
		STC
Das Erste Veilchen	Mendelssohn, F.	FBMS-2
Das Fischermädchen	Schubert, F.	FBTS-2
Das Leben ist ein Traum	Haydn, J.	GAS
Das Verlassene Mägdlein	Wolf, H.	SBSS
Days of Spring, The (Frühlingszeit)	Becker, R.	55AS
Dear Love of Mine (Caro mio ben)	Giordani, G.	ES-2
Dearest and Best (Caro mio ben)	Giordani, Tommaso	SR-1
Dearest Consort	Handel, G. F.	NIE-C
Dearest, believe (Caro mio ben)	Giordani, G.	56S
Death and the Maiden	Schubert, F.	NIE-C
Dedication (Widmung)	Franz, R.	55AS
		56S
		AS-1
		ES-1
		PS-2
		SR-1
		SVR-1
		YS-B
		YS-S
Deep in My Heart	Bishop, Sir H.	NIE-M
Deep River	Burleigh, H. T., arr.	FBBS-2
Deh più a me non v'ascondete	Bononcini, G.	CIS-3
Deh, contentatevi	Carissimi, G.	CIS-2
Deh, rendetemi	Provenzale, F.	CIS-2
Dein Angesicht	Schumann, R.	SBTS

Song Title	Composer	Anthology
Der Blumenstrauss	Mendelssohn, F.	FBMS
Der Gang Zum Liebchen	Brahms, J.	SBTS
Der Jäger		GAS
Der Lindenbaum	Schubert, F.	SBBS
Der Mond	Mendelssohn, F.	FBTS
Der Musikant	Wolf, H.	ES
Der Neugierige	Schubert, F.	FBTS
Der Nussbaum	Schumann, R.	50SS
Der Schmetterling	Schubert, F.	50SS
		GAS
Der Tod, das ist die kühle Nacht	Brahms, J.	50SS
Der Wanderer	Schubert, F.	SBBS
Dewy Violets	Scarlatti, A.	NIE-C
Didn't My Lord Deliver Daniel	Burleigh, H. T., arr.	CCS-S
Dido's Lament	Purcell, H.	ASSV
Dido's Lament from "Dido and Aeneas"		ES-2
Die Allmacht	Schubert, F.	50SS
Die Bekehrte	Stange, M.	FBMS
Die Forelle	Schubert, F.	SBTS
Die Hirten	Cornelius, P.	SBBS
Die Könige		FBBS-2
Die Lotosblume	Schumann, R.	50SS
		STC
Die Mainacht	Brahms, J.	GAS
Die Nacht	Strauss, R.	SBSS
Die Post	Schubert, F.	SBBS
Die Stille	Schumann, R.	ES
		FBMS-2
Die Stille Wasserrose	Fielitz, A. von	FBMS-2
Die Wetterfahne	Schubert, F.	FBBS-2
Dissonance, A	Borodine, A.	56S

Song Title	Composer	Anthology
Do Not Go, My Love	Hageman, R.	15AAS
		56S
		CCS-S
Do-Re-Mi	Rodgers, R.	FS
Doll's Cradle Song	Reinecke, C. H.	SS-Int
Don Juan's Serenade	Tchaikovsky, P.	NIE-Br
Donzelle fuggite	Cavalli, F.	CIS
Dove Sei	Handel, G. F.	ES
Dove sei, amato bene? from "Rodelinda"		GAS
Dove Song, The from "The Wings of the Dove"	Moore, D.	CAS
Down Among the Dead Men	Old English	ASSV
		NIE-Bs
Down by the Salley Gardens	Irish	BS
Down By the Sally Gardens	Hughes, H., arr.	CCS-T
		FBTS-2
Down Harley Street	Kingsford, C.	CAS
		FBBS-2
Down in the Forest	Ronald, L.	SBSS
Dream Valley	Quilter, R.	FBMS-2
		NIE-M
Dream, A	Bartlett, J. C.	YS-T
Dream-Land	V. Williams, R.	SBTS
Dreaming (Träume)	Wagner, R.	55AS
Dreams (Träume)		56S
Drift Down, Drift Down	Ronald, L.	FBSS-2
Drink to Me Only With Thine Eyes	Mellish, Col. R.	ES-1
	Old English	56S
		STC
	Ward, A. E., arr.	SR-1
Drinking	German	NIE-Bs
Droop Not, Young Lover	Handel, G. F.	NIE-Bs

Song Title	Composer	Anthology
Dryads, Sylvans	Handel, G. F.	NIE-M
Du bist die Ruh'	Schubert, F.	SBMS
Du bist wie eine Blume	Liszt, F.	FBBS-2
	Rubinstein, A.	FBTS-2
	Schumann, R.	50SS
		ASSV
		CCS-B
		FBBS-2
Du bist wie eine Blume (E'en as a Lovely Flower)	Willan, H.	SS-6
Dust of Snow	Carter, E.	SS-5
E dove t'aggiri	Cesti, M. A.	CIS-2
E'en As a Lovely Flower	Bridge, F.	NIE-T
Early in the Morning	Rorem, N.	BS
Early One Morning	British	BS
	Hughes, H., arr.	FS
	Willan, H., arr.	SS-3
Earth and Other Minor Things, The	Loewe, F.	FBBS-M
Earth and Sky	Brahms, J.	NIE-Bs
Easter Carol	Shaw, M.	CAS
Echo	Hindemith, P.	ES
Edelweiss	Rodgers, R.	FBBS-B
Edward	Loewe, C.	NIE-Br
		STC
Eileen Aroon	Irish	PS-2
Ein Jüngling Liebt ein Mädchen	Schumann, R.	FBTS
Ein Ton	Cornelius, P.	FBBS-2
El Majo Discreto	Granados, E.	FBSS
El Majo Timido		FBMS
El Tecolote	Paton, J. G., arr.	FS
El tra la la y el punteado	Granados, E.	CCS-S
		FBSS
El Trobador	Mexican	FBTS-2

15

Song Title	Composer	Anthology
Eldorado	Walthew, R. H.	FBBS-2
Elégie	Massenet, J.	56S
		FBMS-2
Elegy (Elégie)		55AS
		ES-2
Elephants	Crawley, C.	SS-Int
Eletelephony	Kasemets, U.	SS-Int
En Barque	Pierné, G.	GAS
En prière	Fauré, G.	50ASMR
Encantadora Maria	Latin American	FBBS
Enchantress, The	Hatton, J. L.	NIE-C
Endless Pleasure, Endless Love	Handel, G. F.	NIE-S
English Usage	Thomson, V.	CAS
Equals (Der Gleichsinn)	Haydn, J.	PS-4
Erhebung	Schoenberg, A.	50ASMR
Erl King, The	Schubert, F.	NIE-Br
Eros	Grieg, E.	GAS
Es Muss ein Wunderbares Sein	Liszt, F.	FBMS-2
Ethiopia Saluting the Colours	Wood, C.	NIE-Bs
Evening	Ives, C. E.	ES
Evening Fair (Beau Soir)	Debussy, C.	ES-2
Evening Prayer, The	Moussorgsky, M. P.	50ASMR
Evensong	Lehmann, L.	FBMS
Every Day is Ladies' Day with Me	Herbert, V.	FBTS-2
Every Night When the Sun Goes In	American	BS
Everybody Says Don't	Sondheim, S.	BR-B
Everyone Sang	Wells, H.	CAS
Everywhere I Look!	Carew, M.	FBSS
Exquisite Hour (L'huere Exquise)	Hahn, R.	55AS
Exquisite Hour, The (L'Heure exquise)		ES-2
Extase	Duparc, H.	50ASMR

Song Title	Composer	Anthology
Extinguish My Eyes	Bernstein, L.	CAS
Eye Hath Not Seen	Gaul, A.	ES-1
		SBMS
Ezekiel's Wheel	Kern, P., arr.	SSS
Fair House of Joy	Quilter, R.	SBTS
Fairy's Lullaby, The	Moffat, A., arr.	FS
Faith in Spring (Frühlingsglaube)	Schubert, F.	AS-2
		ES-1
Falling Dew, The	Czech	PS-1
Falling in Love with Love	Rodgers, R.	FBBS-M
False Phillis	Wilson, H. L., arr.	FBBS
Fame's an Echo	Arne, T.	FBTS-2
Fanny	Rome, H.	BR-T
Far Down in the Valley (Da unten in Tale)	Brahms, J.	ES-1
Far From the Home I Love	Bock, J.	FS
Fare You Well	American	SVR-1
Farewell (Adieu!)	Schubert, F.	PS-1
Farewell! (Gute Nacht!)	Franz, R.	PS-2
Farewell, A	Strauss, R.	NIE-S
Farewell, Lad	O'Neill, J., arr.	FSSS
Farmer by the Sea	Lane, R.	ES
Fate of Gilbert Gim, The	Drynan, M.	SS-2
Feast of Love (Liebesfeier)	Franz, R.	PS-1
Ferryman, The	Helyer, M.	SS-Int
Fiddler, The	Nielsen, C.	SS-2
Fifty Million Years Ago	Schmidt, H.	BR-T
Filli, non t'amo più	Carissimi, G.	CIS-3
Fiocca la neve	Cimara, P.	50ASMR
		SBSS
Fire Down Below	Althouse, J., arr.	FSSS-2
First Concert, The	Mana-Zucca	FBBS-2

Song Title	Composer	Anthology
First Meeting, The (Erstes Begegnen)	Grieg, E.	PS-3
First Primrose, The (Mit einer primula veris)		PS-1
Fleur des Blés	Debussy, C.	GAS
Florian's Song (Chanson de Florian)	Godard, B.	55AS
		AS-1
		ES-2
Flow Gently, Sweet Afton	Scottish	BS
Folk Song (Volksliedchen)	Schumann, R.	SR-1
Follow the Drinking Gourd	Althouse, J., arr.	FSSS-2
For Music (Für Music)	Franz, R.	AS-1
		PS-1
		YS-B
		YS-C
		YS-S
		YS-T
For These Blessings	Sleeth, N.	SunS
Forget Me Not	Bach, J. S.	FBTS-2
Forsake Me Not, My Love, I Pray	Rachmaninoff, S.	GAS
Four Is Wonderful	Henderson, R. W.	SS-3
Free From His Fetters	Sullivan, A.	SBTS
Freudvoll und leidvoll from "Egmont"	Beethoven, L.	GAS
Friar of Orders Grey, The	Shield, W.	FBBS
Friendship and Song	Handel, G. F.	SVR-2
From Far, from Eve and Morning	V. Williams, R.	NIE-T
From the North	Sibelius, J.	50ASMR
Frühlingsglaube	Schubert, F.	ES
Frühlingsnacht	Schumann, R.	50SS
Frühlingsträum	Schubert, F.	SBTS
Fussreise	Wolf, H.	50ASMR
Garland, The	Brahms, J.	NIE-Br
Gefror'ne Thränen	Schubert, F.	SBBS

Song Title	Composer	Anthology
Gentle Shepherd	Pergolesi, G. B.	NIE-S
Gesang Weylas	Wolf, H.	50ASMR
Gesú Bambino	Yon, P.	FBSS-2
Get Me to the Church on Time	Loewe, F.	FBBS-B
Getting to Know You	Rodgers, R.	FBBS-M
Già il sole dal Gange	Scarlatti, A.	26ISAA
		26ISAA
Girl That I Marry, The	Berlin, I.	FBBS-B
Girls' Song	Howells, H.	NIE-M
Give a Man a Horse He Can Ride	O'Hara, G.	CCS-B
		FBBS-2
Gloria Deo	Ouchterlony, D.	SS-3
Glory of God in Nature, The (Die Ehre Grottes in der Natur)	Beethoven, L.	55AS
Go 'Way from My Window	Niles, J. J.	FBMS
	Schram, R. E., arr.	FSSS-2
Go Now In Peace	Sleeth, N.	SunS
Go, Lovely Rose	Quilter, R.	FBTS
Go, Tell it on the Mountain	Simms, P. F., arr.	SSS
God is My Shepherd	Dvořák, A.	FBBS-2
Golden Slumbers	MacMillan, E., arr.	SS-3
Golden Sun Streaming (Die gold'ne Sonne, voll Freud' und Wonne)	Bach, J. S.	PS-4
Gonna Be Another Hot Day	Schmidt, H.	BR-B
		FBBS-B
Good Morning (God Morgen)	Grieg, E.	PS-4
Good-bye	Tosti, F. P.	55AS
Good-bye!		56S
Goodnight, My Someone	Willson, M.	FBBS-S
Gott im Frühling	Schubert, F.	FBMS-2
Grace Thy Fair Brow (Rend' il sereno al ciglio)	Handel, G. F.	PS-1
Grandma	Chanler, T.	FBSS-2

Song Title	Composer	Anthology
Grasshopper Green	Taylor, C.	SS-2
Great Peace Have They Which Love Thy Law	Rogers, J. H.	SBMS
Green Dog, The	Kingsley, H.	20CAS
		FBSS
Green Hills O' Somerset, The	Coates, E.	SBTS
Greensleeves	Kern, P., arr.	FSSS
	Paton, J. G., arr.	ES
Gretchen at the Spinning Wheel	Schubert, F.	NIE-S
Gruss	Mendelssohn, F.	ES
Guitar Player, The	Bennett, C.	SVR-1
Gute Nacht	Franz, R.	ASSV
Habanera	Bizet, G.	56S
Handsome Butcher, The	Seiber, M., arr.	SS-2
Harbour Grace	Bissell, K., arr.	SS-4
Hark! How Still (Still Sicherheit)	Franz, R.	PS-3
Hark! Hark! The Lark	Schubert, F.	AS-2
Hark! The Echoing Air	Purcell, H.	SBSS
Hark! What I Tell to Thee	Haydn, J.	NIE-C
Have You Seen But a Bright Lily Grow?	Old English	ES
Have You Seen But a White Lillie Grow?		ASSV
		CCS-T
		PS-3
Have You Seen But a White Lily Grow		FBSS
Have You Seen But the White Lillie Grow?		SR-2
Have You Seen But the Whyte Lillie Grow?		STC
He Is Noble, He Is Patient	Schumann, R.	NIE-S
He or She That Hopes to Gain	Berger, J.	ES

Song Title	Composer	Anthology
He shall feed His flock	Handel, G. F.	CCS-M
He That Keepeth Israel	Schlösser, A.	FBTS
He Wasn't You She Wasn't You	Lane, B.	FS
He's Gone Away	Schram, R. E., arr.	FSSS-2
He's Got the Whole World in His Hands	Rodgers, R.	FS
Hear My Cry, O God	Franck, C.	FBSS
Hear My Prayer, O Lord	Dvorák, A.	SBSS
Hear! Ye Gods of Britain	Purcell, H.	NIE-Bs
Heard Ye His Voice	Rubinstein, A.	SBMS
Heart Worships, The	Holst, G.	FBBS-2
Heaven-Rays (Himmelsfunken)	Schubert, F.	PS-4
Heavenly Grass	Bowles, P.	15AAS
		CAS
Hebe	Chausson, E.	FS
Hedge-roses (Heidenröslein)	Schubert, F.	AS-1
Heffle Cuckoo Fair	Shaw, M.	FBSS
Heidenröslein	Schubert, F.	50SS
		ES
Heimkehr	Strauss, R.	50SS
		GAS
Heimliche Aufforderung		50SS
Hello, Young Lovers	Rodgers, R.	FBBS-S
Here Amid the Shady Woods	Handel, G. F.	FBSS-2
		NIE-M
		PS-4
Here's to America	Sleeth, N.	WS
Hero, The	Menotti, G. C.	20CAS
High Barbaree	Christy, V. A., arr.	FS
Highland Lullaby, A	Coutts, G.	SS-4
Hinay Ma Tov	Rodgers, R.	FS
His Coming (Er ist gekommen)	Franz, R.	AS-2

Song Title	Composer	Anthology
Holiday Song	Schuman, W.	CAS
Holy Book, The	Sleeth, N.	SunS
Holy City, The	Adams, S.	ES-1
Homeward Bound	Althouse, J., arr.	FSSS
Honey Shun	Schirmer, R.	20CAS
Hör' Ich das Liedchen Klingen	Schumann, R.	FBBS
Horses	Crawley, C.	SS-Int
House to Let	Whitehead, A.	SS-2
How Art Thou Fall'n	Handel, G. F.	NIE-Br
How Calm Is My Spirit	Mozart, W. A.	NIE-S
How Changed the Vision	Handel, G. F.	NIE-C
How Could I Ever Know	Simon, L.	BS
How Do I Love Thee?	Dello Joio, N.	STC
How Do You Preach?	Benton, G.	BR-T
How Fair This Spot	Rachmaninoff, S.	NIE-S
How Few the Joys		NIE-C
How Lovely Are Thy Dwellings	Liddle, S.	FBSS-2
How Soft, upon the Evening Air	Dunhill, T.	SS-3
How to Handle a Woman	Loewe, F.	FBBS-B
Hugh's Song of the Road	V. Williams, R.	CAS
Hush, Be Silent	Purcell, H.	SVR-1
Hushed The Song of the Nightingale	Gretchaninoff, A.	SBMS
I Am a Roamer	Mendelssohn, F.	NIE-Bs
I Attempt From Love's Sickness to Fly	Purcell, H.	ASSV
		CCS-S
		ES
		ES-2
		FBTS
		NIE-M
I Believe In You	Loesser, F.	FBBS-T
I Could Have Danced All Night	Loewe, F.	FBBS-S

Song Title	Composer	Anthology
I Could Write a Book	Rodgers, R.	FBBS-T
I Do Not Know a Day I Did Not Love You		FBBS-T
I Don't Wish to Marry (No quiero casarme)	Spanish	PS-3
I Dreamed That I Was Weeping (Ich hab' im Traum geweinet)	Schumann, R.	ES-2
I Enjoy Being a Girl	Rodgers, R.	FBBS-M
I Got Plenty O' Nuttin'	Gershwin, G.	BR-B
I Had Myself A True Love	Arlen, H.	BR-S
I Have Dreamed	Rodgers, R.	BR-T
		FBBS-S
I Have Twelve Oxen	Ireland, J.	NIE-S
I heard a Cry	Fisher, W. A.	AS-2
I Just Called to Say I Love You	Wonder, S.	FS
I Know Where I'm Goin'	Hughes, H., arr.	FS
I Like Dogs! (J'aime les chiens!)	Ohlin, C. P.	SS-Int
I Love All Graceful Things	Thiman, E. H.	CAS
		FBSS
I Love and I Must	Purcell, H.	FBTS
I Love Paris	Porter, C.	FBBS-M
I Love thee (Ich liebe dich)	Beethoven, L.	56S
		ES-1
		PS-2
	Grieg, E.	56S
		ES-1
		SVR-1
		YS-S
		YS-T
I Loved You Once In Silence	Loewe, F.	BR-S
		FBBS-M
I Said I Will Forget Thee	Brahms, J.	NIE-Bs
I Shall Declare I Love Her	Handel, G. F.	SS-4

Song Title	Composer	Anthology
I Sought the Lord	Stevenson, F.	SBMS
I Talk to the Trees	Loewe, F.	FBBS-B
I Triumph! I Triumph!	Carissimi, G.	NIE-Bs
I wander this Summer morning (Am leuchtenden Sommermorgen)	Franz, R.	AS-2
I Watched the Lady Caroline	Duke, J.	20CAS
I Went to Heaven	Wagner, R.	FS
I Wept, Beloved, As I Dreamed (J'ai pleurè un rêve)	Hüe, G.	ES-2
I Will Make You Brooches	Bury, W.	SS-5
I will Sing New Songs	Dvorák, A.	SBBS
I Wonder As I Wander	Niles, J. J.	FBBS-2
I'll Give My Love an Apple	Ridout, G., arr.	SS-6
I'll Know	Loesser, F.	FBBS-S
I'll Never Ask You to Tell	Fox, O. J.	SR-1
I'll Not Complain (Ich grolle nicht)	Schumann, R.	ES-2
I'll Sail Upon The Dog Star	Purcell, H.	SBTS
I'll Sail upon the Dog-Star		NIE-T
I'm Nobody	Persichetti, V.	ES
I'm Wearing Awa' to the Land O' the Leal	Foote, A.	YS-B
		YS-C
		YS-S
		YS-T
I've Been Roaming	Horn, C. E.	55AS
		YS-C
		YS-S
I've Grown Accustomed To Her Face	Loewe, F.	BR-B
		FBBS-B
Ich atmet' einen linden Duft	Mahler, G.	STC
Ich hab' in Deinem Auge	Schumann, C.	ES
Ich Liebe Dich	Beethoven, L.	FBSS-2

Song Title	Composer	Anthology
Ich Liebe dich	Beethoven, L.	STC
Ich liebe dich so wie du mich		ASSV
Ich trage meine Minne	Strauss, R.	50SS
Ici-Bas!	Fauré, G.	FBMS
		GAS
If All the Seas Were One Sea	McLean, H. J.	SS-6
If Doughty Deeds My Lady Please	Sullivan, A.	NIE-Br
If Ever I Would Leave You	Loewe, F.	BR-B
		FBBS-B
If God left only you	Densmore, J. H.	AS-2
If I Ruled The World	Ornadel, C.	BR-T
		FBBS-M
If Music Be the Food of Love	Purcell, H.	SVR-1
If Thou Be Near (Bist du bei mir)	Bach, J. S.	PS-2
If Thou Love Me (Se tu m'ami)	Pergolesi, G. B.	55AS
If Thou Thy Heart Will Give Me	Bach, J. S.	SR-1
Il mio bel foco	Marcello, B.	28ISAA
Il Neige	Bemberg, H.	SVR-2
Il pleure dans mon coeur	Debussy, C.	50ASMR
		STC
Im Abendroth	Schubert, F.	50SS
Im Herbst	Franz, R.	SBMS
Imagine That	Rosenthal, L.	BR-B
Impatience (Ungeduld)	Schubert, F.	ES-2
Impossible Dream, The	Leigh, M.	FBBS-B
In a Simple Way I Love You	Ford, N.	BS
In a Strange Land	Taubert, W.	NIE-M
In dem Schatten meiner Locken	Wolf, H.	50SS
In Der Fremde	Schumann, R.	FBTS-2
In der Frühe	Wolf, H.	50SS
In einem Kühlen Grunde	German	FBBS-2
In Evening's Glow (Im Abendrot)	Schubert, F.	PS-1

Song Title	Composer	Anthology
In My Own Little Corner	Rodgers, R.	FBBS-M
In Old Donegal	Parke, D.	SS-2
In Summer Fields (Feldeinsamkeit)	Brahms, J.	AS-2
In the Country (Die Landlust)	Haydn, J.	PS-1
In the Silence of Night	Rachmaninoff, S.	50ASMR
In the Silent Night (V'mo Hchányinótchi táïnoi)		SVR-1
In Waldeseinsamkeit	Brahms, J.	50SS
Incline Thine Ear	Charles, E.	FBTS-2
Inn, The	Toye, F.	CAS
Intermezzo	Schumann, R.	FBBS
		GAS
Into the Night	Edwards, C.	FBSS
Intorno All' Idol Mio	Cesti, M. A.	FBSS-2
Invocazione de Orfeo	Peri, J.	CIS
Is It Bliss or is It Sorrow?	Brahms, J.	NIE-T
Is It Really Me?	Schmidt, H.	BR-MS
		FBBS-M
Is She Not Passing Fair?	Elgar, E.	NIE-T
Island, The	Rachmaninoff, S.	50ASMR
		SBBS
It Must Be Me from "Candide"	Bernstein, L.	20CAS
It Must Be Wonderful Indeed (Es muss ein Wunderbares sein)	Liszt, F.	PS-1
It Must Be Wonderful, Indeed (Es muss ein Wunderbares sein)		55AS
It was a Dream	Lassen, E.	55AS
It Was a Lover and His Lass	Coates, E.	FBTS-2
	Morley, T.	CCS-S
		FS
		STC
It Wonders Me	Hague, A.	BR-S
It's a Grand Night for Singing	Rodgers, R.	FBBS-S

Songs by Title

Song Title	Composer	Anthology
J'ai cuelli la belle rose (I Have Culled That Lovely Rosebud)	Ridout, G.	SS-5
J'ai pleuré en rêve	Hüe, G.	50ASMR
Jack and Joan	Campion, T.	SS-2
Jagdlied	Mendelssohn, F.	FBBS
Jailer's Slumber Song, The	Russian	PS-4
Japanese Night Song	Bennett, C.	SVR-2
Jardin d'amour	Keel, J. F., arr.	SS-5
Jeanie With the Light Brown Hair	Foster, S. C.	STC
Jeg elsker Dig	Grieg, E.	ES
Jesu, the Very Thought of Thee	Wesley, S. S.	FBTS
Jesus Walked This Lonesome Valley	Myers, G., arr.	FBMS
Jesus, Fount of Consolation	Bach, J. S.	FBBS-2
Jesus, Jesus, Rest Your Head	American	YS-B
		YS-C
		YS-S
		YS-T
Johnny Doolan's Cat	Irish	BS
Jolly Jolly Breeze, The	Eccles, J.	SBMS
Jolly Roger, The	Robertson, R. R.	FBBS
Joshua Fit the Battle of Jericho	Christy, V. A., arr.	ES-1
Joy of Love, The (Plaisir d'amour)	Martini, G.	55AS
		ES
Joys of Love, The (Plaisir d'amour)		ES-1
Juniper Tree, The	Irish	BS
Júrame	Grever, M.	56S
Just Imagine	DeSylva, B. G.	FBBS-S
Just In Time	Styne, J.	BR-B
		FBBS-B
Just One Person	Grossman, L.	BR-T
Just-Spring	Duke, J.	STC
K'e, The	Dougherty, C.	20CAS
		FBSS

27

Song Title	Composer	Anthology
Kansas City	Rodgers, R.	FBBS-T
Keeping Christmas	Sleeth, N.	WS
Keine Sorg' um den Weg	Raff, J.	FBMS-2
Kelligrews Soiree, The	Burke, J.	SS-2
Kind Fortune Smiles	Purcell, H.	SBMS
King Charles	White, M. V.	NIE-Br
King of Love My Shepherd Is, The	Gounod, C.	FBBS
King of Song, The	Thiman, E. H.	SS-5
Kingdom by the Sea, A	Somervell, A.	FBTS-2
Kiss, The (Der kuss)	Beethoven, L.	PS-3
Kitty of Colerain	Irish	PS-3
Kitty of Coleraine	Easson, J., arr.	SS-4
Knotting Song, The	Purcell, H.	NIE-T
Know'st Thou the Land	Beethoven, L.	NIE-M
Kum Ba Yah	Simms, P. F., arr.	SSS
L'Amour au mois de mai	Lefévre, J.	ES
L'Amour de Moi	French	FBBS-2
L'Amour de mois de mai	Lefevre, J.	ES
L'Anneau D'Argent	Chaminade, C.	FBMS
L'Esclave	Lalo, É.	50ASMR
L'esperto nocchiero	Bononcini, G.	CIS-2
L'Heure exquise	Hahn, R.	50ASMR
		FBSS-2
L'Huere exquise		ASSV
L'Invitation au voyage	Duparc, H.	50ASMR
La donna è mobile	Verdi, G.	56S
La Paloma	Yradier, S.	56S
		FS
La Paloma Blanca	Latin American	FBBS
La Partida	Alvarez, F.	GAS
La Pastorella	Schubert, F.	FBSS-2

Song Title	Composer	Anthology
La petite hirondelle (Oh, Sweet Little Swallow)	Willan, H., arr.	SS-5
La pomme et l'escargot (The Apple and the Snail)	Milhaud, D.	SS-1
La Seña	Latin American	FBTS
La Zingara	Donizetti, G.	SBSS
Lachen und Weinen	Schubert, F.	CCS-S
		FBSS-2
Lamb, The	Chanler, T.	15AAS
		FBMS
Lark, The	Dvořák, A.	50ASMR
Lasciatemi morire	Monteverde, C.	FS
Lasciatemi morire!		26ISAA
		28ISAA
		ASSV
Lascitemi morire		CIS
Lass from the Low Countree, The	Niles, J. J.	15AAS
		FBMS
Lass with the Delicate Air, The	Arne, M.	56S
		STC
	Arne, T.	ES-2
		SR-2
Last Night	Kjerulf, H.	55AS
		SR-1
Last Rose of Summer, The	Irish	56S
	Miliken, R. A.	FBSS-2
Last Toast, The	Schumann, R.	NIE-Bs
Lay of the Imprisoned Huntsman, The	Schubert, F.	NIE-Bs
Lazy Afternoon	Latouche, J.	FBBS-M
	Moross, J.	BR-MS
Lazy Summer	Belyea, W. H.	SS-5
Le Charme	Chausson, E.	SBBS

Song Title	Composer	Anthology
Le Miroir	Ferrari, G.	FBBS-2
		GAS
Le Secret	Fauré, G.	FBBS
Le Soir	Thomas, A.	SBTS
Le Violette	Scarlatti, A.	26ISAA
		28ISAA
		GAS
Leaning on a Lamp-Post	Gay, N.	FBBS-B
Leave Me in Sorrow (Lascia ch'io pianga)	Handel, G. F.	PS-2
Leave Me to Languish (Lascia ch'io pianga) from "Rinaldo"		ES-2
Leave Me, Loathsome Light		FBBS
Leave me, loathsome light! from "Semele"		GAS
Lebe Wohl!	Wolf, H.	50SS
		GAS
Legend, A	Tchaikovsky, P.	50ASMR
		ES-1
		FBMS-2
Les berceaux	Fauré, G.	SBMS
Les Cloches	Debussy, C.	SBSS
Les Paons	Loeffler, C. M.	50ASMR
Les Papillons	Chausson, E.	GAS
Les Roses D'Ispahan	Fauré, G.	SBBS
Let Each Gallant Heart	Purcell, H.	SBBS
Let Me Linger near Thee	Rosa, S.	NIE-M
Let Me Wander Not Unseen	Handel, G. F.	NIE-S
Let My Song Fill Your Heart	Charles, E.	FBSS
Let the Dreadful Engines	Purcell, H.	NIE-Br
Let Us Break Bread Together	Althouse, J., arr.	SSS
	Myers, G., arr.	FBBS
Let Us Dance, Let Us Sing	Purcell, H.	FBSS

Song Title	Composer	Anthology
Let's Make Music	Sleeth, N.	WS
Letter Song	Moore, D.	BR-S
Libera me	Fauré, G.	ASSV
Liebhaber in allen Gestalten	Schubert, F.	50SS
Liebst du um Schönheit	Schumann, C.	BS
Lied	Franck, C.	PS-2
Lied der Mignon	Schubert, F.	FBSS
Light One Candle	Sleeth, N.	SunS
Like Any Foolish Moth I Fly	Scarlatti, A.	NIE-C
Like The Shadow	Handel, G. F.	SBBS
Lilacs	Rachmaninoff, S.	56S
		SBMS
Lime Tree, The	Schubert, F.	NIE-Bs
Linden Lea	V. Williams, R.	FBTS-2
Linnet's Secret, The	Rowley, A.	SS-1
Litany	Schubert, F.	NIE-C
Lithuanian Song (Lithauisches Lied)	Chopin, F.	ES-1
Little Boy Blue	Nevin, E.	ES-1
Little Buttercup	Sullivan, A.	SBMS
Little China Figure, A	Leoni, F.	FBSS
Little Closer, Please, A	Bowles, P.	SS-6
Little David, Play on Your Harp	Kern, P., arr.	SSS
Little Elegy	Duke, J.	FBSS
	Rorem, N.	SS-5
Little Folk Song, A	Schumann, R.	SS-5
Little Irish Girl, The	Lohr, H.	SVR-2
		YS-B
		YS-C
		YS-S
		YS-T
Little Red Lark, The	Nyklicek, G.	SVR-2
Little road to Kerry, The	Cadman, C. W.	AS-1

Song Title	Composer	Anthology
Liza Jane	Althouse, J., arr.	FSSS
Lo! Hear the Gentle Lark	Bishop, Sir H.	STC
Loch Lomond	Crist, B.	SR-1
	Deis, C., arr.	FBTS
Londonderry Air	Irish	56S
Lone and Joyless	Mendelssohn, F.	NIE-S
Lonely House	Weill, K.	BR-S
Lonely Room	Rodgers, R.	BR-B
Lonesome Dove, The from "Down in the Valley"	Weill, K.	20CAS
Lonesome Valley	Christy, V. A., arr.	ES-1
Long Ago	MacDowell, E.	SBTS
Long Time Ago	American	BS
Long, Long Ago	Bayly, T. H.	AS-1
		STC
Longing For Spring	Mozart, W. A.	PS-1
Look at Me, My little dear	McLean, H. J., arr.	SS-2
Look for the Silver Lining	Kern, J.	FBBS-S
Look To The Rainbow	Lane, B.	BR-MS
		FBBS-S
Lord God of Abraham	Mendelssohn, F.	SBBS
Lord Is My Light, The	Speaks, O.	FBTS
Lord Is My Shepherd, The	Liddle, S.	SBTS
	Tchaikovsky, P.	FBMS
Lord, I Want to Be a Christian	Payne, J., arr.	FBBS
Loreley, The	Liszt, F.	NIE-S
Lost Chord, The	Sullivan, A.	55AS
		56S
		ES-1
Lost In The Stars	Weill, K.	BR-B
Lotus Flower, The (Die Lotusblume)	Schumann, R.	55AS
		AS-1
		ES-1

Song Title	Composer	Anthology
Lotus Flower, The (Die Lotusblume)	Schumann, R.	PS-1
Love and a Day	Willan, H.	SS-5
Love Has Eyes	Bishop, Sir H.	55AS
		ES
		ES-2
		FBSS
		PS-3
		YS-B
		YS-C
		YS-S
		YS-T
Love is a Bable	Parry, C. H.	SBBS
Love Is a Bauble	Leveridge, R.	PS-3
Love Is a Many-Splendored Thing	Fain, S.	BS
Love Is Here to Stay	Gershwin, G.	FS
Love Leads to Battle	Bononcini, G.	NIE-Bs
Love Quickly is Pall'd	Purcell, H.	FBTS-2
Love Song	Brahms, J.	NIE-T
Love Song (Minnelied)		AS-2
Love That's True Will Live for Ever	Handel, G. F.	NIE-Bs
Love Triumphant	Brahms, J.	NIE-C
Love's Old, Sweet Song	Molloy, J. L.	56S
Love's Philosophy	Quilter, R.	SBSS
		SVR-2
Love, I Have Won You	Ronald, L.	SBMS
Love, I Hear	Sondheim, S.	BR-T
Loveliest of Trees	Duke, J.	15AAS
		FBMS
Lovely Song My Heart is Singing, The	Goulding, E.	FBMS-2
Lowest Trees Have Tops, The	Dowland, J.	SS-4
Luci vezzose	Gaffi, B.	CIS-3
Lullaby	Brahms, J.	NIE-S

Song Title	Composer	Anthology
Lullaby	Brahms, J.	SR-1
	Godard, B.	56S
	Scott, C.	FBSS
	Sleeth, N.	SunS
	Telfer, N.	SS-1
Lullaby (Wiegenlied)	Mozart, W. A.	55AS
		SR-1
Lullaby from "The Consul"	Menotti, G. C.	CAS
Lullaby, A	Harty, H.	NIE-S
		SBMS
Lungi Dal Caro Bene	Sarti, G.	FBBS
	Secchi, A.	26ISAA
		CIS
Lydia	Fauré, G.	FBTS
Maiden Tell Me	Czech	PS-1
Maiden's Wish, The (Mädchen's Wunch)	Chopin, F.	SVR-2
Make Believe	Kern, J.	FBBS-S
Malìa	Tosti, F. P.	ES
Man and a Woman, A	Schmidt, H.	FBBS-T
Man Is for the Woman Made	Purcell, H.	FS
Mandoline	Debussy, C.	STC
Many a New Day	Rodgers, R.	FBBS-S
March of the Kings (La Marche des Rois)	French	PS-2
Mariä Wiegenlied	Reger, M.	FBMS-2
Marianina	Fletcher, P., arr.	SS-Int
Marianne s'en va-t-au moulin (Marianne Went to the Mill)	Champagne, C., arr.	SS-1
Mary	Richardson, T.	SR-1
Mattinata	Leoncavallo, R.	GAS
		SBBS
May Song	Beethoven, L.	FBTS

Song Title	Composer	Anthology
Me and My Girl	Gay, N.	FBBS-T
Mein Glaubiges Herze	Bach, J. S.	SBSS
Mein schöner Stern!	Schumann, R.	50SS
Meine Liebe ist grün	Brahms, J.	50SS
Meine Lieder		GAS
Melmillo	Carey, C.	NIE-M
Memory	Ireland, J.	SBBS
Memory, A	Ganz, R.	50ASMR
Mermaid's Song, The	Haydn, J.	FBSS
Message, The	Brahms, J.	NIE-Br
Michael, Row the Boat Ashore	Rodgers, R.	FS
Mignon	Wolf, H.	50SS
Mignon's Song	Liszt, F.	NIE-C
Milkmaids	Warlock, P.	SS-6
Mill-Wheel, The (Das Mühlrad)	Germany	PS-2
Miller of Dee, The	Christy, V. A., arr.	ES
		ES-1
Miller of Mansfield, The	Arne, T.	FS
Minnelied	Mendelssohn, F.	FBSS
Minor Bird, A	Dougherty, C.	20CAS
Minstrel Boy, The	Irish	BS
Mister Banjo	Christy, V. A., arr.	ES-1
Mistress Mine	Walthew, R. H.	FBTS
Mit deinen blauen Augen	Strauss, R.	GAS
Mit Einem Gemalten Band	Beethoven, L.	SBTS
Mit Myrthen und Rosen	Schumann, R.	50SS
Mon doux berger/Sweet Shepherd	MacMillan, E., arr.	SS-3
Mondnacht	Schumann, R.	50SS
Money, O!	Head, M.	NIE-Bs
Monk and His Cat, The	Barber, S.	15AAS
Monotone (Ein Ton)	Cornelius, P.	55AS
Moon River	Mancini, H.	BS

Song Title	Composer	Anthology
Moon-Marketing	Weaver, P.	20CAS
Moonlight	Schumann, R.	NIE-T
More Sweet is That Name	Handel, G. F.	SBBS
Morgen	Strauss, R.	50ASMR
		50SS
		YS-B
		YS-C
		YS-S
		YS-T
Morning	Speaks, O.	FBMS
Morning Greeting (Morgengruss)	Schubert, F.	SR-1
Morning Hymn	Henschel, G.	YS-S
Morning Hymn (Morgen-Hymne)		SVR-2
		YS-C
Mother	Palmgren, S.	50ASMR
Mother (Gamle Mor)	Grieg, E.	PS-4
Mother, O Sing Me to Rest (Mutter, O Sing mich zur Ruh)	Franz, R.	SVR-2
Mother-Love	Voigt, H.	56S
Much More	Schmidt, H.	BR-S
Music, When Soft Voices Die	Gold, E.	20CAS
Must the Winter Come so Soon?	Barber, S.	CAS
My Crow Pluto	Thomson, V.	20CAS
My Cup Runneth Over	Schmidt, H.	BR-B
		FBBS-B
My Dear One's Mouth is Like the Rose (Mein Mädel hat einen Rosenmund)	Brahms, J.	PS-2
My Defenses Are Down	Berlin, I.	FBBS-B
My Dog Spot	Curwin, C.	SS-2
My Favorite Things	Rodgers, R.	FBBS-M
My Funny Valentine		BR-MS
		FBBS-M

Song Title	Composer	Anthology
My Heart at thy sweet voice (Mon coeur s'ouvre à ta voix)	Saint-Saëns, C.	56S
My heart ever faithful (Mein gläubiges Herze)	Bach, J. S.	56S
My Heart Is Like a Singing Bird	Parry, C. H.	SBSS
My Heart Stood Still	Rodgers, R.	FBBS-T
My Johann	Grieg, E.	FBSS
My Lady Walks in Loveliness	Charles, E.	FBTS
My Lagan Love	Harty, H.	NIE-Bs
My Last Abode	Schubert, F.	NIE-Bs
My Life's Delight	Quilter, R.	SBTS
My Lord, What a Mornin'	Burleigh, H. T., arr.	CCS-M
	Johnson, H., arr.	FBTS
My Lord, What a Morning	Althouse, J., arr.	SSS
My Love rode by	Calbreath, M. E.	AS-1
My Love's an Arbutus	Irish	AS-1
	MacMillan, E., arr.	SS-3
My Lovely Celia	Monro, G.	55AS
		ES-2
		FBTS-2
		FS
		STC
		SVR-1
		YS-T
My Lover is a Fisherman	Strickland, L.	AS-2
My Mother Bids Me Bind My Hair	Haydn, J.	NIE-M
		SR-2
My Mother Bids Me Bind My Hair (Bind' auf dein Haar)		56S
My Mother Binds My Hair (Bind auf dein Haar)		YS-S
My Native Land (Gesang Weylas)	Wolf, H.	55AS
My Old Kentucky Home	Foster, S. C.	56S

Song Title	Composer	Anthology
My Own Space	Kander, J.	BR-MS
My Romance	Rodgers, R.	FBBS-T
My Soul Is Dark	Schumann, R.	NIE-C
Mystery's Song	Purcell, H.	FBMS-2
Nacht und Träume	Schubert, F.	50SS
Nachtviolen		50SS
Nature Beyond Art	Arne, T.	SBTS
Nature's Adoration	Beethoven, L.	SBBS
Nay, Though My Heart Should Break	Tchaikovsky, P.	NIE-C
Ne'er Shade so Dear (Ombra mai fu)	Handel, G. F.	PS-2
Nebbie	Respighi, O.	50ASMR
		YS-B
		YS-C
		YS-S
		YS-T
Nel cor più non mi sento	Paisiello, G.	26ISAA
		26ISAA
		CIS-3
		CCS-S
		FS
Neue Liebe, neues Leben	Beethoven, L.	GAS
Next Market Day, The	Irish	BS
Next, Winter Comes Slowly	Purcell, H.	FBBS
Night (Die Nacht)	Strauss, R.	PS-4
Night and Dreams (Nacht und Träume)	Schubert, F.	PS-4
Night Has A Thousand Eyes, The	Metcalf, J. W.	SVR-2
		YS-T
Night in May, A	Brahms, J.	NIE-C
Night is Falling	Haydn, J.	FBSS
Night is Mournful	Rachmaninoff, S.	NIE-T
Nightingale and the Rose, The	Rimsky-Korsakoff, N.	55AS

Song Title	Composer	Anthology
Nimmersatte Liebe	Wolf, H.	50SS
		GAS
Nina	Italian	26ISAA
	Pergolesi, G. B.	28ISAA
		ES-2
		FS
		SR-2
Nina (Tre Giorni)		CIS
No Embers, nor a Firebrand (Kein Feuer, Keine Kohle)	Henschel, G.	AS-2
No Flower That Blows	Linley, T.	FBSS-2
No One is Alone	Sondheim, S.	BS
No, no, non si speri!	Carissimi, G.	CIS
Nobody Knows the Trouble I've Seen	Althouse, J., arr.	SSS
	Burleigh, H. T., arr.	FBTS-2
Noche Serena	Latin American	FBTS
Non è ver!	Mattei, T.	GAS
		STC
Non posso disperar	Bononcini, G.	26ISAA
	De Luca, S.	28ISAA
	Luca, S. De	GAS
Non vogl'io se non vederti	Scarlatti, A.	CIS-2
None but the Lonely Heart (Nor wer die Sehnsucht kennt)	Tchaikovsky, P.	ES-1
None by the Lonely Heart (Nur wer die sehnsucht kennt)		AS-2
Novice, The	Schubert, F.	NIE-S
Now is the Month of Maying	Morley, T.	55AS
		CCS-M
		SS-2
Now Love Has Falseley Played Me (Die liebe hat gelogen)	Schubert, F.	PS-4
Now Sleeps the Crimson Petal	Quilter, R.	NIE-T

Song Title	Composer	Anthology
Now Sleeps the Crimson Petal	Quilter, R.	YS-B
		YS-C
		YS-S
		YS-T
Now Suffer Me, Fair Maiden (Er laube mir, fein's Mädchen)	Brahms, J., arr.	PS-4
Now the Dancing Sunbeams Play	Haydn, J.	NIE-M
Nuit d'Etoiles	Debussy, C.	GAS
		SVR-2
Nun Takes the Veil, A	Barber, S.	FBSS-2
Nun Wandre, Maria	Wolf, H.	50SS
		GAS
Nur Wer die Sehnsucht Kennt	Tchaikovsky, P.	FBSS-2
Nymphs and Shepherds	Purcell, H.	CCS-M
		FBMS-2
		GAS
		NIE-M
		YS-C
		YS-S
O bellissimi capelli	Falconieri, A.	CIS-2
O Calm of Night (In stiller Nacht)	Brahms, J.	ES-1
O Can Ye Sew Cushions	Britten, B.	NIE-C
O cessate di piagarmi	Scarlatti, A.	26ISAA
		28ISAA
		BS
		CIS
		CCS-B
O Come, O Come, My Dearest	Arne, T.	FBTS-2
O Death Now Come (Lasciatemi morire) from "Ariana"	Monteverde, C.	ES-2
O Del Mio Amato Ben	Donaudy, S.	FBTS-2
O del mio dolce ardor	Gluck, C. W. von	26ISAA
		28ISAA
		ASSV

Song Title	Composer	Anthology
O Divine Redeemer	Gounod, C.	SBSS
O genti tutte	Marcello, B.	ES
O komme, holde Sommernacht	Brahms, J.	50SS
O Lord, Have Mercy (Pietà, Signore)	Stradella, A.	ES-2
O Lovely Peace from "Judas Maccabaeus"	Handel, G. F.	ES-2
O Mistress Mine	Quilter, R.	ASSV
		ES
		FBBS
		NIE-Br
		SVR-2
O My Deir Hert	Howells, H.	NIE-C
O No, John!	English	AS-1
O Peace, Thou Fairest Child of Heaven	Arne, T.	FBSS
O rest in the Lord	Mendelssohn, F.	56S
		ES-1
		FBMS
O Saviour So Meek	Schemelli, G. C.	SS-3
O Saviour, Hear Me!	Gluck, C. W. von	FBSS-2
O Sing the Glories of Our Lord	Ridout, A.	SS-2
O sole mio	di Capua, E.	56S
O Thou Billowy Harvest-Field!	Rachmaninoff, S.	SBTS
O'er the Hills	Hopkinson, F.	FBBS-2
O, Bid Your Faithful Ariel Fly	Linley, T.	NIE-S
O, Divine Redeemer (Repentir)	Gounod, C.	ES-2
Obstination	Fontenailles, H.	ASSV
Offrande	Hahn, R.	GAS
Oft Have I Sighed	Campion, T.	NIE-C
Oh Sleep, Why Dost Thou Leave Me?	Handel, G. F.	ASSV
		ES
		FBMS

Song Title	Composer	Anthology
Oh Sleep, Why Dost Thou Leave Me?	Handel, G. F.	PS-3
		SR-2
Oh Sleep, Why Dost Thou Leave Me? from "Semele"		ES-2
Oh! Had I Jubal's Lyre		SBSS
Oh, Tis the Melody	Bayly, T. H.	PS-2
Oh, What a Beautiful City!	Boatner, E., arr.	FBSS
Oh, What a Beautiful Mornin'	Rodgers, R.	FBBS-T
Oh, When I Was in Love With You	V. Williams, R.	ES
Oklahoma	Rodgers, R.	FBBS-B
Ol' Jim	Edwards, C.	FBTS
Ol' Man River	Kern, J.	BR-B
Old Dan Tucker	Althouse, J., arr.	FSSS-2
Old Devil Moon	Lane, B.	BR-T
		FBBS-T
Old Folks at Home	Foster, S. C.	STC
Old Smokey	Rodgers, R.	FS
Old Woman and the Peddler, The	Christy, V. A., arr.	ES-1
Ombra cara, amorosa	Traetta, T.	CIS-3
Ombra mai fù	Handel, G. F.	ASSV
		BS
Ombra mai fu'		CCS-M
Omnipotence	Schubert, F.	NIE-S
Omnipotence (Die Allmacht)		55AS
On A Clear Day	Lane, B.	BR-B
On My Own	Schönberg, C. M.	FBBS-M
On Richmond Hill There Lives a Lass	Hook, J.	FBTS-2
On the Road to Mandalay	Speaks, O.	FBBS
On The Street Where You Live	Lerner, A. J.	BR-T
	Loewe, F.	FBBS-T

Songs by Title

Song Title	Composer	Anthology
On Wings of Song (Auf Flügeln des Gesanges)	Mendelssohn, F.	55AS
		ES-1
		NIE-T
		YS-B
		YS-C
		YS-S
		YS-T
Once in Love with Amy	Loesser, F.	FBBS-T
Once You Lose Your Heart	Gay, N.	FBBS-S
One Day at a Time	Sleeth, N.	WS
One Sweetly Solemn Thought	Ambrose, R. S.	56S
One who has yearn'd alone (Nur, wer die Sehnsucht kennt)	Tchaikovsky, P.	56S
Only Home I Know, The	Geld, G.	FBBS-T
Open Our Eyes	Macfarlane, W. C.	FBMS
Open Thy Lattice, Love	Foster, S. C.	55AS
Orpheus with His Lute	Coates, E.	FBTS
	Schuman, W.	15AAS
		20CAS
		FBSS-2
	Sullivan, A.	ES-2
		NIE-M
		SBMS
	V. Williams, R.	SBTS
		SS-4
Os Tormentos de Amor	Brasilian	FBBS-2
Out of My Dreams	Rodgers, R.	FBBS-S
Out of My Soul's Great Sadness (Aus meinen grossen schmerzen)	Franz, R.	AS-1
		ES-1
Ouvre Tes Yeux Bleus	Massenet, J.	SBTS
Over the Rainbow	Arlen, H.	BS
Owl Is Abroad, The	Smith, J. S.	NIE-Bs

Song Title	Composer	Anthology
Panis Angelicus	Franck, C.	FBTS-2
		PS-1
Part of the Plan	Sleeth, N.	SunS
Parting	Brahms, J.	NIE-M
	Gold, E.	20CAS
Passing By	Purcell, E. C.	55AS
		56S
		AS-1
		ES
		ES-1
		PS-1
		STC
		SVR-1
		YS-B
		YS-C
		YS-S
		YS-T
Pastoral, A	Carey, H.	55AS
		ES-2
		YS-C
		YS-S
	Veracini, F. M.	SBSS
Pastorale	Bizet, G.	SBMS
	Stravinsky, I.	50ASMR
Pastorale addane, A	Carey, H.	STC
Pastorella, spera, spera	Bononcini, M. A.	BS
Patiently Have I Waited	Saint-Saëns, C.	SBMS
Peace	Schubert, F.	NIE-M
Peace Prayer of St. Francis of Assisi	Christy, V. A., arr.	ES
Peaceful Evening (Beau Soir)	Debussy, C.	55AS
Peggy Mitchell	Duke, J.	CAS
People	Styne, J.	BR-MS
		FBBS-M
People Will Say We're In Love	Rodgers, R.	BR-S

Song Title	Composer	Anthology
Per la gloria d'adorarvi from "Griselda"	Bononcini, G.	26ISAA
		28ISAA
		GAS
		STC
Per Non Penar	d'Astorga, E.	FBSS-2
Per pietà	Stradella, A.	CIS-3
Petit Jean (Little John)	Champagne, C., arr.	SS-2
Petit Noël	Louis, E.	FBSS-2
Phillis Has Such Charming Graces	Young, A.	FBTS-2
Pie Jesu	Fauré, G.	ASSV
Piercing Eyes	Haydn, J.	BS
		FBSS
Pietà, Signore!	Stradella, A.	26ISAA
Pilgrim's Song	Tchaikovsky, P.	FBBS-2
		YS-B
		YS-T
Piper's Song	Inness, G.	SS-4
Pirate Song, A	Smith, W. R.	SS-3
Più Vaga e Vezzosetta	Bononcini, G.	SBBS
Plague of Love, The	Arne, T.	NIE-Br
		SBTS
Plaint	Czech	PS-3
Plaisir D'Amour	Martini, G.	SBBS
		STC
Plant a Radish	Schmidt, H.	FBBS-T
Pleading (Bitte)	Franz, R.	YS-C
		YS-S
		YS-T
Pleasure's Gentle Zephyrs Play	Handel, G. F.	SBMS
Policeman's Song, The	Sullivan, A.	SBBS
Polly Willis	Arne, T.	SBTS
Poor Boy	Schram, R. E., arr.	FSSS-2

Song Title	Composer	Anthology
Poor Wayfaring Stranger	Althouse, J., arr.	FSSS-2
Porque toco el pandero	Rodrigo, J.	CCS-M
Prairie Lily, The	Adaskin, M.	SS-4
Praise of God, The	Beethoven, L.	NIE-C
Praise the Lord	Sleeth, N.	SunS
Prayer	Guion, D. W.	FBMS
Prayer Perfect, The	Speaks, O.	FBSS-2
Pregúntale a Las Estrellas	Latin American	FBMS
Press Thy Cheek Against Mine Own	Jensen, A.	AS-2
Presto, presto lo m'innamoro	Mazzaferrata, G. B.	CIS-2
Pretty as a Picture	Herbert, V.	FBBS-2
Pretty Creature, The	Wilson, H. L., arr.	ES-1
		FBBS-2
Pretty Polly Oliver	Old English	AS-1
Pretty Ring Time	Warlock, P.	ASSV
Psalm XXIII	Creston, P.	20CAS
Psyche	Paladilhe, E.	55AS
Pur dicesti, o bocca bella	Lotti, A.	26ISAA
		28ISAA
		CIS
Put On a Happy Face	Adams, L.	BS
Quella Barbara Catena	Ciampi, F.	FBSS-2
Quella fiamma che m'accende	Marcello, B.	26ISAA
Qui sedes ad dexteram	Vivaldi, A.	ASSV
Rabbits	Belyea, W. H.	SS-Int
Rastlose Liebe	Schubert, F.	50SS
Rataplan	Grever, M.	50ASMR
Red, Red, Rose, A	Schumann, R.	FS
Reign Here a Queen within the Heart	Brahms, J.	NIE-T
Religion Is a Fortune	Johnson, H., arr.	FBTS
Remembrance	Ives, C. E.	FS
Rend'il Sereno Al Cigilo	Handel, G. F.	FBMS-2

Song Title	Composer	Anthology
Rend'il Sereno Al Cigilo	Handel, G. F.	SVR-2
Request (Bitte)	Franz, R.	AS-2
		PS-2
Requiem	Homer, S.	YS-B
		YS-T
Resolve, A (Obstination)	de Fontainailles, H.	56S
		SR-1
	Fontenailles, H.	ES-1
Rest, Sweet Nymph	Pilkington, F.	NIE-T
Return to the Mountain Home (Auf der Reise zur Heimat)	Grieg, E.	PS-4
Revenge! Timotheus Cries	Handel, G. F.	NIE-Br
Ridente la Calma	Mozart, W. A.	STC
Rio Grande	Dougherty, C., arr.	FBTS
Rise Up, Shepherd, and Follow	Hayes, M., arr.	SSS
Road to Home, The	Strickland, L.	AS-1
Roadside Fire, The	V. Williams, R.	FBBS-2
		YS-B
Rolling Down to Rio	German, E.	FBBS-2
		YS-B
		YS-T
Romance	Debussy, C.	ASSV
		FBSS-2
Rose and the Lily, The (Die Rose, die Lilie, die Taube)	Schumann, R.	PS-4
Rose Chérie, Aimable Fleur	Grétry, A. E. M.	SBTS
Rose Complained, The (es hat die Rosesich beklagt)	Franz, R.	AS-1
Rose Complains, The (Es hat die Rose sich beklagt)		PS-3
Rose Softly Blooming	Spohr, L.	FBSS
Rose, The	Clokey, J. W.	AS-1
	McBroom, A.	BS

Song Title	Composer	Anthology
Rose-Lipt Maid	Brahms, J., arr.	SS-5
Round of Greeting, A	Sleeth, N.	WS
Rovin' Gambler, The	Niles, J. J.	FBBS
Rugiadose, odorose	Scarlatti, A.	CIS
Ruhe, meine Seele!	Strauss, R.	50SS
Rules and Regulations	Wuensch, G.	SS-2
Russian Picnic	Enders, H.	FBTS-2
Sailor's Song	Haydn, J.	SVR-1
Sainte Marguerite	Willan, H., arr.	SS-4
Salvation Belongeth Unto The Lord	Greene, M.	SBBS
Sandman, The	German	PS-1
Santa Lucia	Italian	BS
Sapphic Ode (Sapphische Ode)	Brahms, J.	56S
		AS-2
		ES-2
		NIE-C
		YS-C
		YS-S
Sapphische Ode		ASSV
Scarborough Fair	Althouse, J., arr.	FSSS
	Smith, J. S.	FS
Schneeglöckchen	Schumann, R.	50SS
Se Florinda è fedele	Scarlatti, A.	26ISAA
		28ISAA
Se Florindo è fedele		ASSV
Se i miei sospiri	Fétis, F. J.	26ISAA
Se il mio nome saper	García, M.	ES
Se l'aura spira	Frescobaldi, G.	CIS
Se nel ben	Stradella, A.	ES
Se tu m'ami	Parisotti, A.	26ISAA
		CCS-S
	Pergolesi, G. B.	ASSV
		CIS-3

Song Title	Composer	Anthology
Se tu m'ami, se sospiri	Pergolesi, G. B.	28ISAA
Sea Fever	Andrews, M.	FBBS-2
	Ireland, J.	FBTS-2
Sea Moods	Tyson, M. L.	FBBS
Sea Wrack	Harty, H.	NIE-C
Sea, The	MacDowell, E.	55AS
		CCS-B
		ES-1
		FBBS
Sea-Shell	Engel, C.	50ASMR
Searching for a Gift	Telfer, N.	SS-Int
Sebben crudele	Caldara, A.	ASSV
Sebben, crudele		26ISAA
		28ISAA
		CCS-T
Secrecy (Verborgenheit)	Wolf, H.	ES-2
Secret Love	Czech	PS-1
Secret, The	Schubert, F.	NIE-T
Segador	Chávez, C.	CAS
Self-Banished, The	Blow, Dr. J.	NIE-Bs
Seligkeit	Schubert, F.	FBSS-2
Selve amiche, ombrose piante	Caldara, A.	CIS-3
Selve, voi che le speranze	Rosa, S.	28ISAA
		CIS
Seminarian, The	Moussorgsky, M. P.	GAS
Sento nel core	Scarlatti, A.	26ISAA
		26ISAA
		CIS-2
		FBTS
Separazione	Sgambati, G., arr.	FBMS-2
		FS
		GAS
Serenade	Gounod, C.	NIE-C

Song Title	Composer	Anthology
Serenade	Haydn, J.	SVR-2
		YS-T
Sérénade	Gounod, C.	ES
		FBMS-2
Serenade (La Serenata)	Tosti, F. P.	SR-2
Serenade (Liebes Mädchen, hör' mir zu)	Haydn, J.	PS-2
Serenade (Standchen)	Schubert, F.	ES-2
Serenade (Ständchen)		56S
Serenata Gitana	Sandoval, M.	GAS
Serenity	Ives, C. E.	15AAS
Shaded with Olive Trees	Greaves, T.	SS-6
Sharing it with me	Sleeth, N.	WS
She Never Told Her Love	Haydn, J.	55AS
		ES
		ES-1
		GAS
		SVR-1
		YS-C
		YS-S
She Wasn't You	Lane, B.	BR-T
She's Like the Swallow	Strommen, C., arr.	FSSS
Shenandoah	Althouse, J., arr.	FSSS-2
	Christy, V. A., arr.	ES-1
	Dougherty, C.	ASSV
	Dougherty, C., arr.	FBBS
Shepherd! Thy Demeanour Vary	Brown, T.	SBSS
		STC
Should He Upbraid	Bishop, Sir H.	NIE-S
Show Me	Loewe, F.	BR-MS
Si mes vers avaient des ailes	Hahn, R.	ES
Si Mes Vers Avaient Des Ailes!		FBSS
Si, tra i ceppi	Handel, G. F.	SBBS

Songs by Title

Song Title	Composer	Anthology
Si, tra i ceppi from "Bernice"	Handel, G. F.	GAS
Sigh No More, Ladies	Stevens, R. J.	FS
		NIE-T
Sight in Camp, A	Symons, D. T.	CAS
Silent Noon	V. Williams, R.	50ASMR
		CCS-M
		FBMS
		SVR-2
		YS-B
		YS-T
Silent Worship	Handel, G. F.	FBTS
Silver	Duke, J.	20CAS
Silver Swan, The	Gibbons, O.	55AS
Silver'd is the Raven Hair	Sullivan, A.	SBMS
Simple Gifts	American	ASSV
	Hayes, M., arr.	FSSS-2
	Holman, D., arr.	SS-3
Simple Joys of Maidenhood, The	Loewe, F.	FBBS-S
Simple Little Things	Schmidt, H.	FBBS-M
Sin tu amor	Sandoval, M.	50ASMR
		GAS
Since From My Dear	Purcell, H.	SBBS
Sing Noel	Sleeth, N.	SunS
Sing, Smile, Slumber (Sérénade)	Gounod, C.	55AS
Singer, The	Head, M.	NIE-S
Sir Niketty Nox	Marchant, S.	SS-4
Skye Boat Song	Lawson, M., arr.	SS-1
Slave, The (L'Esclave)	Lalo, É.	55AS
Sleep	Gurney, I.	NIE-T
sleep that flits on baby's eyes, The	Carpenter, J. A.	50ASMR
		FBMS-2
Sleep, Gentle Cherub, Sleep Descend	Arne, T.	SBSS

Song Title	Composer	Anthology
Sleep, Little Angel (Hajej, mujandilku)	Czech	PS-4
Sleeping Princess, The	Borodine, A.	50ASMR
Slighted Swain, The	Wilson, H. L., arr.	CCS-B
		FBBS-2
Slow March (Procession triste)	Ives, C. E.	SS-Int
Slumber Song	Gretchaninoff, A.	55AS
		AS-1
	Wagner, R.	NIE-M
Slumber-Song	Gretchaninoff, A.	50ASMR
Smiling Hours, The	Handel, G. F.	SBMS
Snowbells (Schneeglöckchen)	Schumann, R.	PS-1
Snowdrops	Prokofieff, S.	50ASMR
Snowflakes		50ASMR
So In Love	Porter, C.	BR-S
So Sweet Is Thy Discourse	Campion, T.	NIE-S
Solitary "Yes", A	Conti, F.	SS-5
Solitary One, The	Strauss, R.	NIE-Bs
Solveig's Song	Grieg, E.	NIE-S
Solvejg's Lied		56S
Solvejg's Song		CCS-S
		FBSS-2
Solvejg's Song (Solvejgs Lied)		AS-2
Sombre Woods (Bois épais)	Lully, J. B.	ES-1
Some Day	Ouchterlony, D.	SS-1
Some Enchanted Evening	Rodgers, R.	BR-B
		FBBS-B
Some Folks	Foster, S. C.	FS
		SS-1
Somebody	Schumann, R.	NIE-M
Something Wonderful	Rodgers, R.	FBBS-M
Sometimes a Day Goes By	Kander, J.	BS

Song Title	Composer	Anthology
Sometimes I Feel like a Motherless Child	Frey, H., arr.	SS-5
Somewhere	Bernstein, L.	BS
Song for Bedtime, A	McLean, H. J.	SS-3
Song Is You, The	Kern, J.	FBBS-M
Song of Devotion	Beck, J. N.	CAS
Song of India (Chanson indoue)	Rimsky-Korsakoff, N.	56S
Song of Khivria, The	Moussorgsky, M. P.	GAS
Song of Momus to Mars, The	Boyce, W.	FBBS-2
Song of Praise	Somer, H.	SS-2
Song of the Blackbird	Quilter, R.	SBSS
Song of the Carter, The	McLean, H. J., arr.	SS-1
Song of the Drummer, The (La chanson du Tambourineur)	French	PS-2
Song of the Flea, The	Beethoven, L.	NIE-Bs
Song of the Girl at the Window	Szymanowski, K.	50ASMR
Song of the Nightingale, The (Wehmut)	Schumann, R.	PS-4
Song of the Palanquin Bearers	Shaw, M.	20CAS
Song of the Seagull (Chant de la mouette)	McLean, H. J., arr.	SS-Int
Song of the Volga Boatmen	Russian	56S
Songs My Mother Taught Me (Als die alte Mutter)	Dvořák, A.	55AS
		56S
		ES-1
		ES-1
		YS-C
		YS-S
Sonntag	Brahms, J.	FBTS-2
Sonntags am Rhein	Schumann, R.	GAS
Soon It's Gonna Rain	Schmidt, H.	BR-B
		FBBS-B

Song Title	Composer	Anthology
Soul of My Heart (Alma del core)	Caldara, A.	PS-4
Sound of Music, The	Rodgers, R.	FBBS-S
Sound the Flute!	Dougherty, C.	CAS
Sound the Trumpet	Purcell, H.	ES-2
Speak Once More, Dear (Pur dicesti, o bocca bella)	Lotti, A.	ES-2
Spesso vibra per suo gioco	Scarlatti, A.	ES
Spirate Pur, Spirate	Donaudy, S.	SBTS
Spirit Flower, A	Campbell-Tipton, L.	FBSS-2
Splendour Falls, The	Walthew, R. H.	FBBS
Spring	Henschel, G.	NIE-S
Spring Day	McArthur, E.	STC
Spring Is at the Door	Quilter, R.	FBMS-2
Spring Is upon Us	Mendelssohn, F.	SS-6
Spring Morning, A	Carey, H.	SBSS
Spring Song	Schubert, F.	SS-2
Spring Song, A	Parry, C. H.	SS-6
Spring's Secret	Brahms, J.	NIE-M
Ständchen		50SS
		GAS
	Schubert, F.	FBTS
	Strauss, R.	50SS
Star vicino	Italian	26ISAA
	Rosa, S.	28ISAA
		CIS-2
Star-Spangled Banner, The	Smith, J. S.	FS
Starting Here, Starting Now	Shire, D.	BR-MS
Statue at Czarskoe-Selo, The	Cui, C.	FBMS
Stay Well	Weill, K.	BR-S
Steal Away	Burleigh, H. T., arr.	CCS-T
Still as the Night (Still wie die Nacht)	Bohm, C.	55AS
		AS-1
		ES-1

Song Title	Composer	Anthology
Still wie die Nacht	Bohm, C.	ASSV
Still wie die Nacht (Still as the Night)		STC
Stille Sicherheit	Franz, R.	FBTS-2
Stille Thränen	Schumann, R.	GAS
Stopping by Woods on a Snowy Evening	Sargent, P.	CAS
Stranger in Paradise	Wright, R.	FBBS-T
Strike the Viol	Purcell, H.	SVR-1
Such a li'l' fellow	Dichmont, W.	AS-1
Suleika's Song	Schumann, R.	NIE-S
Summer on the Prairie	Anderson, W. H.	SS-1
Summertime	Gershwin, G.	BR-S
Sun O'er the Ganges, The (Già il sole dal Gange)	Scarlatti, A.	PS-3
Sun Shall Be No More Thy Light, The	Greene, M.	SBSS
Sun Whose Rays, The	Sullivan, A.	SBSS
Sunday Morning	Brahms, J.	NIE-Br
Sunrise of The Ganges (Già il sole dal Gange)	Scarlatti, A.	55AS
Suo-Gan	Rowley, A., arr.	SS-3
Sure On This Shining Night	Barber, S.	15AAS
Surrey with the Fringe on Top, The	Rodgers, R.	FBBS-B
Swan, A	Grieg, E.	YS-C
Swan, A (Ein Schwan)		AS-2
		YS-B
		YS-S
		YS-T
Sweetest Flower That Blows, The	Hawley, C. B.	SVR-2
		YS-S
Swing Low, Sweet Chariot	American	BS
	Burleigh, H. T., arr.	CCS-B
Sylvelin	Sinding, C.	56S

Song Title	Composer	Anthology
Sylvelin	Sinding, C.	AS-2
		YS-C
		YS-S
		YS-T
Symphony in Yellow	Griffes, C. T.	20CAS
Take Me To The World	Sondheim, S.	BR-T
Take, O Take Those Lips Away	Beach, Mrs. H. H. A.	SBSS
Take, O, Take Those Lips Away	Thomson, V.	ES
Tally-Ho!	Leoni, F.	FBBS
Tanto sospirerò	Bencini, P. P.	CIS
Te Deum	Handel, G. F.	FBMS-2
		GAS
Te souviens-tu?	Godard, B.	SBMS
Tears of Autumn	Bártok, B.	50ASMR
Tell, O tell her	Rimsky-Korsakoff, N.	50ASMR
That Dirty Old Man	Sondheim, S.	BR-S
That's Good	Sleeth, N.	SunS
That's the Way It Happens	Rodgers, R.	FBBS-T
Then you'll remember me	Balfe, M. W.	56S
There is a Lady Sweet and Kind	Dello Joio, N.	STC
There Is Nothin' Like a Dame	Rodgers, R.	FBBS-B
There Stands a Little Man	MacMillan, E., arr.	SS-1
There Was a Mighty Monarch	Beethoven, L.	FBBS
There's Weeping in My Heart (Il pleure dans mon coeur)	Debussy, C.	PS-3
These Are They Which Came	Gaul, A.	SBSS
They Call The Wind Maria	Loewe, F.	BR-B
		FBBS-B
Think On Me	Scott, A. A.	ES-1
		SVR-1
		YS-C
This is the Day	Sleeth, N.	SunS
This Little Rose	Roy, W.	15AAS

Song Title	Composer	Anthology
This Little Rose	Roy, W.	FBMS
This Nearly Was Mine	Rodgers, R.	FBBS-B
Those Happy Days (O Schönezeit)	Goetze, C.	SR-1
Thou Art A Tender Blossom (Du bist wie eine Blume)	Schumann, R.	PS-4
Thou Art Near (Bist du bei mir)	Bach, J. S.	55AS
Thou art so like a flower (Du bist wie eine Blume)	Schumann, R.	56S
Thou Knowest Well (Tu to sai)	Torelli, G.	PS-3
Thou Shalt Bring Them In	Handel, G. F.	SBMS
Thou'rt Like a Lovely Flower	Schumann, R.	NIE-T
Thou'rt Like unto a Flower (Du bist wie eine Blume)	Rubinstein, A.	SR-1
Thou'rt Lovely as a Flower (Du bist wie eine Blume)	Schumann, R.	AS-1
		ES-1
Thoughts at Eventide	Mozart, W. A.	NIE-Bs
Three	Bowles, P.	SS-3
Three Fine Ships	Dunhill, T.	SS-5
Thrice Happy the Monarch	Handel, G. F.	NIE-Br
Through the Eyes of Love	Hamlisch, M.	FS
Thy Beaming Eyes	MacDowell, E.	YS-C
		YS-S
		YS-T
Thy Fingers Make Early Flowers	Dougherty, C.	20CAS
Thy Lovely Face	Schumann, R.	NIE-Br
Tiger, The	Thomson, V.	CAS
Till There Was You	Willson, M.	FBBS-S
Tirana del Caramba	Spanish	ES
Tis the Last Rose of Summer	Flotow, F.	CCS-S
To a Brown Girl, Dead	Bonds, M.	FS
To a Wild Rose	MacDowell, E.	FBSS-2
To Anthea	Hatton, J. L.	NIE-Br

Song Title	Composer	Anthology
To Be Near Thee (Star vicino)	Rosa, S.	ES-2
		PS-3
To brune øjne	Grieg, E.	ES
To Friendship (An die Freundschaft)	Haydn, J.	PS-2
To Mary	White, M. V.	NIE-T
To Music	Schubert, F.	NIE-C
To Music (An die Musik)		SR-1
To One Who Passed Whistling Through the Night	Gibbs, C. A.	20CAS
To Part, Ah Grief Unending (Ach Gott, wie weh tut Scheiden)	Brahms, J., arr.	PS-4
To the Beloved (An die Geliebte)	Beethoven, L.	PS-2
To The Birds (A des Oiseaux)	Hüe, G.	SBSS
To the Children	Rachmaninoff, S.	GAS
		NIE-M
		SBMS
To the Distant Beloved (An die fern Geliebte)	Beethoven, L.	ES-2
To the Faithless One		NIE-Br
To the Forest	Tchaikovsky, P.	NIE-Bs
To the Lute	Schubert, F.	SS-3
To the Moon		SS-4
To the Nightingale		SS-5
To the Queen of Heaven	Dunhill, T.	CAS
To the Sky	Strommen, C., arr.	FSSS
To the Sunshine	Schumann, R.	SS-6
To The Sunshine (An den Sonnenschein)		PS-1
To Thy Fair Charm	Colasse, P.	PS-1
To You	Strauss, R.	ES-2
To You (Zueignung)		56S
Tobacco	Hume, T.	NIE-Bs
Toglietemi la Vita Ancor	Scarlatti, A.	FBBS-2

Song Title	Composer	Anthology
Tomorrow	Strauss, R.	ES-2
Tomorrow (Morgen)		55AS
		PS-4
Total Eclipse	Handel, G. F.	SBTS
Tout Est Si Beau	Rachmaninoff, S.	SVR-2
		YS-T
Tra La La	Granados, E.	SS-5
Tragic Story, A	Mozart, W. A.	ES-1
Traum durch die Dämmerung	Strauss, R.	50SS
Trumpeter, The	Dix, J. A.	YS-B
		YS-T
Try Again	Sleeth, N.	WS
Try to Remember	Schmidt, H.	FBBS-B
Tschaikowsky	Weill, K.	BR-T
Tu lo sai	Torelli, G.	26ISAA
		26ISAA
		ASSV
		CIS
Turn Thee To Me	Dvorák, A.	SBTS
Turn Then Thine Eyes	Purcell, H.	FBMS
Turn Ye to Me	McLean, H. J., arr.	SS-4
	Scottish	BS
Tus ojillos negros	de Falla, M.	50ASMR
Tutu Maramba	Christy, V. A., arr.	ES-1
Twas April	Tchaikovsky, P.	NIE-T
Twas in the Lovely Month of May (Im wunderschönen Monat Mai)	Schumann, R.	AS-2
Twas in the Moon of Wintertime (Jesous Ahatouhia)	Willan, H., arr.	SS-1
Two Grenadiers, The	Schumann, R.	NIE-Bs
Two Grenadiers, The (Die beiden Grenadiere)		56S
		AS-2

Song Title	Composer	Anthology
Two Roads	Sleeth, N.	WS
Un certo non so che	Vivaldi, A.	CIS-3
		SBMS
Un Doux Lien	Delbruck, A.	FBTS-2
Un Moto Di Gioja	Mozart, W. A.	SBSS
Und willst du deinen Liebsten sterben sehen	Wolf, H.	50SS
Under the Green Wood Tree	Arne, T.	STC
Under the Greenwood Tree		NIE-T
Under the Rose	Fisher, W. A.	AS-1
Under The Tree	Schmidt, H.	BR-MS
Under the Willow Tree from "Vanessa"	Barber, S.	20CAS
Undiscovered Country, The	Berlioz, H.	NIE-M
Ungeduld	Schubert, F.	50SS
		ASSV
		GAS
Unicorn, The	Corigliano, J.	CAS
Vaaren	Grieg, E.	GAS
		SBMS
Vado ben spesso	Bononcini, G.	FS
Vaga luna	Bellini, V.	ES
Vagabond, The	V. Williams, R.	SBBS
Vaghissima Sembianza	Donaudy, S.	SBTS
Vain Suit, The	Brahms, J.	NIE-S
Valentine Wish, A	Sleeth, N.	WS
Valley, The	Gounod, C.	NIE-Bs
Veille Chanson	Bizet, G.	SBSS
Verborgenheit	Wolf, H.	50SS
		SBMS
Verdant Meadows	Handel, G. F.	PS-1
Verdant Meadows (Verdi prati)		ES-1
Verdant-Meadows		NIE-C

Song Title	Composer	Anthology
Vergebliches Ständchen	Brahms, J.	50SS
		SBSS
Vergin, tutt'amor/Solfeggio	Durante, F.	26ISAA
Vergin, tutta amor		CIS
Vergin, tutto amor		28ISAA
		ASSV
		CCS-M
Verrathene Liebe	Schumann, R.	FBBS-2
Verschwiegene Liebe	Wolf, H.	50ASMR
Very Commonplace Story, A (Ein sehr gewohnlische Geschichte)	Haydn, J.	ES-1
Very Ordinary Story, A (Eine sehr gewöhnliche Geschichte)		PS-4
Very Soft Shoes	Barer, M.	FBBS-T
Villanelle	Dell'Acqua, E.	SBSS
Violet, The	Mozart, W. A.	NIE-M
		SR-2
Violet, The (Das Veilchen)		56S
		SVR-2
Virgin, Fount of Love (Vergin, tutto amor)	Durante, F.	ES-2
Vittoria, mio core!	Carissimi, G.	26ISAA
		28ISAA
		ASSV
		CIS
		STC
Vive la Canadienne! (My Canadian Girl)	McLean, H. J., arr.	SS-1
Vocalise	Chenoweth, W.	CAS
	Rachmaninoff, S.	GAS
Volksliedchen	Schumann, R.	FBMS
Von ewiger Liebe	Brahms, J.	50SS
Vouchsafe, O Lord	Handel, G. F.	PS-4

Song Title	Composer	Anthology
Wade in the Water	Hayes, M., arr.	SSS
Waiting	Deis, C.	50ASMR
Waldeinsamkeit	Reger, M.	FBSS
Walk Together, Children	Christy, V. A., arr.	FS
Walking the Woods	Warlock, P.	NIE-Br
Wanderer, The	Schubert, F.	NIE-Br
Wanderer, The (Der Wanderer)	Haydn, J.	SVR-1
Wanderers Nachtlied	Schubert, F.	FBTS-2
		FS
Was Ist Sylvia?		FBBS-2
Watchman's Song	Hefferman, I.	PS-2
Water is Wide, The	British	BS
	Hayes, M., arr.	FSSS-2
Water Parted from the Sea	Arne, T.	FBSS
Wayfaring Stranger	Niles, J. J.	FBTS
We Kiss In A Shadow	Rodgers, R.	BR-T
		FBBS-T
We Sing to Him	Purcell, H.	SBMS
We're on Our Way	Sleeth, N.	WS
Weep No More	Handel, G. F.	FBMS-2
Weep No More from "Hercules"		ES-2
Weep You No More	Quilter, R.	CCS-T
		FBTS-2
Weep You No More, Sad Fountains		ES
Welcome Vision, A	Strauss, R.	NIE-Br
Well Thou Knowest	Torelli, G.	ES-2
Were My Songs With Wings Provided (Si mes vers avaient des ailes)	Hahn, R.	56S
		ES-2
What Are You Doing the Rest of Your Life?	LeGrand, M.	BS
What I Did For Love	Hamlisch, M.	BR-MS

Song Title	Composer	Anthology
What I Did for Love	Hamlisch, M.	FS
What if a Day	Campion, T.	FS
What Is A Woman?	Schmidt, H.	BR-MS
What Shall I Do to Show How Much I Love Her?	Purcell, H.	FBTS
What Songs Were Sung	Niles, J. J.	FBTS-2
What's the Use of Wond'rin'	Rodgers, R.	FBBS-M
When Daisies Pied	Arne, T.	FBSS-2
		NIE-M
When First My Old	Sullivan, A.	SBTS
When First We Met	Handel, G. F.	YS-B
		YS-T
When First We Met (Non Io dirò col labbro)		SVR-1
When from My Love	Bartlet, J.	BS
When I Am Dead, My Dearest	Coleridge-Taylor, S.	ES
When I Bring to You Colour'd Toys	Carpenter, J. A.	CAS
When I Have Often Heard Young Maids Complaining	Purcell, H.	FBMS-2
When I Have Sung My Songs	Charles, E.	15AAS
		FBSS
When I was a Lad I Served a Term	Sullivan, A.	SBBS
When I was One-and-Twenty	Gibbs, C. A.	CAS
When I was Seventeen	Swedish	AS-2
		FBSS-2
	Swedish Folk Song	YS-S
When Laura Smiles	Rosseter, P.	FS
When Love is Kind	Old English	AS-1
		PS-3
		STC
		YS-C
		YS-S
When My Soul Touches Yours	Bernstein, L.	CAS

63

Song Title	Composer	Anthology
When on the Surging Wave (Come raggio di sol)	Caldara, A.	ES-2
When the Children Are Asleep	Rodgers, R.	FBBS-T
When the Roses Bloom	Reichardt, L.	YS-C
		YS-S
		YS-T
When the roses bloom (Hoffnung)		56S
		SVR-1
		YS-B
When the Saints Go Marchin' In	Smith, J. S.	FS
When To Her Lute Corinna Sings	Campion, T.	55AS
When Yesterday We Met	Rachmaninoff, S.	NIE-Br
Where Corals Lie	Elgar, E.	NIE-C
		SBMS
Where E'er You Walk	Handel, G. F.	56S
		BS
		CCS-T
		ES-1
		FBTS-2
		NIE-T
		SR-1
		SVR-1
		YS-B
		YS-T
Where I Believed	Caccini, F.	SS-6
Where or When	Rodgers, R.	FBBS-M
Where the Bee Sucks	Arne, T.	NIE-S
	Sullivan, A.	NIE-S
Whispering Hope	Hawthorne, A.	56S
Whither	Schubert, F.	NIE-T
Whither Must I Wander?	V. Williams, R.	SBTS
Who Are You Now?	Styne, J.	BR-MS
Who Ever Thinks or Hopes of Love	Dowland, J.	NIE-M
Who Has Seen the Wind?	Kasemets, U.	SS-1

Song Title	Composer	Anthology
Who is Sylvia (Was ist Sylvia)	Schubert, F.	AS-1
Who is Sylvia?	Coates, E.	FBTS-2
	Schubert, F.	NIE-T
Who'll Buy My Lavender?	German, E.	YS-C
		YS-S
Why Blame Thee Now?	Schumann, R.	NIE-Br
Why Do I Love Thee?	Gibbs, C. A.	NIE-S
Why Do I Love You?	Kern, J.	FBBS-S
Why So Pale and Wan	Arne, T.	FBBS
Widmung	Franz, R.	BS
		FBBS
		FS
	Schumann, R.	50SS
		STC
Wie Melodien	Brahms, J.	FBMS
Wie Melodien zieht es mir		50SS
Wiegenlied	Flies, J. B.	STC
	Mozart, W. A.	STC
Wild Rose, The	Schubert, F.	NIE-M
Willow Song, The	Sullivan, A.	FBMS-2
		NIE-C
Wilt Thou Thy Heart Surrender	Giovannini	PS-3
(Willst du dein Herz mir schenken)		
Wind of the Western Sea	Peel, G.	FBMS
Wind of the Wheat	Phillips, M. F.	FBMS-2
Wind Speaks, The	Grant-Schaefer, G. A.	AS-1
Wind, The	Sharman, C.	SS-1
Winter Dedication, A	Strauss, R.	NIE-T
Winter's a Drag Rag, The	Sleeth, N.	WS
Wish, The	Chopin, F.	SS-4
Witchcraft		SS-3
With a Primrose	Grieg, E.	SS-6
With a Song in My Heart	Rodgers, R.	FBBS-S

Song Title	Composer	Anthology
With a Swanlike Beauty Gliding	Mozart, W. A.	NIE-C
With A Water Lily (Mit einer Wasser lilie)	Grieg, E.	PS-3
With Cunning Conniving (Che fiero costume)	Legrenzi, G.	ES-2
Without Thee!	Gounod, C.	NIE-S
Wohin?	Schubert, F.	50SS
Wonderful Day Like Today, A	Bricusse, L.	FBBS-T
Wonderful Guy, A	Rodgers, R.	FBBS-M
Woodland Journey, A (Waldfahrt)	Franz, R.	PS-1
Would You Gain the Tender Creature	Handel, G. F.	NIE-T
Wouldn't It Be Loverly?	Loewe, F.	FBBS-S
Wraith, The	Schubert, F.	NIE-Br
Wunderbar	Porter, C.	FBBS-B
Ye Twice Ten Hundred Deities	Purcell, H.	NIE-Br
Ye Verdant Hills	Handel, G. F.	NIE-T
Year's At the Spring, The	Beach, Mrs. H. H. A.	YS-S
Yesterday	Lennon & McCartney	FS
Yesterday I Loved You	Rodgers, M.	BR-T
Yo no se que decir	Mexican	ES
You and I	Sleeth, N.	SunS
You Never Stop Learning		WS
You'll Never Walk Alone	Rodgers, R.	BR-S
		FBBS-S
You've Got to Be Carefully Taught		FBBS-T
Young And Foolish	Hague, A.	BR-T
Younger Than Springtime	Rodgers, R.	BR-T
		FBBS-T
Youth and Love	V. Williams, R.	NIE-Br
Zärtliche Liebe	Beethoven, L.	ES
Zueignung	Strauss, R.	50SS

Songs by Composer

Composer	Song Title	Anthology
Abt, F.	Ave Maria	FBSS-2
Adam, A.	Cantique de Noël	STC
Adams, L.	Put On a Happy Face	BS
Adams, S.	Holy City, The	ES-1
Adaskin, M.	Prairie Lily, The	SS-4
Althouse, J., arr.	Amazing Grace	FSSS
		SSS
	Camptown Races	FSSS-2
	Cindy	FSSS-2
	Fire Down Below	FSSS-2
	Follow the Drinking Gourd	FSSS-2
	Homeward Bound	FSSS
	Let Us Break Bread Together	SSS
	Liza Jane	FSSS
	My Lord, What a Morning	SSS
	Nobody Knows the Trouble I've Seen	SSS
	Old Dan Tucker	FSSS-2
	Poor Wayfaring Stranger	FSSS-2
	Scarborough Fair	FSSS
	Shenandoah	FSSS-2
Alvarez, F.	La Partida	GAS
Ambrose, R. S.	One Sweetly Solemn Thought	56S
American	All the Pretty Little Horses	BS
	Black is the Color of My True Love's Hair	BS
	Every Night When the Sun Goes In	BS
	Fare You Well	SVR-1
	Jesus, Jesus, Rest Your Head	YS-B
		YS-C
		YS-S
		YS-T

Composer	Song Title	Anthology
American	Long Time Ago	BS
	Simple Gifts	ASSV
	Swing Low, Sweet Chariot	BS
Anderson, W. H.	Summer on the Prairie	SS-1
Andrews, M.	Build Thee More Stately Mansions	FBBS-2
	Sea Fever	FBBS-2
Archer, V.	April Weather	SS-6
Arlen, H.	I Had Myself A True Love	BR-S
	Over the Rainbow	BS
Arne, M.	Lass with the Delicate Air, The	56S
		STC
Arne, T.	Air from Comus	STC
		SVR-1
	Bacchus, God of Mirth and Wine	NIE-Bs
	Blow, Blow, Thou Winter Wind	55AS
		ASSV
		ES
		FBBS-2
	Fame's an Echo	FBTS-2
	Lass with the Delicate Air, The	ES-2
		SR-2
	Miller of Mansfield, The	FS
	Nature Beyond Art	SBTS
	O Come, O Come, My Dearest	FBTS-2
	O Peace, Thou Fairest Child of Heaven	FBSS
	Plague of Love, The	NIE-Br
		SBTS
	Polly Willis	SBTS
	Sleep, Gentle Cherub, Sleep Descend	SBSS
	Under the Green Wood Tree	STC
	Under the Greenwood Tree	NIE-T

Composer	Song Title	Anthology
Arne, T.	Water Parted from the Sea	FBSS
	When Daisies Pied	FBSS-2
		NIE-M
	Where the Bee Sucks	NIE-S
	Why So Pale and Wan	FBBS
Bach, J. S.	Bist du bei mir	FBMS-2
		STC
	Blessed Redeemer (Liebster Herr Jesu)	PS-4
	Come Sweet Repose	SR-2
	Come, Sweet Death (Komm, Süsser Tod)	PS-3
	Forget Me Not	FBTS-2
	Golden Sun Streaming (Die gold'ne Sonne, voll Freud' und Wonne)	PS-4
	If Thou Be Near (Bist du bei mir)	PS-2
	If Thou Thy Heart Will Give Me	SR-1
	Jesus, Fount of Consolation	FBBS-2
	Mein Glaubiges Herze	SBSS
	My heart ever faithful (Mein gläubiges Herze)	56S
	Thou Art Near (Bist du bei mir)	55AS
Bachelet, A.	Chère Nuit	GAS
Balfe, M. W.	Then you'll remember me	56S
Barber, S.	Crucifixion, The	15AAS
		FBSS
	Daisies, The	15AAS
		FBTS
	Monk and His Cat, The	15AAS
	Must the Winter Come so Soon?	CAS
	Nun Takes the Veil, A	FBSS-2
	Sure On This Shining Night	15AAS

Composer	Song Title	Anthology
Barber, S.	Under the Willow Tree from "Vanessa"	20CAS
Barer, M.	Very Soft Shoes	FBBS-T
Bart, L.	As Long as He Needs Me	FBBS-M
Bartlet, J.	When from My Love	BS
Bartlett, J. C.	Dream, A	YS-T
Bártok, B.	Tears of Autumn	50ASMR
Bayly, T. H.	Long, Long Ago	AS-1
		STC
	Oh, Tis the Melody	PS-2
Beach, Mrs. H. H. A.	Take, O Take Those Lips Away	SBSS
	Year's At the Spring, The	YS-S
Beaulieu, J.	Boy's Song, A	SS-3
Beck, J. N.	Song of Devotion	CAS
Becker, R.	Days of Spring, The (Frühlingszeit)	55AS
Beethoven, L.	Adelaide	NIE-T
	An die Geliebte	CCS-T
		FBTS-2
	Andenken	FBSS-2
	Bitten	FS
	Freudvoll und leidvoll from "Egmont"	GAS
	Glory of God in Nature, The (Die Ehre Grottes in der Natur)	55AS
	I Love thee (Ich liebe dich)	56S
		ES-1
		PS-2
	Ich Liebe Dich	FBSS-2
		STC
	Ich liebe dich so wie du mich	ASSV
	Kiss, The (Der kuss)	PS-3
	Know'st Thou the Land	NIE-M
	May Song	FBTS

Composer	Song Title	Anthology
Beethoven, L.	Mit Einem Gemalten Band	SBTS
	Nature's Adoration	SBBS
	Neue Liebe, neues Leben	GAS
	Praise of God, The	NIE-C
	Song of the Flea, The	NIE-Bs
	There Was a Mighty Monarch	FBBS
	To the Beloved (An die Geliebte)	PS-2
	To the Distant Beloved (An die fern Geliebte)	ES-2
	To the Faithless One	NIE-Br
	Zärtliche Liebe	ES
Bellini, V.	Vaga luna	ES
Belyea, W. H.	Lazy Summer	SS-5
	Rabbits	SS-Int
Bemberg, H.	Il Neige	SVR-2
Bencini, P. P.	Tanto sospirerò	CIS
Bennett, C.	Guitar Player, The	SVR-1
	Japanese Night Song	SVR-2
Benton, G.	How Do You Preach?	BR-T
Berger, J.	He or She That Hopes to Gain	ES
Berlin, I.	Girl That I Marry, The	FBBS-B
	My Defenses Are Down	FBBS-B
Berlioz, H.	Absence	GAS
	Undiscovered Country, The	NIE-M
Bernstein, L.	Extinguish My Eyes	CAS
	It Must Be Me from "Candide"	20CAS
	Somewhere	BS
	When My Soul Touches Yours	CAS
Besig, D., arr.	Cross the Wide Missouri	FSSS
Bishop, Sir H.	Deep in My Heart	NIE-M
	Lo! Hear the Gentle Lark	STC
	Love Has Eyes	55AS

Composer	Song Title	Anthology
Bishop, Sir H.	Love Has Eyes	ES
		ES-2
		FBSS
		PS-3
		YS-B
		YS-C
		YS-S
		YS-T
	Should He Upbraid	NIE-S
Bissell, K., arr.	Harbour Grace	SS-4
Bizet, G.	Habanera	56S
	Pastorale	SBMS
	Veille Chanson	SBSS
Bland, J. A.	Carry me back to old Virginny	56S
Bliss, A.	Buckle, The	20CAS
Blow, Dr. J.	Self-Banished, The	NIE-Bs
Boardman, R., arr	Cindy	SVR-2
Boatner, E., arr.	Oh, What a Beautiful City!	FBSS
Bock, J.	Far From the Home I Love	FS
Bohm, C.	Calm as the Night (Still wie die Nacht)	56S
	Still as the Night (Still wie die Nacht)	55AS
		AS-1
		ES-1
	Still wie die Nacht	ASSV
	Still wie die Nacht (Still as the Night)	STC
Bonds, M.	To a Brown Girl, Dead	FS
Bononcini, G.	Bella vittoria	ES
	Deh più a me non v'ascondete	CIS-3
	L'esperto nocchiero	CIS-2
	Love Leads to Battle	NIE-Bs
	Non posso disperar	26ISAA

Composer	Song Title	Anthology
Bononcini, G.	Per la gloria d'adorarvi from "Griselda"	26ISAA
		28ISAA
		GAS
		STC
	Più Vaga e Vezzosetta	SBBS
	Vado ben spesso	FS
Bononcini, M. A.	Pastorella, spera, spera	BS
Borodine, A.	Dissonance, A	56S
	Sleeping Princess, The	50ASMR
Bowles, P.	Cabin	15AAS
		20CAS
	Heavenly Grass	15AAS
		CAS
	Little Closer, Please, A	SS-6
	Three	SS-3
Boyce, W.	Song of Momus to Mars, The	FBBS-2
Brahe, M. H.	As I Went A-Roaming	FBMS-2
Brahms, J.	Alone in the Fields (Wäldeinsamkeit)	55AS
	An die Nachtigall	SBMS
	At Last	NIE-S
	Auf dem Kirchhofe	50SS
	Below in the Valley (Da unten im Tale)	PS-2
	Blacksmith, The	NIE-M
	Botschaft	50SS
		GAS
	Cradle Song (Wiegenlied)	AS-1
		PS-2
	Cradle-song (Wiegenlied)	56S
	Da unten im Tale	ES
	Der Gang Zum Liebchen	SBTS
	Der Jäger	GAS

Composer	Song Title	Anthology
Brahms, J.	Der Tod, das ist die kühle Nacht	50SS
	Die Mainacht	GAS
	Earth and Sky	NIE-Bs
	Far Down in the Valley (Da unten in Tale)	ES-1
	Garland, The	NIE-Br
	I Said I Will Forget Thee	NIE-Bs
	In Summer Fields (Feldeinsamkeit)	AS-2
	In Waldeseinsamkeit	50SS
	Is It Bliss or is It Sorrow?	NIE-T
	Love Song	NIE-T
	Love Song (Minnelied)	AS-2
	Love Triumphant	NIE-C
	Lullaby	NIE-S
		SR-1
	Meine Liebe ist grün	50SS
	Meine Lieder	GAS
	Message, The	NIE-Br
	My Dear One's Mouth is Like the Rose (Mein Mädel hat einen Rosenmund)	PS-2
	Night in May, A	NIE-C
	O Calm of Night (In stiller Nacht)	ES-1
	O komme, holde Sommernacht	50SS
	Parting	NIE-M
	Reign Here a Queen within the Heart	NIE-T
	Sapphic Ode (Sapphische Ode)	56S
		AS-2
		ES-2
		NIE-C
		YS-C
		YS-S
	Sapphische Ode	ASSV

Composer	Song Title	Anthology
Brahms, J.	Sonntag	FBTS-2
	Spring's Secret	NIE-M
	Ständchen	50SS
		GAS
	Sunday Morning	NIE-Br
	Vain Suit, The	NIE-S
	Vergebliches Ständchen	50SS
		SBSS
	Von ewiger Liebe	50SS
	Wie Melodien	FBMS
	Wie Melodien zieht es mir	50SS
Brahms, J., arr.	Now Suffer Me, Fair Maiden (Er laube mir, fein's Mädchen)	PS-4
	Rose-Lipt Maid	SS-5
	To Part, Ah Grief Unending (Ach Gott, wie weh tut Scheiden)	PS-4
Brasilian	Os Tormentos de Amor	FBBS-2
Bricusse, L.	Wonderful Day Like Today, A	FBBS-T
Bridge, F.	E'en As a Lovely Flower	NIE-T
British	Early One Morning	BS
	Water is Wide, The	BS
Britten, B.	O Can Ye Sew Cushions	NIE-C
Brook, H.	Colours	SS-Int
Brown, T.	Shepherd! Thy Demeanour Vary	SBSS
		STC
Burke, J.	Kelligrews Soiree, The	SS-2
Burleigh, H. T., arr.	Deep River	FBBS-2
	Didn't My Lord Deliver Daniel	CCS-S
	My Lord, What a Mornin'	CCS-M
	Nobody Knows the Trouble I've Seen	FBTS-2
	Steal Away	CCS-T

Composer	Song Title	Anthology
Burleigh, H. T., arr.	Swing Low, Sweet Chariot	CCS-B
Bury, W.	I Will Make You Brooches	SS-5
Caccini, F.	Where I Believed	SS-6
Caccini, G.	Amarilli	CIS
		PS-3
	Amarilli, mia bella	26ISAA
		28ISAA
		STC
	Amarylis	NIE-T
Cadman, C. W.	Little road to Kerry, The	AS-1
Calbreath, M. E.	My Love rode by	AS-1
Caldara, A.	Alma del core	26ISAA
		28ISAA
		CIS-2
		CCS-B
	As a Sunbeam at Morn	NIE-C
	As From the Sun A Ray (Come raggio di sole)	PS-4
	Come raggio di sol	26ISAA
		28ISAA
		CIS-2
	Sebben crudele	ASSV
	Sebben, crudele	26ISAA
		28ISAA
		CCS-T
	Selve amiche, ombrose piante	CIS-3
	Soul of My Heart (Alma del core)	PS-4
	When on the Surging Wave (Come raggio di sol)	ES-2
Campbell-Tipton, L.	Crying of Water, The	FBSS-2
	Spirit Flower, A	FBSS-2
Campion, T.	Jack and Joan	SS-2
	Oft Have I Sighed	NIE-C

Composer	Song Title	Anthology
Campion, T.	So Sweet Is Thy Discourse	NIE-S
	What if a Day	FS
	When To Her Lute Corinna Sings	55AS
Campra, A.	Charmant Papillon	FBSS-2
Carew, M.	Everywhere I Look!	FBSS
Carey, C.	Melmillo	NIE-M
Carey, H.	Pastoral, A	55AS
		ES-2
		YS-C
		YS-S
	Pastorale addane, A	STC
	Spring Morning, A	SBSS
Carissimi, G.	Deh, contentatevi	CIS-2
	Filli, non t'amo più	CIS-3
	I Triumph! I Triumph!	NIE-Bs
	No, no, non si speri!	CIS
	Vittoria, mio core!	26ISAA
		28ISAA
		ASSV
		CIS
		STC
Carpenter, J. A.	sleep that flits on baby's eyes, The	50ASMR
		FBMS-2
	When I Bring to You Colour'd Toys	CAS
Carter, E.	Dust of Snow	SS-5
Cavalli, F.	Donzelle fuggite	CIS
Cesti, M. A.	Ah! quanto è vero	CIS-2
	E dove t'aggiri	CIS-2
	Intorno All' Idol Mio	FBSS-2
Chaminade, C.	L'Anneau D'Argent	FBMS
Champagne, C., arr.	Marianne s'en va-t-au moulin (Marianne Went to the Mill)	SS-1
	Petit Jean (Little John)	SS-2

Composer	Song Title	Anthology
Chanler, T.	Grandma	FBSS-2
	Lamb, The	15AAS
		FBMS
Charles, E.	Clouds	FBMS-2
	Incline Thine Ear	FBTS-2
	Let My Song Fill Your Heart	FBSS
	My Lady Walks in Loveliness	FBTS
	When I Have Sung My Songs	15AAS
		FBSS
Chausson, E.	Hebe	FS
	Le Charme	SBBS
	Les Papillons	GAS
Chávez, C.	Segador	CAS
Chenoweth, W.	Vocalise	CAS
Chopin, F.	Lithuanian Song (Lithauisches Lied)	ES-1
	Maiden's Wish, The (Mädchen's Wunch)	SVR-2
	Wish, The	SS-4
	Witchcraft	SS-3
Christy, V. A., arr.	All Through the Night	ES-1
	Away Over Yandro	ES-1
	Beautiful Savior	ES-1
	Begone Dull Care	ES-1
	Cockles and Mussels	FS
	High Barbaree	FS
	Joshua Fit the Battle of Jericho	ES-1
	Lonesome Valley	ES-1
	Miller of Dee, The	ES
		ES-1
	Mister Banjo	ES-1
	Old Woman and the Peddler, The	ES-1
	Peace Prayer of St. Francis of Assisi	ES

Composer	Song Title	Anthology
Christy, V. A., arr.	Shenandoah	ES-1
	Tutu Maramba	ES-1
	Walk Together, Children	FS
Ciampi, F.	Quella Barbara Catena	FBSS-2
Cimador, G. B.	Bel nume	ES
Cimara, P.	Fiocca la neve	50ASMR
		SBSS
Clarke, R. C.	Blind Ploughman, The	FBBS
Clokey, J. W.	Rose, The	AS-1
Coates, E.	By Mendip Side	FBTS
	Green Hills O' Somerset, The	SBTS
	It Was a Lover and His Lass	FBTS-2
	Orpheus with His Lute	FBTS
	Who is Sylvia?	FBTS-2
Colasse, P.	To Thy Fair Charm	PS-1
Coleridge-Taylor, S.	When I Am Dead, My Dearest	ES
Conti, F.	Solitary "Yes", A	SS-5
Corigliano, J.	Christmas at the Cloisters	CAS
	Unicorn, The	CAS
Cornelius, P.	Christkind	SBTS
	Die Hirten	SBBS
	Die Könige	FBBS-2
	Ein Ton	FBBS-2
	Monotone (Ein Ton)	55AS
Coutts, G.	Highland Lullaby, A	SS-4
Crawley, C.	Elephants	SS-Int
	Horses	SS-Int
Creston, P.	Psalm XXIII	20CAS
Crist, B.	Blue Bird	SR-1
	Loch Lomond	SR-1
Crist, B., arr.	C'est Mon Ami	FBMS-2
Cui, C.	Statue at Czarskoe-Selo, The	FBMS

Composer	Song Title	Anthology
Curwin, C.	My Dog Spot	SS-2
Czech	Dance Song	PS-1
	Falling Dew, The	PS-1
	Maiden Tell Me	PS-1
	Plaint	PS-3
	Secret Love	PS-1
	Sleep, Little Angel (Hajej, mujandilku)	PS-4
d'Astorga, E.	Per Non Penar	FBSS-2
D'Hardelot, G.	Because	SVR-1
de Falla, M.	Asturiana	ES
	Tus ojillos negros	50ASMR
de Fontainailles, H.	Resolve, A (Obstination)	56S
		SR-1
De Luca, S.	Non posso disperar	28ISAA
Debussy, C.	Beau Soir	56S
		ASSV
		ES
	Bells, The (Les Cloches)	PS-4
	C'est l'extase langoureuse	50ASMR
	Clair de lune	GAS
	Evening Fair (Beau Soir)	ES-2
	Fleur des Blés	GAS
	Il pleure dans mon coeur	50ASMR
		STC
	Les Cloches	SBSS
	Mandoline	STC
	Nuit d'Etoiles	GAS
		SVR-2
	Peaceful Evening (Beau Soir)	55AS
	Romance	ASSV
		FBSS-2

Composer	Song Title	Anthology
Debussy, C.	There's Weeping in My Heart (Il pleure dans mon coeur)	PS-3
Deis, C.	Waiting	50ASMR
Deis, C., arr.	Loch Lomond	FBTS
Delbruck, A.	Un Doux Lien	FBTS-2
Delibes, L.	Bonjour Suzon	YS-S
	Bonjour, Suzon!	FBTS-2
Dell'Acqua, E.	Villanelle	SBSS
Dello Joio, N.	How Do I Love Thee?	STC
	There is a Lady Sweet and Kind	STC
Densmore, J. H.	If God left only you	AS-2
DeSylva, B. G.	Just Imagine	FBBS-S
di Capua, E.	O sole mio	56S
Dibdin, C.	Blow High, Blow Low	55AS
		FBBS
Dichmont, W.	Such a li'l' fellow	AS-1
Dix, J. A.	Trumpeter, The	YS-B
		YS-T
Donaudy, S.	O Del Mio Amato Ben	FBTS-2
	Spirate Pur, Spirate	SBTS
	Vaghissima Sembianza	SBTS
Donizetti, G.	La Zingara	SBSS
Dougherty, C.	K'e, The	20CAS
		FBSS
	Minor Bird, A	20CAS
	Shenandoah	ASSV
	Sound the Flute!	CAS
	Thy Fingers Make Early Flowers	20CAS
Dougherty, C., arr.	Across the Western Ocean	20CAS
		FBBS
	Blow, Ye Winds	FBBS-2
	Rio Grande	FBTS

Composer	Song Title	Anthology
Dougherty, C., arr.	Shenandoah	FBBS
Dowland, J.	Come Again, Sweet Love	55AS
		BS
		CCS-T
		FBTS
		NIE-Br
	Lowest Trees Have Tops, The	SS-4
	Who Ever Thinks or Hopes of Love	NIE-M
Drynan, M.	Fate of Gilbert Gim, The	SS-2
Duke, J.	I Watched the Lady Caroline	20CAS
	Just-Spring	STC
	Little Elegy	FBSS
	Loveliest of Trees	15AAS
		FBMS
	Peggy Mitchell	CAS
	Silver	20CAS
Duncan, C.	Beautiful	SS-4
Dunhill, T.	Cloths of Heaven, The	FBTS-2
	Curliest Thing, The	SS-1
	How Soft, upon the Evening Air	SS-3
	Three Fine Ships	SS-5
	To the Queen of Heaven	CAS
Duparc, H.	Extase	50ASMR
	L'Invitation au voyage	50ASMR
Durante, F.	Dance, Maiden, Dance (Danza, danza Fanciulla)	PS-3
	Danza, danza, fanciulla gentile	26ISAA
		28ISAA
		CIS-2
		STC
	Vergin, tutt'amor/Solfeggio	26ISAA
	Vergin, tutta amor	CIS
	Vergin, tutto amor	28ISAA

Composer	Song Title	Anthology
Durante, F.	Vergin, tutto amor	ASSV
		CCS-M
	Virgin, Fount of Love (Vergin, tutto amor)	ES-2
Dvořák, A.	God is My Shepherd	FBBS-2
	Hear My Prayer, O Lord	SBSS
	I will Sing New Songs	SBBS
	Lark, The	50ASMR
	Songs My Mother Taught Me (Als die alte Mutter)	55AS
		56S
		ES-1
		ES-1
		YS-C
		YS-S
	Turn Thee To Me	SBTS
Easson, J., arr.	Kitty of Coleraine	SS-4
Eccles, J.	Jolly Jolly Breeze, The	SBMS
Edwards, C.	Into the Night	FBSS
	Ol' Jim	FBTS
Elgar, E.	Is She Not Passing Fair?	NIE-T
	Where Corals Lie	NIE-C
		SBMS
Enders, H.	Russian Picnic	FBTS-2
Engel, C.	Sea-Shell	50ASMR
English	O No, John!	AS-1
Fain, S.	Love Is a Many-Splendored Thing	BS
Falconieri, A.	Bella porta di rubini	CIS-3
	O bellissimi capelli	CIS-2
Fauré, G.	Adieu	FBTS-2
	After a Dream (Après un rêve)	ES-2
	Après un rêve	50ASMR
		55AS

Composer	Song Title	Anthology
Fauré, G.	Après un rêve	ASSV
		BS
	Au bord de l'eau	SBMS
	Aurore	50ASMR
		GAS
	Chanson d'Amour	ES
	Cradles, The (Les Berceaux)	ES-2
		PS-2
	Dans les Ruines d'une Abbaye	GAS
	En prière	50ASMR
	Ici-Bas!	FBMS
		GAS
	Le Secret	FBBS
	Les berceaux	SBMS
	Les Roses D'Ispahan	SBBS
	Libera me	ASSV
	Lydia	FBTS
	Pie Jesu	ASSV
Ferrari, G.	Le Miroir	FBBS-2
		GAS
Fétis, F. J.	Se i miei sospiri	26ISAA
Fielitz, A. von	Die Stille Wasserrose	FBMS-2
Fisher, W. A.	I heard a Cry	AS-2
	Under the Rose	AS-1
Fletcher, P., arr.	Marianina	SS-Int
Flies, J. B.	Cradle Song	SS-Int
	Wiegenlied	STC
Flotow, F.	Tis the Last Rose of Summer	CCS-S
Fontenailles, H.	Obstination	ASSV
	Resolve, A (Obstination)	ES-1
Foote, A.	I'm Wearing Awa' to the Land O' the Leal	YS-B
		YS-C

Composer	Song Title	Anthology
Foote, A.	I'm Wearing Awa' To the Land O' the Leal	YS-S
		YS-T
Ford, N.	In a Simple Way I Love You	BS
Foss, H.	As I Walked Forth	SS-6
Foster, S. C.	Ah, May the Red Rose Live Always	ES
	Beautiful Dreamer	CCS-B
		SR-1
	Come Where My Love Lies Dreaming	STC
	Jeanie With the Light Brown Hair	STC
	My Old Kentucky Home	56S
	Old Folks at Home	STC
	Open Thy Lattice, Love	55AS
	Some Folks	FS
		SS-1
Fox, O. J.	I'll Never Ask You to Tell	SR-1
Franck, C.	Bread of Angels (Panis Angelicus)	ES-1
	Hear My Cry, O God	FBSS
	Lied	PS-2
	Panis Angelicus	FBTS-2
		PS-1
Franz, R.	Auf dem Meere	FBMS-2
	Dedication (Widmung)	55AS
		56S
		AS-1
		ES-1
		PS-2
		SR-1
		SVR-1
		YS-B
		YS-S
	Farewell! (Gute Nacht!)	PS-2

Composer	Song Title	Anthology
Franz, R.	Feast of Love (Liebesfeier)	PS-1
	For Music (Für Music)	AS-1
		PS-1
		YS-B
		YS-C
		YS-S
		YS-T
	Gute Nacht	ASSV
	Hark! How Still (Still Sicherheit)	PS-3
	His Coming (Er ist gekommen)	AS-2
	I wander this Summer morning (Am leuchtenden Sommermorgen)	AS-2
	Im Herbst	SBMS
	Mother, O Sing Me to Rest (Mutter, O Sing mich zur Ruh)	SVR-2
	Out of My Soul's Great Sadness (Aus meinen grossen schmerzen)	AS-1
		ES-1
	Pleading (Bitte)	YS-C
		YS-S
		YS-T
	Request (Bitte)	AS-2
		PS-2
	Rose Complained, The (es hat die Rosesich beklagt)	AS-1
	Rose Complains, The (Es hat die Rose sich beklagt)	PS-3
	Stille Sicherheit	FBTS-2
	Widmung	BS
		FBBS
		FS
	Woodland Journey, A (Waldfahrt)	PS-1
Fraser-Simson, H.	Christopher Robin is Saying His Prayers	FBMS

Composer	Song Title	Anthology
French	L'Amour de Moi	FBBS-2
	March of the Kings (La Marche des Rois)	PS-2
	Song of the Drummer, The (La chanson du Tambourineur)	PS-2
Frescobaldi, G.	Se l'aura spira	CIS
Frey, H., arr.	Sometimes I Feel like a Motherless Child	SS-5
Gaffi, B.	Luci vezzose	CIS-3
Ganz, R.	Memory, A	50ASMR
García, M.	Se il mio nome saper	ES
Gaul, A.	Come Ye Blessed	FBMS-2
	Eye Hath Not Seen	ES-1
		SBMS
	These Are They Which Came	SBSS
Gay, N.	Leaning on a Lamp-Post	FBBS-B
	Me and My Girl	FBBS-T
	Once You Lose Your Heart	FBBS-S
Geld, G.	Only Home I Know, The	FBBS-T
German	Drinking	NIE-Bs
	In einem Kühlen Grunde	FBBS-2
	Sandman, The	PS-1
German, E.	Rolling Down to Rio	FBBS-2
		YS-B
		YS-T
	Who'll Buy My Lavender?	YS-C
		YS-S
Germany	Mill-Wheel, The (Das Mühlrad)	PS-2
Gershwin, G.	I Got Plenty O' Nuttin'	BR-B
	Love Is Here to Stay	FS
	Summertime	BR-S
Gibbons, O.	Silver Swan, The	55AS
Gibbs, C. A.	Cherry Tree, The	FBMS

Composer	Song Title	Anthology
Gibbs, C. A.	To One Who Passed Whistling Through the Night	20CAS
	When I was One-and-Twenty	CAS
	Why Do I Love Thee?	NIE-S
Giordani, G.	Ah, Love of Mine (Caro mio ben)	55AS
	Caro mio ben	26ISAA
		28ISAA
		CIS
		CCS-T
	Dear Love of Mine (Caro mio ben)	ES-2
	Dearest, believe (Caro mio ben)	56S
Giordani, Tommaso	Dearest and Best (Caro mio ben)	SR-1
Giovannini	Wilt Thou Thy Heart Surrender (Willst du dein Herz mir schenken)	PS-3
Glick, S. I.	Baruch and Hamakom	SS-5
Gluck, C. W. von	Author of All My Joys	NIE-C
	Beloved Strand (Spiagge Amate)	PS-3
	O del mio dolce ardor	26ISAA
		28ISAA
		ASSV
	O Saviour, Hear Me!	FBSS-2
Godard, B.	Florian's Song (Chanson de Florian)	55AS
		AS-1
		ES-2
	Lullaby	56S
	Te souviens-tu?	SBMS
Goetze, C.	Those Happy Days (O Schönezeit)	SR-1
Gold, E.	Music, When Soft Voices Die	20CAS
	Parting	20CAS
Gonzalez, L. J.	Canción del niño por nacer	ES
Goodhart, A. M.	Bells of Clermont Town, The	FBBS
Goulding, E.	Lovely Song My Heart is Singing, The	FBMS-2

Songs by Composer

Composer	Song Title	Anthology
Gounod, C.	King of Love My Shepherd Is, The	FBBS
	O Divine Redeemer	SBSS
	O, Divine Redeemer (Repentir)	ES-2
	Serenade	NIE-C
	Sérénade	ES
		FBMS-2
	Sing, Smile, Slumber (Sérénade)	55AS
	Valley, The	NIE-Bs
	Without Thee!	NIE-S
Granados, E.	El Majo Discreto	FBSS
	El Majo Timido	FBMS
	El tra la la y el punteado	CCS-S
		FBSS
	Tra La La	SS-5
Grant-Schaefer, G. A.	Wind Speaks, The	AS-1
Greaves, T.	Shaded with Olive Trees	SS-6
Greene, M.	Salvation Belongeth Unto The Lord	SBBS
	Sun Shall Be No More Thy Light, The	SBSS
Gretchaninoff, A.	Hushed The Song of the Nightingale	SBMS
	Slumber Song	55AS
		AS-1
	Slumber-Song	50ASMR
Grétry, A. E. M.	Rose Chérie, Aimable Fleur	SBTS
Grever, M.	Júrame	56S
	Rataplan	50ASMR
Grieg, E.	Boat Song (Im Kahne)	55AS
	By the Brook	50ASMR
	Eros	GAS
	First Meeting, The (Erstes Begegnen)	PS-3
	First Primrose, The (Mit einer primula veris)	PS-1

89

Composer	Song Title	Anthology
Grieg, E.	Good Morning (God Morgen)	PS-4
	I love thee (Ich liebe dich)	56S
		ES-1
		SVR-1
		YS-S
		YS-T
	Jeg elsker Dig	ES
	Mother (Gamle Mor)	PS-4
	My Johann	FBSS
	Return to the Mountain Home (Auf der Reise zur Heimat)	PS-4
	Solveig's Song	NIE-S
	Solvejg's Lied	56S
	Solvejg's Song	CCS-S
		FBSS-2
	Solvejg's Song (Solvejgs Lied)	AS-2
	Swan, A	YS-C
	Swan, A (Ein Schwan)	AS-2
		YS-B
		YS-S
		YS-T
	To brune øjne	ES
	Vaaren	GAS
		SBMS
	With a Primrose	SS-6
	With A Water Lily (Mit einer Wasser lilie)	PS-3
Griffes, C. T.	Auf geheimem Waldespfade	50ASMR
	Symphony in Yellow	20CAS
Grossman, L.	Just One Person	BR-T
Guion, D. W.	All Day on the Prairie	FBTS
	At the Cry of the First Bird	20CAS
	Prayer	FBMS

Composer	Song Title	Anthology
Gurney, I.	Bonnie Earl of Murray, The	NIE-Br
	Sleep	NIE-T
Hageman, R.	Animal Crackers	FBSS-2
	At the Well	50ASMR
	Do Not Go, My Love	15AAS
		56S
		CCS-S
Hague, A.	It Wonders Me	BR-S
	Young And Foolish	BR-T
Hahn, R.	D'Une Prison	GAS
	Exquisite Hour (L'huere Exquise)	55AS
	Exquisite Hour, The (L'Heure exquise)	ES-2
	L'Heure exquise	50ASMR
		FBSS-2
	L'Huere exquise	ASSV
	Offrande	GAS
	Si mes vers avaient des ailes	ES
	Si Mes Vers Avaient Des Ailes!	FBSS
	Were My Songs With Wings Provided (Si mes vers avaient des ailes)	56S
		ES-2
Hamlisch, M.	Through the Eyes of Love	FS
	What I Did For Love	BR-MS
		FS
Handel, G. F.	Ah! mio cor	ASSV
		FBMS-2
	Ah, Poor Heart (Ah! mio cor from "Alcina")	ES-2
	Air (Care Selve)	PS-3
	Angels, Ever Bright and Fair	NIE-M
	Arm, Arm, Ye Brave	SBBS

Composer	Song Title	Anthology
Handel, G. F.	Art Thou Troubled?	SS-6
	Bel Piacere	FBSS
	Care Selve	NIE-S
		STC
		SVR-2
		YS-S
		YS-T
	Come and Trip It	FBSS-2
	Con Rauco Mormorio	SBMS
	Dank sei Dir, Herr	GAS
	Dearest Consort	NIE-C
	Dove Sei	ES
	Dove sei, amato bene? from "Rodelinda"	GAS
	Droop Not, Young Lover	NIE-Bs
	Dryads, Sylvans	NIE-M
	Endless Pleasure, Endless Love	NIE-S
	Friendship and Song	SVR-2
	Grace Thy Fair Brow (Rend' il sereno al ciglio)	PS-1
	He shall feed His flock	CCS-M
	Here Amid the Shady Woods	FBSS-2
		NIE-M
		PS-4
	How Art Thou Fall'n	NIE-Br
	How Changed the Vision	NIE-C
	I Shall Declare I Love Her	SS-4
	Leave Me in Sorrow (Lascia ch'io pianga)	PS-2
	Leave Me to Languish (Lascia ch'io pianga) from "Rinaldo"	ES-2
	Leave Me, Loathsome Light	FBBS

Composer	Song Title	Anthology
Handel, G. F.	Leave me, loathsome light! from "Semele"	GAS
	Let Me Wander Not Unseen	NIE-S
	Like The Shadow	SBBS
	Love That's True Will Live for Ever	NIE-Bs
	More Sweet is That Name	SBBS
	Ne'er Shade so Dear (Ombra mai fu)	PS-2
	O Lovely Peace from "Judas Maccabaeus"	ES-2
	Oh Sleep, Why Dost Thou Leave Me?	ASSV
		ES
		FBMS
		PS-3
		SR-2
	Oh Sleep, Why Dost Thou Leave Me? from "Semele"	ES-2
	Oh! Had I Jubal's Lyre	SBSS
	Ombra mai fù	ASSV
		BS
	Ombra mai fu'	CCS-M
	Pleasure's Gentle Zephyrs Play	SBMS
	Rend'il Sereno Al Cigilo	FBMS-2
		SVR-2
	Revenge! Timotheus Cries	NIE-Br
	Si, tra i ceppi	SBBS
	Si, tra i ceppi from "Bernice"	GAS
	Silent Worship	FBTS
	Smiling Hours, The	SBMS
	Te Deum	FBMS-2
		GAS
	Thou Shalt Bring Them In	SBMS
	Thrice Happy the Monarch	NIE-Br

Composer	Song Title	Anthology
Handel, G. F.	Total Eclipse	SBTS
	Verdant Meadows	PS-1
	Verdant Meadows (Verdi prati)	ES-1
	Verdant-Meadows	NIE-C
	Vouchsafe, O Lord	PS-4
	Weep No More	FBMS-2
	Weep No More from "Hercules"	ES-2
	When First We Met	YS-B
		YS-T
	When First We Met (Non Io dirò col labbro)	SVR-1
	Where E'er You Walk	56S
		BS
		CCS-T
		ES-1
		FBTS-2
		NIE-T
		SR-1
		SVR-1
		YS-B
		YS-T
	Would You Gain the Tender Creature	NIE-T
	Ye Verdant Hills	NIE-T
Harty, H.	Lullaby, A	NIE-S
		SBMS
	My Lagan Love	NIE-Bs
	Sea Wrack	NIE-C
Hatton, J. L.	Enchantress, The	NIE-C
	To Anthea	NIE-Br
Hawley, C. B.	Sweetest Flower That Blows, The	SVR-2
		YS-S
Hawthorne, A.	Whispering Hope	56S

Composer	Song Title	Anthology
Haydn, J.	Bald wehen uns des Frühlings Lüfte	FS
	Das Leben ist ein Traum	GAS
	Equals (Der Gleichsinn)	PS-4
	Hark! What I Tell to Thee	NIE-C
	In the Country (Die Landlust)	PS-1
	Mermaid's Song, The	FBSS
	My Mother Bids Me Bind My Hair	NIE-M
		SR-2
	My Mother Bids Me Bind My Hair (Bind' auf dein Haar)	56S
	My Mother Binds My Hair (Bind auf dein Haar)	YS-S
	Night is Falling	FBSS
	Now the Dancing Sunbeams Play	NIE-M
	Piercing Eyes	BS
		FBSS
	Sailor's Song	SVR-1
	Serenade	SVR-2
		YS-T
	Serenade (Liebes Mädchen, hör' mir zu)	PS-2
	She Never Told Her Love	55AS
		ES
		ES-1
		GAS
		SVR-1
		YS-C
		YS-S
	To Friendship (An die Freundschaft)	PS-2
	Very Commonplace Story, A (Ein sehr gewohnlische Geschichte)	ES-1
	Very Ordinary Story, A (Eine sehr gewöhnliche Geschichte)	PS-4
	Wanderer, The (Der Wanderer)	SVR-1

Composer	Song Title	Anthology
Hayes, M., arr.	Rise Up, Shepherd, and Follow	SSS
	Simple Gifts	FSSS-2
	Wade in the Water	SSS
	Water is Wide, The	FSSS-2
Head, M.	Money, O!	NIE-Bs
	Singer, The	NIE-S
Hefferman, I.	Watchman's Song	PS-2
Helyer, M.	Ferryman, The	SS-Int
Henderson, R. W.	Four Is Wonderful	SS-3
Henschel, G.	Morning Hymn	YS-S
	Morning Hymn (Morgen-Hymne)	SVR-2
		YS-C
	No Embers, nor a Firebrand (Kein Feuer, Keine Kohle)	AS-2
	Spring	NIE-S
Herbert, V.	Art Is Calling For Me	SBSS
	Every Day is Ladies' Day with Me	FBTS-2
	Pretty as a Picture	FBBS-2
Hilton, J., arr.	Come Follow!	FS
Hindemith, P.	Echo	ES
Hoiby, L.	An Immorality	CAS
Holman, D., arr.	Simple Gifts	SS-3
Holst, G.	Heart Worships, The	FBBS-2
Homer, S.	Country of the Camisards, The	FS
	Requiem	YS-B
		YS-T
Hook, J.	On Richmond Hill There Lives a Lass	FBTS-2
Hopkinson, F.	Beneath a Weeping Willow's Shade	55AS
		BS
		FBMS-2
	O'er the Hills	FBBS-2

Composer	Song Title	Anthology
Horn, C. E.	Cherry Ripe	SR-1
	I've Been Roaming	55AS
		YS-C
		YS-S
Horrocks, A. E.	Bird and the Rose, The	SR-1
Howells, H.	Girls' Song	NIE-M
	O My Deir Hert	NIE-C
Hüe, G.	I Wept, Beloved, As I Dreamed (J'ai pleurè un rêve)	ES-2
	J'ai pleuré en rêve	50ASMR
	To The Birds (A des Oiseaux)	SBSS
Hughes, H., arr.	Down By the Sally Gardens	CCS-T
		FBTS-2
	Early One Morning	FS
	I Know Where I'm Goin'	FS
Hume, T.	Tobacco	NIE-Bs
Inness, G.	Piper's Song	SS-4
Ireland, J.	I Have Twelve Oxen	NIE-S
	Memory	SBBS
	Sea Fever	FBTS-2
Irish	Cockles and Mussels	SVR-1
	Danny Boy	FBMS-2
	Down by the Salley Gardens	BS
	Eileen Aroon	PS-2
	Johnny Doolan's Cat	BS
	Juniper Tree, The	BS
	Kitty of Colerain	PS-3
	Last Rose of Summer, The	56S
	Londonderry Air	56S
	Minstrel Boy, The	BS
	My Love's an Arbutus	AS-1
	Next Market Day, The	BS

Composer	Song Title	Anthology
Italian	Cicerenella	PS-4
	Nina	26ISAA
	Santa Lucia	BS
	Star vicino	26ISAA
Ives, C. E.	At Sea	ES
	Evening	ES
	Remembrance	FS
	Serenity	15AAS
	Slow March (Procession triste)	SS-Int
Jensen, A.	Press Thy Cheek Against Mine Own	AS-2
Johnson, H., arr.	My Lord, What a Mornin'	FBTS
	Religion Is a Fortune	FBTS
Kander, J.	And All That Jazz	BR-MS
	My Own Space	BR-MS
	Sometimes a Day Goes By	BS
Karlin, F.	Come Saturday Morning	BS
Kasemets, U.	Eletelephony	SS-Int
	Who Has Seen the Wind?	SS-1
Kasha, A.	Candle on the Water	BS
Keel, J. F., arr.	Jardin d'amour	SS-5
Kern, J.	All the Things You Are	FBBS-S
	Can't Help Lovin' Dat Man	BR-S
		FBBS-S
	Look for the Silver Lining	FBBS-S
	Make Believe	FBBS-S
	Ol' Man River	BR-B
	Song Is You, The	FBBS-M
	Why Do I Love You?	FBBS-S
Kern, P., arr.	Angels through the Night	FSSS
	Ezekiel's Wheel	SSS
	Greensleeves	FSSS
	Little David, Play on Your Harp	SSS

Composer	Song Title	Anthology
Kingsford, C.	Down Harley Street	CAS
		FBBS-2
Kingsley, H.	Green Dog, The	20CAS
		FBSS
Kjerulf, H.	Last Night	55AS
		SR-1
Knowles, J., arr.	Danny Boy	FSSS
Kurth, B.	Circus Clown, The	SS-Int
Lalo, É.	Captive, The (L'Esclave)	ES-2
	L'Esclave	50ASMR
	Slave, The (L'Esclave)	55AS
Lane, B.	He Wasn't You She Wasn't You	FS
	Look To The Rainbow	BR-MS
		FBBS-S
	Old Devil Moon	BR-T
		FBBS-T
	On A Clear Day	BR-B
	She Wasn't You	BR-T
Lane, R.	Farmer by the Sea	ES
Lassen, E.	It was a Dream	55AS
Latin American	Encantadora Maria	FBBS
	La Paloma Blanca	FBBS
	La Seña	FBTS
	Noche Serena	FBTS
	Pregúntale a Las Estrellas	FBMS
Latouche, J.	Lazy Afternoon	FBBS-M
Lawes, H.	Bid me To Live	55AS
Lawson, M., arr.	Skye Boat Song	SS-1
Lefevre, J.	L'Amour de mois de mai	ES
Lefévre, J.	L'Amour au mois de mai	ES
LeGrand, M.	What Are You Doing the Rest of Your Life?	BS

Composer	Song Title	Anthology
Legrenzi. G.	Che fiero costume	26ISAA
		28ISAA
		CIS-2
	With Cunning Conniving (Che fiero costume)	ES-2
Lehmann, L.	Cuckoo, The	SVR-1
		YS-C
		YS-S
	Evensong	FBMS
Leigh, M.	Impossible Dream, The	FBBS-B
Lennon & McCartney	Yesterday	FS
Leoncavallo, R.	Mattinata	GAS
		SBBS
Leoni, F.	Little China Figure, A	FBSS
	Tally-Ho!	FBBS
Lerner, A. J.	On The Street Where You Live	BR-T
Leveridge, R.	Love Is a Bauble	PS-3
Liddle, S.	How Lovely Are Thy Dwellings	FBSS-2
	Lord Is My Shepherd, The	SBTS
Liliuokalani, Queen	Aloha oe	56S
Linley, T.	No Flower That Blows	FBSS-2
	O, Bid Your Faithful Ariel Fly	NIE-S
Liszt, F.	Du bist wie eine Blume	FBBS-2
	Es Muss ein Wunderbares Sein	FBMS-2
	It Must Be Wonderful Indeed (Es muss ein Wunderbares sein)	PS-1
	It Must Be Wonderful, Indeed (Es muss ein Wunderbares sein)	55AS
	Loreley, The	NIE-S
	Mignon's Song	NIE-C
Loder, E. J.	Brooklet, The	NIE-T
Loeffler, C. M.	Adieu pour jamais	50ASMR
	Les Paons	50ASMR

Composer	Song Title	Anthology
Loesser, F.	I Believe In You	FBBS-T
	I'll Know	FBBS-S
	Once in Love with Amy	FBBS-T
Loewe, C.	Edward	NIE-Br
		STC
Loewe, F.	Almost Like Being in Love	BS
	Earth and Other Minor Things, The	FBBS-M
	Get Me to the Church on Time	FBBS-B
	How to Handle a Woman	FBBS-B
	I Could Have Danced All Night	FBBS-S
	I Loved You Once In Silence	BR-S
		FBBS-M
	I Talk to the Trees	FBBS-B
	I've Grown Accustomed To Her Face	BR-B
		FBBS-B
	If Ever I Would Leave You	BR-B
		FBBS-B
	On the Street Where You Live	FBBS-T
	Show Me	BR-MS
	Simple Joys of Maidenhood, The	FBBS-S
	They Call The Wind Maria	BR-B
		FBBS-B
	Wouldn't It Be Loverly?	FBBS-S
Lohr, H.	Little Irish Girl, The	SVR-2
		YS-B
		YS-C
		YS-S
		YS-T
Lotti, A.	Pur dicesti, o bocca bella	26ISAA
		28ISAA
		CIS

Composer	Song Title	Anthology
Lotti, A.	Speak Once More, Dear (Pur dicesti, o bocca bella)	ES-2
Louis, E.	Petit Noël	FBSS-2
Lowry, R. R.	At the River	FS
Luca, S. De	Non posso disperar	GAS
Lully, J. B.	All Your Shades	NIE-Bs
	Bois épais	ASSV
		ES
		FBBS-2
		SVR-2
	By the Light of The Moon (Au clair de la lune)	PS-2
	Sombre Woods (Bois épais)	ES-1
MacDowell, E.	Blue-Bell, The	CCS-M
		FBMS-2
	Long Ago	SBTS
	Sea, The	55AS
		CCS-B
		ES-1
		FBBS
	Thy Beaming Eyes	YS-C
		YS-S
		YS-T
	To a Wild Rose	FBSS-2
Macfarlane, W. C.	Open Our Eyes	FBMS
MacMillan, E., arr.	Bells of Aberdovey, The	SS-2
	Golden Slumbers	SS-3
	Mon doux berger/Sweet Shepherd	SS-3
	My Love's an Arbutus	SS-3
	There Stands a Little Man	SS-1
Mahler, G.	Ich atmet' einen linden Duft	STC
Malotte, A. H.	Beatitudes, The	FBSS
Mana-Zucca	First Concert, The	FBBS-2

Composer	Song Title	Anthology
Mancini, H.	Moon River	BS
Manney, C. F.	Consecration	AS-2
Marcello, B.	Il mio bel foco	28ISAA
	O genti tutte	ES
	Quella fiamma che m'accende	26ISAA
Marchant, S.	Sir Niketty Nox	SS-4
Martin, E.	Come to the Fair	FBSS-2
Martini, G.	Joy of Love, The (Plaisir d'amour)	55AS
		ES
	Joys of Love, The (Plaisir d'amour)	ES-1
	Plaisir D'Amour	SBBS
		STC
Massenet, J.	Bonne Nuit	FBSS
	Crépuscule	FBMS-2
	Elégie	56S
		FBMS-2
	Elegy (Elégie)	55AS
		ES-2
	Ouvre Tes Yeux Bleus	SBTS
Mattei, T.	Non è ver!	GAS
		STC
Mazzaferrata, G. B.	Presto, presto lo m'innamoro	CIS-2
McArthur, E.	Spring Day	STC
McBroom, A.	Rose, The	BS
McLean, H. J.	If All the Seas Were One Sea	SS-6
	Song for Bedtime, A	SS-3
McLean, H. J., arr.	Look at Me, My little dear	SS-2
	Song of the Carter, The	SS-1
	Song of the Seagull (Chant de la mouette)	SS-Int
	Turn Ye to Me	SS-4
	Vive la Canadienne! (My Canadian Girl)	SS-1

Composer	Song Title	Anthology
Mellish, Col. R.	Drink to Me Only With Thine Eyes	ES-1
Mendelssohn, F.	Be Thou Faithful Unto Death	SBTS
	Cradle Song	NIE-C
	Das Erste Veilchen	FBMS-2
	Der Blumenstrauss	FBMS
	Der Mond	FBTS
	Gruss	ES
	I Am a Roamer	NIE-Bs
	Jagdlied	FBBS
	Lone and Joyless	NIE-S
	Lord God of Abraham	SBBS
	Minnelied	FBSS
	O rest in the Lord	56S
		ES-1
		FBMS
	On Wings of Song (Auf Flügeln des Gesanges)	55AS
		ES-1
		NIE-T
		YS-B
		YS-C
		YS-S
		YS-T
	Spring Is upon Us	SS-6
Menotti, G. C.	Black Swan, The from "The Medium"	20CAS
	Hero, The	20CAS
	Lullaby from "The Consul"	CAS
Metcalf, J. W.	Night Has A Thousand Eyes, The	SVR-2
		YS-T
Mexican	El Trobador	FBTS-2
	Yo no se que decir	ES

Composer	Song Title	Anthology
Milhaud, D.	La pomme et l'escargot (The Apple and the Snail)	SS-1
Miliken, R. A.	Last Rose of Summer, The	FBSS-2
Moffat, A., arr.	Fairy's Lullaby, The	FS
Molloy, J. L.	Love's Old, Sweet Song	56S
Monro, G.	My Lovely Celia	55AS
		ES-2
		FBTS-2
		FS
		STC
		SVR-1
		YS-T
Monteverde, C.	Ahi, troppo è duro	CIS
	Lasciatemi morire	FS
	Lasciatemi morire!	26ISAA
		28ISAA
		ASSV
	Lascitemi morire	CIS
	O Death Now Come (Lasciatemi morire) from "Ariana"	ES-2
Moore, D.	Dove Song, The from "The Wings of the Dove"	CAS
	Letter Song	BR-S
Morley, T.	It Was a Lover and His Lass	CCS-S
		FS
		STC
	Now is the Month of Maying	55AS
		CCS-M
		SS-2
Moross, J.	Lazy Afternoon	BR-MS
Moussorgsky, M. P.	Cradlesong of the Poor	55AS
	Evening Prayer, The	50ASMR
	Seminarian, The	GAS
	Song of Khivria, The	GAS

Composer	Song Title	Anthology
Mozart, W. A.	Adieu	NIE-C
	Ave Verum	FBMS-2
	Cradle Song	PS-1
	How Calm Is My Spirit	NIE-S
	Longing For Spring	PS-1
	Lullaby (Wiegenlied)	55AS
		SR-1
	Ridente la Calma	STC
	Thoughts at Eventide	NIE-Bs
	Tragic Story, A	ES-1
	Un Moto Di Gioja	SBSS
	Violet, The	NIE-M
		SR-2
	Violet, The (Das Veilchen)	56S
		SVR-2
	Wiegenlied	STC
	With a Swanlike Beauty Gliding	NIE-C
Mueller, C. F.	Create in Me a Clean Heart, O God	FBBS
Myers, G., arr.	Jesus Walked This Lonesome Valley	FBMS
	Let Us Break Bread Together	FBBS
Neidlinger, W. H.	Birthday of a King, The	FBTS-2
Nevin, E.	Little Boy Blue	ES-1
Nielsen, C.	Fiddler, The	SS-2
Niles, J. J.	Black Dress, The	FBTS
	Black Is the Color of My True Love's Hair	FBTS
	Carol of the Birds, The	FBMS-2
	Go 'Way from My Window	FBMS
	I Wonder As I Wander	FBBS-2
	Lass from the Low Countree, The	15AAS
		FBMS
	Rovin' Gambler, The	FBBS

Composer	Song Title	Anthology
Niles, J. J.	Wayfaring Stranger	FBTS
	What Songs Were Sung	FBTS-2
Nyklicek, G.	Little Red Lark, The	SVR-2
O'Hara, G.	Give a Man a Horse He Can Ride	CCS-B
		FBBS-2
O'Neill, J., arr.	Farewell, Lad	FSSS
Obradors, F. J.	Con amores, la mi madre	BS
Offenbach, J.	Barcarolle	56S
Ohlin, C. P.	I Like Dogs! (J'aime les chiens!)	SS-Int
Old English	Alleluia!	SBTS
	Come Let's be Merry	YS-B
	Down Among the Dead Men	ASSV
		NIE-Bs
	Drink to me only with thine eyes	56S
		STC
	Have You Seen But a Bright Lily Grow?	ES
	Have You Seen But a White Lillie Grow?	ASSV
		CCS-T
		PS-3
	Have You Seen But a White Lily Grow	FBSS
	Have You Seen But the White Lillie Grow?	SR-2
	Have You Seen But the Whyte Lillie Grow?	STC
	Pretty Polly Oliver	AS-1
	When Love is Kind	AS-1
		PS-3
		STC
		YS-C
		YS-S
Old Welsh	All Through the Night	CCS-B

Composer	Song Title	Anthology
Old Welsh	All through the Night	FBTS
Ornadel, C.	If I Ruled The World	BR-T
		FBBS-M
Ouchterlony, D.	Cradle Carol (Berceuse)	SS-4
	Gloria Deo	SS-3
	Some Day	SS-1
Paisiello, G.	Chi vuol la zingarella	ES
		FBMS
	Nel cor più non mi sento	26ISAA
		26ISAA
		CIS-3
		CCS-S
		FS
Paladilhe, E.	Psyche	55AS
Palmgren, S.	Mother	50ASMR
Parisotti, A.	Se tu m'ami	26ISAA
		CCS-S
Parke, D.	In Old Donegal	SS-2
Parry, C. H.	Love is a Bable	SBBS
	My Heart Is Like a Singing Bird	SBSS
	Spring Song, A	SS-6
Paton, J. G., arr.	Aupres de ma Blonde	FS
	El Tecolote	FS
	Greensleeves	ES
Payne, J., arr.	Crucifixion	FBMS
	Lord, I Want to Be a Christian	FBBS
Peel, G.	Wind of the Western Sea	FBMS
Pergolesi, G. B.	Gentle Shepherd	NIE-S
	If Thou Love Me (Se tu m'ami)	55AS
	Nina	28ISAA
		ES-2
		FS
		SR-2

Composer	Song Title	Anthology
Pergolesi, G. B.	Nina (Tre Giorni)	CIS
	Se tu m'ami	ASSV
		CIS-3
	Se tu m'ami, se sospiri	28ISAA
Peri, J.	Invocazione de Orfeo	CIS
Persichetti, V.	I'm Nobody	ES
Perti, J. A.	Begli occhi, io non mi pento	CIS-3
Phillips, M. F.	Wind of the Wheat	FBMS-2
Pierné, G.	En Barque	GAS
Pilkington, F.	Rest, Sweet Nymph	NIE-T
Porter, C.	Brush Up Your Shakespeare	FS
	I Love Paris	FBBS-M
	So In Love	BR-S
	Wunderbar	FBBS-B
Prokofieff, S.	Snowdrops	50ASMR
	Snowflakes	50ASMR
Provenzale, F.	Deh, rendetemi	CIS-2
Purcell, E. C.	Passing By	55AS
		56S
		AS-1
		ES
		ES-1
		PS-1
		STC
		SVR-1
		YS-B
		YS-C
		YS-S
		YS-T
Purcell, H.	Arise Ye Subterranean Winds	NIE-Bs
		SBBS
	Arrival of the Royal Barge, The	SVR-1
	Come Unto These Yellow Sands	55AS

Composer	Song Title	Anthology
Purcell, H.	Come Unto These Yellow Sands	ES-2
		SS-6
	Dido's Lament	ASSV
	Dido's Lament from "Dido and Aeneas"	ES-2
	Hark! The Echoing Air	SBSS
	Hear! Ye Gods of Britain	NIE-Bs
	Hush, Be Silent	SVR-1
	I Attempt From Love's Sickness to Fly	ASSV
		CCS-S
		ES
		ES-2
		FBTS
		NIE-M
	I Love and I Must	FBTS
	I'll Sail Upon The Dog Star	SBTS
	I'll Sail upon the Dog-Star	NIE-T
	If Music Be the Food of Love	SVR-1
	Kind Fortune Smiles	SBMS
	Knotting Song, The	NIE-T
	Let Each Gallant Heart	SBBS
	Let the Dreadful Engines	NIE-Br
	Let Us Dance, Let Us Sing	FBSS
	Love Quickly is Pall'd	FBTS-2
	Man Is for the Woman Made	FS
	Mystery's Song	FBMS-2
	Next, Winter Comes Slowly	FBBS
	Nymphs and Shepherds	CCS-M
		FBMS-2
		GAS
		NIE-M
		YS-C

Composer	Song Title	Anthology
Purcell, H.	Nymphs and Shepherds	YS-S
	Since From My Dear	SBBS
	Sound the Trumpet	ES-2
	Strike the Viol	SVR-1
	Turn Then Thine Eyes	FBMS
	We Sing to Him	SBMS
	What Shall I Do to Show How Much I Love Her?	FBTS
	When I Have Often Heard Young Maids Complaining	FBMS-2
	Ye Twice Ten Hundred Deities	NIE-Br
Quilter, R.	Autumn Evening	SBTS
	Blow, Blow, Thou Winter Wind	FBBS
	Dream Valley	FBMS-2
		NIE-M
	Fair House of Joy	SBTS
	Go, Lovely Rose	FBTS
	Love's Philosophy	SBSS
		SVR-2
	My Life's Delight	SBTS
	Now Sleeps the Crimson Petal	NIE-T
		YS-B
		YS-C
		YS-S
		YS-T
	O Mistress Mine	ASSV
		ES
		FBBS
		NIE-Br
		SVR-2
	Song of the Blackbird	SBSS
	Spring Is at the Door	FBMS-2
	Weep You No More	CCS-T

Composer	Song Title	Anthology
Quilter, R.	Weep You No More	FBTS-2
	Weep You No More, Sad Fountains	ES
Rachmaninoff, S.	By the Grave	NIE-Bs
	Forsake Me Not, My Love, I Pray	GAS
	How Fair This Spot	NIE-S
	How Few the Joys	NIE-C
	In the Silence of Night	50ASMR
	In the Silent Night (V'mo Hchányinótchi táïnoi)	SVR-1
	Island, The	50ASMR
		SBBS
	Lilacs	56S
		SBMS
	Night is Mournful	NIE-T
	O Thou Billowy Harvest-Field!	SBTS
	To the Children	GAS
		NIE-M
		SBMS
	Tout Est Si Beau	SVR-2
		YS-T
	Vocalise	GAS
	When Yesterday We Met	NIE-Br
Raff, J.	Keine Sorg' um den Weg	FBMS-2
Ravel, M.	Chanson espagnole	50ASMR
	D'Anne jouant de l'espinette	50ASMR
Reger, M.	Mariä Wiegenlied	FBMS-2
	Waldeinsamkeit	FBSS
Reichardt, L.	When the Roses Bloom	YS-C
		YS-S
		YS-T
	When the roses bloom (Hoffnung)	56S
		SVR-1
		YS-B

Composer	Song Title	Anthology
Reinecke, C. H.	Doll's Cradle Song	SS-Int
Respighi, O.	Nebbie	50ASMR
		YS-B
		YS-C
		YS-S
		YS-T
Rich, G.	American Lullaby	15AAS
		FBMS
Richardson, T.	Mary	SR-1
Ridout, A.	O Sing the Glories of Our Lord	SS-2
Ridout, G.	J'ai cuelli la belle rose (I Have Culled That Lovely Rosebud)	SS-5
Ridout, G., arr.	I'll Give My Love an Apple	SS-6
Rimsky-Korsakoff, N.	Nightingale and the Rose, The	55AS
	Song of India (Chanson indoue)	56S
	Tell, O tell her	50ASMR
Roberton, H. S.	All in the April Evening	20CAS
Robertson, R. R.	Jolly Roger, The	FBBS
Rodgers, M.	Yesterday I Loved You	BR-T
Rodgers, R.	Bali Ha'I	BR-MS
		FBBS-M
	Bewitched	BR-S
	Climb Ev'ry Mountain	BR-S
		FBBS-S
	Cock-Eyed Optimist, A	FBBS-M
		FS
	Do-Re-Mi	FS
	Edelweiss	FBBS-B
	Falling in Love with Love	FBBS-M
	Getting to Know You	FBBS-M
	He's Got the Whole World in His Hands	FS
	Hello, Young Lovers	FBBS-S

Composer	Song Title	Anthology
Rodgers, R.	Hinay Ma Tov	FS
	I Could Write a Book	FBBS-T
	I Do Not Know a Day I Did Not Love You	FBBS-T
	I Enjoy Being a Girl	FBBS-M
	I Have Dreamed	BR-T
		FBBS-S
	In My Own Little Corner	FBBS-M
	It's a Grand Night for Singing	FBBS-S
	Kansas City	FBBS-T
	Lonely Room	BR-B
	Many a New Day	FBBS-S
	Michael, Row the Boat Ashore	FS
	My Favorite Things	FBBS-M
	My Funny Valentine	BR-MS
		FBBS-M
	My Heart Stood Still	FBBS-T
	My Romance	FBBS-T
	Oh, What a Beautiful Mornin'	FBBS-T
	Oklahoma	FBBS-B
	Old Smokey	FS
	Out of My Dreams	FBBS-S
	People Will Say We're In Love	BR-S
	Some Enchanted Evening	BR-B
		FBBS-B
	Something Wonderful	FBBS-M
	Sound of Music, The	FBBS-S
	Surrey with the Fringe on Top, The	FBBS-B
	That's the Way It Happens	FBBS-T
	There Is Nothin' Like a Dame	FBBS-B
	This Nearly Was Mine	FBBS-B
	We Kiss In A Shadow	BR-T

Composer	Song Title	Anthology
Rodgers, R.	We Kiss in a Shadow	FBBS-T
	What's the Use of Wond'rin'	FBBS-M
	When the Children Are Asleep	FBBS-T
	Where or When	FBBS-M
	With a Song in My Heart	FBBS-S
	Wonderful Guy, A	FBBS-M
	You'll Never Walk Alone	BR-S
		FBBS-S
	You've Got to Be Carefully Taught	FBBS-T
	Younger Than Springtime	BR-T
		FBBS-T
Rodrigo, J.	Adela	CCS-B
		CCS-T
	Porque toco el pandero	CCS-M
Rogers, J. H.	Cloud-Shadows	FBMS
	Great Peace Have They Which Love Thy Law	SBMS
Rome, H.	Fanny	BR-T
Ronald, L.	Down in the Forest	SBSS
	Drift Down, Drift Down	FBSS-2
	Love, I Have Won You	SBMS
Rorem, N.	Christmas Carol, A	FS
	Early in the Morning	BS
	Little Elegy	SS-5
Rosa, S.	Let Me Linger near Thee	NIE-M
	Selve, voi che le speranze	28ISAA
		CIS
	Star vicino	28ISAA
		CIS-2
	To Be Near Thee (Star vicino)	ES-2
		PS-3
Rosenthal, L.	Imagine That	BR-B
Rosseter, P.	When Laura Smiles	FS

Composer	Song Title	Anthology
Rowley, A.	Linnet's Secret, The	SS-1
Rowley, A., arr.	Suo-Gan	SS-3
Roy, W.	This Little Rose	15AAS
		FBMS
Rubinstein, A.	Asra, The (Der Asra)	55AS
	Du bist wie eine Blume	FBTS-2
	Heard Ye His Voice	SBMS
	Thou'rt Like unto a Flower (Du bist wie eine Blume)	SR-1
Russian	Ah, No Stormy Wind	PS-4
	Jailer's Slumber Song, The	PS-4
	Song of the Volga Boatmen	56S
Sacco, J.	Brother Will, Brother John	20CAS
		FBTS
Saint-Saëns, C.	Ave Maria	FBTS-2
	My Heart at thy sweet voice (Mon coeur s'ouvre à ta voix)	56S
	Patiently Have I Waited	SBMS
Sandoval, M.	Serenata Gitana	GAS
	Sin tu amor	50ASMR
		GAS
Sargent, P.	Stopping by Woods on a Snowy Evening	CAS
Sarti, G.	Lungi Dal Caro Bene	FBBS
Scarlatti, A.	Cara e dolce	BS
	Cease, Oh Maiden	NIE-Br
	Chi vuole innomorarsi	CIS-3
	Dewy Violets	NIE-C
	Già il sole dal Gange	26ISAA
		26ISAA
	Le Violette	26ISAA
		28ISAA
		GAS

Composer	Song Title	Anthology
Scarlatti, A.	Like Any Foolish Moth I Fly	NIE-C
	Non vogl'io se non vederti	CIS-2
	O cessate di piagarmi	26ISAA
		28ISAA
		BS
		CIS
		CCS-B
	Rugiadose, odorose	CIS
	Se Florinda è fedele	26ISAA
		28ISAA
	Se Florindo è fedele	ASSV
	Sento nel core	26ISAA
		26ISAA
		CIS-2
		FBTS
	Spesso vibra per suo gioco	ES
	Sun O'er the Ganges, The (Già il sole dal Gange)	PS-3
	Sunrise of The Ganges (Già il sole dal Gange)	55AS
	Toglietemi la Vita Ancor	FBBS-2
Schemelli, G. C.	Come, Let Us All This Day	SS-5
	O Saviour So Meek	SS-3
Schirmer, R.	Honey Shun	20CAS
Schlösser, A.	He That Keepeth Israel	FBTS
Schmidt, H.	Fifty Million Years Ago	BR-T
	Gonna Be Another Hot Day	BR-B
		FBBS-B
	Is It Really Me?	BR-MS
		FBBS-M
	Man and a Woman, A	FBBS-T
	Much More	BR-S
	My Cup Runneth Over	BR-B

Composer	Song Title	Anthology
Schmidt, H.	My Cup Runneth Over	FBBS-B
	Plant a Radish	FBBS-T
	Simple Little Things	FBBS-M
	Soon It's Gonna Rain	BR-B
		FBBS-B
	Try to Remember	FBBS-B
	Under The Tree	BR-MS
	What Is A Woman?	BR-MS
Schoenberg, A.	Erhebung	50ASMR
Schönberg, C. M.	Bring Him Home	FBBS-T
	On My Own	FBBS-M
Schram, R. E., arr.	All My Trials	FSSS-2
	All Through the Night	FSSS-2
	Go 'Way From My Window	FSSS-2
	He's Gone Away	FSSS-2
	Poor Boy	FSSS-2
Schubert, F.	An die Leier	GAS
	An die Musik	CCS-M
		FS
		SBMS
		STC
	Ave Maria	56S
		AS-2
		STC
	Bei Dir!	GAS
	Benedictus	ASSV
	Calm at Sea (Meeresstille)	PS-2
	Cradle Song	NIE-M
	Cradle Song (Wiegenlied)	PS-3
	Das Fischermädchen	FBTS-2
	Death and the Maiden	NIE-C
	Der Lindenbaum	SBBS

Composer	Song Title	Anthology
Schubert, F.	Der Neugierige	FBTS
	Der Schmetterling	50SS
		GAS
	Der Wanderer	SBBS
	Die Allmacht	50SS
	Die Forelle	SBTS
	Die Post	SBBS
	Die Wetterfahne	FBBS-2
	Du bist die Ruh'	SBMS
	Erl King, The	NIE-Br
	Faith in Spring (Frühlingsglaube)	AS-2
		ES-1
	Farewell (Adieu!)	PS-1
	Frühlingsglaube	ES
	Frühlingsträum	SBTS
	Gefror'ne Thränen	SBBS
	Gott im Frühling	FBMS-2
	Gretchen at the Spinning Wheel	NIE-S
	Hark! Hark! The Lark	AS-2
	Heaven-Rays (Himmelsfunken)	PS-4
	Hedge-roses (Heidenröslein)	AS-1
	Heidenröslein	50SS
		ES
	Im Abendroth	50SS
	Impatience (Ungeduld)	ES-2
	In Evening's Glow (Im Abendrot)	PS-1
	La Pastorella	FBSS-2
	Lachen und Weinen	CCS-S
		FBSS-2
	Lay of the Imprisoned Huntsman, The	NIE-Bs
	Liebhaber in allen Gestalten	50SS

Composer	Song Title	Anthology
Schubert, F.	Lied der Mignon	FBSS
	Lime Tree, The	NIE-Bs
	Litany	NIE-C
	Morning Greeting (Morgengruss)	SR-1
	My Last Abode	NIE-Bs
	Nacht und Träume	50SS
	Nachtviolen	50SS
	Night and Dreams (Nacht und Träume)	PS-4
	Novice, The	NIE-S
	Now Love Has Falseley Played Me (Die liebe hat gelogen)	PS-4
	Omnipotence	NIE-S
	Omnipotence (Die Allmacht)	55AS
	Peace	NIE-M
	Rastlose Liebe	50SS
	Secret, The	NIE-T
	Seligkeit	FBSS-2
	Serenade (Standchen)	ES-2
	Serenade (Ständchen)	56S
	Spring Song	SS-2
	Ständchen	FBTS
	To Music	NIE-C
	To Music (An die Musik)	SR-1
	To the Lute	SS-3
	To the Moon	SS-4
	To the Nightingale	SS-5
	Ungeduld	50SS
		ASSV
		GAS
	Wanderer, The	NIE-Br
	Wanderers Nachtlied	FBTS-2

Composer	Song Title	Anthology
Schubert, F.	Wanderers Nachtlied	FS
	Was Ist Sylvia?	FBBS-2
	Whither	NIE-T
	Who is Sylvia (Was ist Sylvia)	AS-1
	Who Is Sylvia?	NIE-T
	Wild Rose, The	NIE-M
	Wohin?	50SS
	Wraith, The	NIE-Br
Schuman, W.	Holiday Song	CAS
	Orpheus with His Lute	15AAS
		20CAS
		FBSS-2
Schumann, C.	Ich hab' in Deinem Auge	ES
	Liebst du um Schönheit	BS
Schumann, R.	Aufträge	50SS
		GAS
	Belshazzar	NIE-Br
	Blacksmith's Song, A	SS-1
	Bride's Song, The	NIE-M
	Chestnut, The	NIE-S
	Children's Bedtime	SS-Int
	Dein Angesicht	SBTS
	Der Nussbaum	50SS
	Die Lotosblume	50SS
		STC
	Die Stille	ES
		FBMS-2
	Du bist wie eine Blume	50SS
		ASSV
		CCS-B
		FBBS-2
	Ein Jüngling Liebt ein Mädchen	FBTS
	Folk Song (Volksliedchen)	SR-1

Composer	Song Title	Anthology
Schumann, R.	Frühlingsnacht	50SS
	He Is Noble, He Is Patient	NIE-S
	Hör' Ich das Liedchen Klingen	FBBS
	I Dreamed That I Was Weeping (Ich hab' im Traum geweinet)	ES-2
	I'll Not Complain (Ich grolle nicht)	ES-2
	In Der Fremde	FBTS-2
	Intermezzo	FBBS
		GAS
	Last Toast, The	NIE-Bs
	Little Folk Song, A	SS-5
	Lotus Flower, The (Die Lotusblume)	55AS
		AS-1
		ES-1
		PS-1
	Mein schöner Stern!	50SS
	Mit Myrthen und Rosen	50SS
	Mondnacht	50SS
	Moonlight	NIE-T
	My Soul Is Dark	NIE-C
	Red, Red, Rose, A	FS
	Rose and the Lily, The (Die Rose, die Lilie, die Taube)	PS-4
	Schneeglöckchen	50SS
	Snowbells (Schneeglöckchen)	PS-1
	Somebody	NIE-M
	Song of the Nightingale, The (Wehmut)	PS-4
	Sonntags am Rhein	GAS
	Stille Thränen	GAS
	Suleika's Song	NIE-S
	Thou Art A Tender Blossom (Du bist wie eine Blume)	PS-4

Composer	Song Title	Anthology
Schumann, R.	Thou art so like a flower (Du bist wie eine Blume)	56S
	Thou'rt Like a Lovely Flower	NIE-T
	Thou'rt Lovely as a Flower (Du bist wie eine Blume)	AS-1
		ES-1
	Thy Lovely Face	NIE-Br
	To the Sunshine	SS-6
	To The Sunshine (An den Sonnenschein)	PS-1
	Twas in the Lovely Month of May (Im wunderschönen Monat Mai)	AS-2
	Two Grenadiers, The	NIE-Bs
	Two Grenadiers, The (Die beiden Grenadiere)	56S
		AS-2
	Verrathene Liebe	FBBS-2
	Volksliedchen	FBMS
	Why Blame Thee Now?	NIE-Br
	Widmung	50SS
		STC
Schwartz, S.	Corner Of The Sky	BR-T
Scott, A. A.	Think On Me	ES-1
		SVR-1
		YS-C
Scott, C.	Lullaby	FBSS
Scott, J. P.	Come Ye Blessed	SBBS
Scott, Lady John	Annie Laurie	SBBS
Scottish	Flow Gently, Sweet Afton	BS
	Turn Ye To Me	BS
Secchi, A.	Lungi dal caro bene	26ISAA
		CIS
Seiber, M., arr.	Handsome Butcher, The	SS-2

Composer	Song Title	Anthology
Sgambati, G., arr.	Separazione	FBMS-2
		FS
		GAS
Sharman, C.	Wind, The	SS-1
Shaw, M.	Child of The Flowing Tide	SBBS
	Easter Carol	CAS
	Heffle Cuckoo Fair	FBSS
	Song of the Palanquin Bearers	20CAS
Shield, W.	Friar of Orders Grey, The	FBBS
Shire, D.	Starting Here, Starting Now	BR-MS
Sibelius, J.	Black Roses	SVR-1
	Black Roses (Svarta rosor)	SVR-2
	From the North	50ASMR
Simms, P. F., arr.	Climbin' Up the Mountain	SSS
	Go, Tell it on the Mountain	SSS
	Kum Ba Yah	SSS
Simon, L.	How Could I Ever Know	BS
Sinding, C.	Sylvelin	56S
		AS-2
		YS-C
		YS-S
		YS-T
Sleeth, N.	Children of the Lord	SunS
	For These Blessings	SunS
	Go Now In Peace	SunS
	Here's to America	WS
	Holy Book, The	SunS
	Keeping Christmas	WS
	Let's Make Music	WS
	Light One Candle	SunS
	Lullaby	SunS
	One Day at a Time	WS

Composer	Song Title	Anthology
Sleeth, N.	Part of the Plan	SunS
	Praise the Lord	SunS
	Round of Greeting, A	WS
	Sharing it with me	WS
	Sing Noel	SunS
	That's Good	SunS
	This is the Day	SunS
	Try Again	WS
	Two Roads	WS
	Valentine Wish, A	WS
	We're on Our Way	WS
	Winter's a Drag Rag, The	WS
	You and I	SunS
	You Never Stop Learning	WS
Smith, J. S.	Owl Is Abroad, The	NIE-Bs
	Scarborough Fair	FS
	Star-Spangled Banner, The	FS
	When the Saints Go Marchin' In	FS
Smith, L.	Butterflies (Les papillons)	SS-Int
Smith, W. R.	Pirate Song, A	SS-3
Somer, H.	Song of Praise	SS-2
Somervell, A.	Birds in the High Hall-garden	NIE-Br
	Kingdom by the Sea, A	FBTS-2
Sondheim, S.	Anyone Can Whistle	BR-MS
		FS
	Broadway Baby	FS
	Comedy Tonight	FBBS-B
	Everybody Says Don't	BR-B
	Love, I Hear	BR-T
	No One is Alone	BS
	Take Me To The World	BR-T
	That Dirty Old Man	BR-S

Composer	Song Title	Anthology
Spanish	I Don't Wish to Marry (No quiero casarme)	PS-3
	Tirana del Caramba	ES
Speaks, O.	Lord Is My Light, The	FBTS
	Morning	FBMS
	On the Road to Mandalay	FBBS
	Prayer Perfect, The	FBSS-2
Spohr, L.	Rose Softly Blooming	FBSS
Stange, M.	Die Bekehrte	FBMS
Stevens, R. J.	Sigh No More, Ladies	FS
		NIE-T
Stevenson, F.	I Sought the Lord	SBMS
Stradella, A.	Col mio sangue comprerei	CIS-2
	Cosi, amor, mi fai languir!	CIS-3
	O Lord, Have Mercy (Pietà, Signore)	ES-2
	Per pietà	CIS-3
	Pietà, Signore!	26ISAA
	Se nel ben	ES
Strauss, R.	Ach Lieb, ich muss nun scheiden	FS
	All Soul's Day (Allerseelen)	56S
		ES-2
	Allerseelen	50SS
		ASSV
	Alone in the Forest	NIE-M
	Cäcilie	50ASMR
		50SS
	Die Nacht	SBSS
	Farewell, A	NIE-S
	Heimkehr	50SS
		GAS
	Heimliche Aufforderung	50SS
	Ich trage meine Minne	50SS

Composer	Song Title	Anthology
Strauss, R.	Mit deinen blauen Augen	GAS
	Morgen	50ASMR
		50SS
		YS-B
		YS-C
		YS-S
		YS-T
	Night (Die Nacht)	PS-4
	Ruhe, meine Seele!	50SS
	Solitary One, The	NIE-Bs
	Ständchen	50SS
	To You	ES-2
	To You (Zueignung)	56S
	Tomorrow	ES-2
	Tomorrow (Morgen)	55AS
		PS-4
	Traum durch die Dämmerung	50SS
	Welcome Vision, A	NIE-Br
	Winter Dedication, A	NIE-T
	Zueignung	50SS
Stravinsky, I.	Pastorale	50ASMR
Strickland, L.	My Lover is a Fisherman	AS-2
	Road to Home, The	AS-1
Strommen, C., arr.	She's Like the Swallow	FSSS
	To the Sky	FSSS
Strozzi, B.	Amor dormiglione	CIS-3
Styne, J.	Just In Time	BR-B
		FBBS-B
	People	BR-MS
		FBBS-M
	Who Are You Now?	BR-MS
Sullivan, A.	Free From His Fetters	SBTS
	If Doughty Deeds My Lady Please	NIE-Br

Composer	Song Title	Anthology
Sullivan, A.	Little Buttercup	SBMS
	Lost Chord, The	55AS
		56S
		ES-1
	Orpheus With His Lute	ES-2
		NIE-M
		SBMS
	Policeman's Song, The	SBBS
	Silver'd is the Raven Hair	SBMS
	Sun Whose Rays, The	SBSS
	When First My Old	SBTS
	When I was a Lad I Served a Term	SBBS
	Where the Bee Sucks	NIE-S
	Willow Song, The	FBMS-2
		NIE-C
Swedish	When I was Seventeen	AS-2
		FBSS-2
Swedish Folk Song		YS-S
Symons, D. T.	Sight in Camp, A	CAS
Szymanowski, K.	Song of the Girl at the Window	50ASMR
Taubert, W.	In a Strange Land	NIE-M
Taylor, C.	Grasshopper Green	SS-2
Tchaikovsky, P.	At the Ball	50ASMR
		55AS
		FBTS
	Don Juan's Serenade	NIE-Br
	Legend, A	50ASMR
		ES-1
		FBMS-2
	Lord is My Shepherd, The	FBMS
	Nay, Though My Heart Should Break	NIE-C

Composer	Song Title	Anthology
Tchaikovsky, P.	None but the Lonely Heart (Nor wer die Sehnsucht kennt)	ES-1
	None by the Lonely Heart (Nur wer die sehnsucht kennt)	AS-2
	Nur Wer die Sehnsucht Kennt	FBSS-2
	One who has yearn'd alone (Nur, wer die Sehnsucht kennt)	56S
	Pilgrim's Song	FBBS-2
		YS-B
		YS-T
	To the Forest	NIE-Bs
	Twas April	NIE-T
Telfer, N.	Blessing, A	SS-6
	Lullaby	SS-1
	Searching for a Gift	SS-Int
Thiman, E. H.	I Love All Graceful Things	CAS
		FBSS
	King of Song, The	SS-5
Thomas, A.	Le Soir	SBTS
Thomson, V.	English Usage	CAS
	My Crow Pluto	20CAS
	Take, O, Take Those Lips Away	ES
	Tiger, The	CAS
Torelli, G.	Thou Knowest Well (Tu to sai)	PS-3
	Tu lo sai	26ISAA
		26ISAA
		ASSV
		CIS
	Well Thou Knowest	ES-2
Tosti, F. P.	Could I (Vorrei)	SR-2
	Good-bye	55AS
	Good-bye!	56S
	Malìa	ES

Composer	Song Title	Anthology
Tosti, F. P.	Serenade (La Serenata)	SR-2
Toye, F.	Inn, The	CAS
Traetta, T.	Ombra cara, amorosa	CIS-3
Treharne, B.	Corals	50ASMR
Tyson, M. L.	Sea Moods	FBBS
V. Williams, R.	Bright Is the Ring of Words	BS
		FBBS-2
	Call, The	SBTS
	Dream-Land	SBTS
	From Far, from Eve and Morning	NIE-T
	Hugh's Song of the Road	CAS
	Linden Lea	FBTS-2
	Oh, When I Was in Love With You	ES
	Orpheus With His Lute	SBTS
		SS-4
	Roadside Fire, The	FBBS-2
		YS-B
	Silent Noon	50ASMR
		CCS-M
		FBMS
		SVR-2
		YS-B
		YS-T
	Vagabond, The	SBBS
	Whither Must I Wander?	SBTS
	Youth and Love	NIE-Br
Van Heusen, J.	Call Me Irresponsible	BS
Veracini, F. M.	Pastoral, A	SBSS
Verdi, G.	La donna è mobile	56S
Vivaldi, A.	Qui sedes ad dexteram	ASSV
	Un certo non so che	CIS-3
		SBMS
Voigt, H.	Mother-Love	56S

Composer	Song Title	Anthology
Wagner, R.	Dreaming (Träume)	55AS
	Dreams (Träume)	56S
	I Went to Heaven	FS
	Slumber Song	NIE-M
Waller & Brooks	Ain't Misbehavin'	FS
Walthew, R. H.	Eldorado	FBBS-2
	Mistress Mine	FBTS
	Splendour Falls, The	FBBS
Ward, A. E., arr.	Drink to Me Only with Thine Eyes	SR-1
Ward, S. A.	America the Beautiful	FS
	Auld Lang Syne	FS
Warlock, P.	As Ever I Saw	NIE-T
	Milkmaids	SS-6
	Pretty Ring Time	ASSV
	Walking the Woods	NIE-Br
Watts, W.	Blue are Her Eyes	AS-2
Weaver, P.	Moon-Marketing	20CAS
Weill, K.	Lonely House	BR-S
	Lonesome Dove, The from "Down in the Valley"	20CAS
	Lost In The Stars	BR-B
	Stay Well	BR-S
	Tschaikowsky	BR-T
Wells, H.	Everyone Sang	CAS
Wesley, S. S.	Jesu, the Very Thought of Thee	FBTS
White, M. V.	Crabbed Age and Youth	FBMS
	King Charles	NIE-Br
	To Mary	NIE-T
Whitehead, A.	House to Let	SS-2
Willan, H.	Du bist wie eine Blume (E'en as a Lovely Flower)	SS-6
	Love and a Day	SS-5

Composer	Song Title	Anthology
Willan, H., arr.	Early One Morning	SS-3
	La petite hirondelle (Oh, Sweet Little Swallow)	SS-5
	Sainte Marguerite	SS-4
	Twas in the Moon of Wintertime (Jesous Ahatouhia)	SS-1
Willson, M.	Goodnight, My Someone	FBBS-S
	Till There Was You	FBBS-S
Wilson, H. L.	Carmeña	FBMS-2
Wilson, H. L., arr.	Ah! Willow	SBBS
	False Phillis	FBBS
	Pretty Creature, The	ES-1
		FBBS-2
	Slighted Swain, The	CCS-B
		FBBS-2
Wolf, H.	Auf dem grünen Balcon	50SS
		GAS
	Bescheidene Liebe	50SS
		SBSS
	Das Verlassene Mägdlein	SBSS
	Der Musikant	ES
	Fussreise	50ASMR
	Gesang Weylas	50ASMR
	In dem Schatten meiner Locken	50SS
	In der Frühe	50SS
	Lebe Wohl!	50SS
		GAS
	Mignon	50SS
	My Native Land (Gesang Weylas)	55AS
	Nimmersatte Liebe	50SS
		GAS
	Nun Wandre, Maria	50SS
		GAS

Composer	Song Title	Anthology
Wolf, H.	Secrecy (Verborgenheit)	ES-2
	Und willst du deinen Liebsten sterben sehen	50SS
	Verborgenheit	50SS
		SBMS
	Verschwiegene Liebe	50ASMR
Wonder, S.	I Just Called to Say I Love You	FS
Wood, C.	Ethiopia Saluting the Colours	NIE-Bs
Wright, R.	And This Is My Beloved	FBBS-S
	Stranger in Paradise	FBBS-T
Wuensch, G.	Rules and Regulations	SS-2
Yon, P.	Gesú Bambino	FBSS-2
Young, A.	Phillis Has Such Charming Graces	FBTS-2
Yradier, S.	La Paloma	56S
		FS

Section 2

Level 1 Songs

Song Title	Composer	Anthology
Adela	Rodrigo, J.	CCS-B
		CCS-T
Adieu	Fauré, G.	FBTS-2
Ah! Willow	Wilson, H. L., arr.	SBBS
Ah, May the Red Rose Live Always	Foster, S. C.	ES
Ain't Misbehavin'	Waller & Brooks	FS
All Day on the Prairie	Guion, D. W.	FBTS
All in the April Evening	Roberton, H. S.	20CAS
All My Trials	Schram, R. E., arr.	FSSS-2
All the Things You Are	Kern, J.	FBBS-S
All Through the Night	Christy, V. A., arr.	ES-1
	Old Welsh	CCS-B
		FBTS
	Schram, R. E., arr.	FSSS-2
Alleluia!	Old English	SBTS
Alma del core	Caldara, A.	CCS-B
Almost Like Being in Love	Loewe, F.	BS
Amazing Grace	Althouse, J., arr.	SSS
America the Beautiful	Ward, S. A.	FS
American Lullaby	Rich, G.	15AAS
		FBMS
An die Geliebte	Beethoven, L.	CCS-T
Angels, Ever Bright and Fair	Handel, G. F.	NIE-M
Animal Crackers	Hageman, R.	FBSS-2
Annie Laurie	Scott, Lady John	SBBS
Anyone Can Whistle	Sondheim, S.	BR-MS
		FS
Arm, Arm, Ye Brave	Handel, G. F.	SBBS
Art Thou Troubled?		SS-6
As Ever I Saw	Warlock, P.	NIE-T
As I Went A-Roaming	Brahe, M. H.	FBMS-2
As Long as He Needs Me	Bart, L.	FBBS-M

Song Title	Composer	Anthology
Asra, The (Der Asra)	Rubinstein, A.	55AS
At the Ball	Tchaikovsky, P.	50ASMR
		55AS
		FBTS
At the River	Lowry, R. R.	FS
Aufträge	Schumann, R.	50SS
Auld Lang Syne	Ward, S. A.	FS
Aupres de ma Blonde	Paton, J. G., arr.	FS
Author of All My Joys	Gluck, C. W. von	NIE-C
Bacchus, God of Mirth and Wine	Arne, T.	NIE-Bs
Bald wehen uns des Frühlings Lüfte	Haydn, J.	FS
Baruch and Hamakom	Glick, S. I.	SS-5
Beautiful	Duncan, C.	SS-4
Beautiful Dreamer	Foster, S. C.	CCS-B
		SR-1
Beautiful Savior	Christy, V. A., arr.	ES-1
Begone Dull Care		ES-1
Bella porta di rubini	Falconieri, A.	CIS-3
Bella vittoria	Bononcini, G.	ES
Below in the Valley (Da unten im Tale)	Brahms, J.	PS-2
Beneath a Weeping Willow's Shade	Hopkinson, F.	55AS
		BS
		FBMS-2
Bewitched	Rodgers, R.	BR-S
Bid me To Live	Lawes, H.	55AS
Birthday of a King, The	Neidlinger, W. H.	FBTS-2
Black Dress, The	Niles, J. J.	FBTS
Black is the Color of My True Love's Hair	American	BS
	Niles, J. J.	FBTS
Black Roses (Svarta rosor)	Sibelius, J.	SVR-2
Blacksmith's Song, A	Schumann, R.	SS-1

Song Title	Composer	Anthology
Blacksmith, The	Brahms, J.	NIE-M
Blessing, A	Telfer, N.	SS-6
Blow High, Blow Low	Dibdin, C.	55AS
		FBBS
Blow, Blow, Thou Winter Wind	Arne, T.	55AS
		ES
		FBBS-2
Blue-Bell, The	MacDowell, E.	CCS-M
Boy's Song, A	Beaulieu, J.	SS-3
Broadway Baby	Sondheim, S.	FS
Brush Up Your Shakespeare	Porter, C.	FS
Butterflies (Les papillons)	Smith, L.	SS-Int
By the Light of The Moon (Au clair de la lune)	Lully, J. B.	PS-2
C'est Mon Ami	Crist, B., arr.	FBMS-2
Cabin	Bowles, P.	15AAS
		20CAS
Call Me Irresponsible	Van Heusen, J.	BS
Can't Help Lovin' Dat Man	Kern, J.	FBBS-S
Candle on the Water	Kasha, A.	BS
Cara e dolce	Scarlatti, A.	BS
Caro mio ben	Giordani, G.	26ISAA
		28ISAA
Carol of the Birds, The	Niles, J. J.	FBMS-2
Carry me back to old Virginny	Bland, J. A.	56S
Cherry Ripe	Horn, C. E.	SR-1
Cherry Tree, The	Gibbs, C. A.	FBMS
Chestnut, The	Schumann, R.	NIE-S
Children of the Lord	Sleeth, N.	SunS
Children's Bedtime	Schumann, R.	SS-Int
Christopher Robin is Saying His Prayers	Fraser-Simson, H.	FBMS
Cindy	Boardman, R., arr	SVR-2

Song Title	Composer	Anthology
Circus Clown, The	Kurth, B.	SS-Int
Cock-Eyed Optimist, A	Rodgers, R.	FS
Cockles and Mussels	Christy, V. A., arr.	FS
	Irish	SVR-1
Colours	Brook, H.	SS-Int
Come Again, Sweet Love	Dowland, J.	55AS
		BS
		CCS-T
		FBTS
		NIE-Br
Come and Trip It	Handel, G. F.	FBSS-2
Come Follow!	Hilton, J., arr.	FS
Come Saturday Morning	Karlin, F.	BS
Come to the Fair	Martin, E.	FBSS-2
Come Unto These Yellow Sands	Purcell, H.	55AS
		SS-6
Come Where My Love Lies Dreaming	Foster, S. C.	STC
Come Ye Blessed	Gaul, A.	FBMS-2
Come, Let Us All This Day	Schemelli, G. C.	SS-5
Con Rauco Mormorio	Handel, G. F.	SBMS
Consecration	Manney, C. F.	AS-2
Corner Of The Sky	Schwartz, S.	BR-T
Country of the Camisards, The	Homer, S.	FS
Cradle Carol (Berceuse)	Ouchterlony, D.	SS-4
Cradle Song	Flies, J. B.	SS-Int
	Mozart, W. A.	PS-1
Cradle Song (Wiegenlied)	Brahms, J.	AS-1
		PS-2
Cradle-song (Wiegenlied)		56S
Curliest Thing, The	Dunhill, T.	SS-1
Daisies, The	Barber, S.	15AAS
Dance Song	Czech	PS-1

Song Title	Composer	Anthology
Dedication (Widmung)	Franz, R.	55AS
		SR-1
		SVR-1
		YS-S
Dewy Violets	Scarlatti, A.	NIE-C
Didn't My Lord Deliver Daniel	Burleigh, H. T., arr.	CCS-S
Die Wetterfahne	Schubert, F.	FBBS-2
Do-Re-Mi	Rodgers, R.	FS
Doll's Cradle Song	Reinecke, C. H.	SS-Int
Donzelle fuggite	Cavalli, F.	CIS
Down Among the Dead Men	Old English	ASSV
		NIE-Bs
Down by the Salley Gardens	Irish	BS
Down By the Sally Gardens	Hughes, H., arr.	CCS-T
		FBTS-2
Down Harley Street	Kingsford, C.	CAS
		FBBS-2
Dream Valley	Quilter, R.	FBMS-2
		NIE-M
Drink to Me Only With Thine Eyes	Mellish, Col. R.	ES-1
	Old English	56S
		STC
	Ward, A. E., arr.	SR-1
Du bist wie eine Blume	Rubinstein, A.	FBTS-2
Early One Morning	British	BS
	Hughes, H., arr.	FS
	Willan, H., arr.	SS-3
Eileen Aroon	Irish	PS-2
Ein Jüngling Liebt ein Mädchen	Schumann, R.	FBTS
El Majo Discreto	Granados, E.	FBSS
El Tecolote	Paton, J. G., arr.	FS
Elephants	Crawley, C.	SS-Int
Eletelephony	Kasemets, U.	SS-Int

Song Title	Composer	Anthology
Equals (Der Gleichsinn)	Haydn, J.	PS-4
Every Day is Ladies' Day with Me	Herbert, V.	FBTS-2
Every Night When the Sun Goes In	American	BS
Fairy's Lullaby, The	Moffat, A., arr.	FS
Falling Dew, The	Czech	PS-1
Falling in Love with Love	Rodgers, R.	FBBS-M
Fame's an Echo	Arne, T.	FBTS-2
Far Down in the Valley (Da unten in Tale)	Brahms, J.	ES-1
Far From the Home I Love	Bock, J.	FS
Farewell! (Gute Nacht!)	Franz, R.	PS-2
Farewell, Lad	O'Neill, J., arr.	FSSS
Fate of Gilbert Gim, The	Drynan, M.	SS-2
Fiddler, The	Nielsen, C.	SS-2
First Concert, The	Mana-Zucca	FBBS-2
Florian's Song (Chanson de Florian)	Godard, B.	55AS
Flow Gently, Sweet Afton	Scottish	BS
Folk Song (Volksliedchen)	Schumann, R.	SR-1
Follow the Drinking Gourd	Althouse, J., arr.	FSSS-2
For Music (Für Music)	Franz, R.	YS-C
		YS-S
For These Blessings	Sleeth, N.	SunS
Forget Me Not	Bach, J. S.	FBTS-2
Four Is Wonderful	Henderson, R. W.	SS-3
Free From His Fetters	Sullivan, A.	SBTS
Friar of Orders Grey, The	Shield, W.	FBBS
Friendship and Song	Handel, G. F.	SVR-2
Get Me to the Church on Time	Loewe, F.	FBBS-B
Getting to Know You	Rodgers, R.	FBBS-M
Girl That I Marry, The	Berlin, I.	FBBS-B
Give a Man a Horse He Can Ride	O'Hara, G.	CCS-B
		FBBS-2

Song Title	Composer	Anthology
Gloria Deo	Ouchterlony, D.	SS-3
Go 'Way From My Window	Schram, R. E., arr.	FSSS-2
Go Now In Peace	Sleeth, N.	SunS
Go, Tell it on the Mountain	Simms, P. F., arr.	SSS
Golden Slumbers	MacMillan, E., arr.	SS-3
Golden Sun Streaming (Die gold'ne Sonne, voll Freud' und Wonne)	Bach, J. S.	PS-4
Gonna Be Another Hot Day	Schmidt, H.	FBBS-B
Goodnight, My Someone	Willson, M.	FBBS-S
Great Peace Have They Which Love Thy Law	Rogers, J. H.	SBMS
Greensleeves	Kern, P., arr.	FSSS
	Paton, J. G., arr.	ES
Gruss	Mendelssohn, F.	ES
Guitar Player, The	Bennett, C.	SVR-1
Habanera	Bizet, G.	56S
Handsome Butcher, The	Seiber, M., arr.	SS-2
Harbour Grace	Bissell, K., arr.	SS-4
Hark! The Echoing Air	Purcell, H.	SBSS
Have You Seen But a Bright Lily Grow?	Old English	ES
Have You Seen But a White Lillie Grow?		CCS-T
		PS-3
Have You Seen But a White Lily Grow		FBSS
Have You Seen But the White Lillie Grow?		SR-2
Have You Seen But the Whyte Lillie Grow?		STC
He shall feed His flock	Handel, G. F.	CCS-M
He's Got the Whole World in His Hands	Rodgers, R.	FS

Song Title	Composer	Anthology
Hear! Ye Gods of Britain	Purcell, H.	NIE-Bs
Hebe	Chausson, E.	FS
Heffle Cuckoo Fair	Shaw, M.	FBSS
Hello, Young Lovers	Rodgers, R.	FBBS-S
Here Amid the Shady Woods	Handel, G. F.	FBSS-2
		NIE-M
		PS-4
Here's to America	Sleeth, N.	WS
High Barbaree	Christy, V. A., arr.	FS
Highland Lullaby, A	Coutts, G.	SS-4
Hinay Ma Tov	Rodgers, R.	FS
Holy Book, The	Sleeth, N.	SunS
Holy City, The	Adams, S.	ES-1
Hör' Ich das Liedchen Klingen	Schumann, R.	FBBS
Horses	Crawley, C.	SS-Int
House to Let	Whitehead, A.	SS-2
How Changed the Vision	Handel, G. F.	NIE-C
How Do You Preach?	Benton, G.	BR-T
How Lovely Are Thy Dwellings	Liddle, S.	FBSS-2
How to Handle a Woman	Loewe, F.	FBBS-B
Hushed The Song of the Nightingale	Gretchaninoff, A.	SBMS
I Attempt From Love's Sickness to Fly	Purcell, H.	ASSV
		CCS-S
		ES
		FBTS
		NIE-M
I Could Have Danced All Night	Loewe, F.	FBBS-S
I Could Write a Book	Rodgers, R.	FBBS-T
I Do Not Know a Day I Did Not Love You		FBBS-T
I Don't Wish to Marry (No quiero casarme)	Spanish	PS-3

Song Title	Composer	Anthology
I Enjoy Being a Girl	Rodgers, R.	FBBS-M
I Have Dreamed		BR-T
I Have Twelve Oxen	Ireland, J.	NIE-S
I Just Called to Say I Love You	Wonder, S.	FS
I Know Where I'm Goin'	Hughes, H., arr.	FS
I Like Dogs! (J'aime les chiens!)	Ohlin, C. P.	SS-Int
I Love All Graceful Things	Thiman, E. H.	CAS
		FBSS
I Love Paris	Porter, C.	FBBS-M
I Love Thee (Ich liebe dich)	Beethoven, L.	ES-1
	Grieg, E.	56S
I Loved You Once in Silence	Loewe, F.	FBBS-M
I Shall Declare I Love Her	Handel, G. F.	SS-4
I Talk to the Trees	Loewe, F.	FBBS-B
I wander this Summer morning (Am leuchtenden Sommermorgen)	Franz, R.	AS-2
I Went to Heaven	Wagner, R.	FS
I Will Make You Brooches	Bury, W.	SS-5
I will Sing New Songs	Dvořák, A.	SBBS
I Wonder As I Wander	Niles, J. J.	FBBS-2
I'll Give My Love an Apple	Ridout, G., arr.	SS-6
I'll Know	Loesser, F.	FBBS-S
I've Been Roaming	Horn, C. E.	55AS
		YS-S
I've Grown Accustomed To Her Face	Loewe, F.	BR-B
		FBBS-B
Ich Liebe Dich	Beethoven, L.	FBSS-2
If Doughty Deeds My Lady Please	Sullivan, A.	NIE-Br
If Ever I Would Leave You	Loewe, F.	FBBS-B
If I Ruled The World	Ornadel, C.	BR-T
		FBBS-M
Imagine That	Rosenthal, L.	BR-B

Song Title	Composer	Anthology
Impossible Dream, The	Leigh, M.	FBBS-B
In a Simple Way I Love You	Ford, N.	BS
In My Own Little Corner	Rodgers, R.	FBBS-M
In Old Donegal	Parke, D.	SS-2
In the Country (Die Landlust)	Haydn, J.	PS-1
Is It Really Me?	Schmidt, H.	BR-MS
		FBBS-M
Is She Not Passing Fair?	Elgar, E.	NIE-T
It Was a Lover and His Lass	Morley, T.	CCS-S
		FS
		STC
It Wonders Me	Hague, A.	BR-S
It's a Grand Night for Singing	Rodgers, R.	FBBS-S
J'ai cuelli la belle rose (I Have Culled That Lovely Rosebud)	Ridout, G.	SS-5
Jack and Joan	Campion, T.	SS-2
Jagdlied	Mendelssohn, F.	FBBS
Jeanie With the Light Brown Hair	Foster, S. C.	STC
Jesu, the Very Thought of Thee	Wesley, S. S.	FBTS
Jesus, Fount of Consolation	Bach, J. S.	FBBS-2
Jesus, Jesus, Rest Your Head	American	YS-S
		YS-T
Johnny Doolan's Cat	Irish	BS
Joy of Love, The (Plaisir d'amour)	Martini, G.	55AS
Juniper Tree, The	Irish	BS
Just Imagine	DeSylva, B. G.	FBBS-S
Just In Time	Styne, J.	BR-B
		FBBS-B
Kansas City	Rodgers, R.	FBBS-T
Keeping Christmas	Sleeth, N.	WS
Kelligrews Soiree, The	Burke, J.	SS-2
Knotting Song, The	Purcell, H.	NIE-T

Song Title	Composer	Anthology
L'Amour au mois de mai	Lefévre, J.	ES
La Paloma	Yradier, S.	56S
La petite hirondelle (Oh, Sweet Little Swallow)	Willan, H., arr.	FS SS-5
La pomme et l'escargot (The Apple and the Snail)	Milhaud, D.	SS-1
Lachen und Weinen	Schubert, F.	FBSS-2
Lamb, The	Chanler, T.	15AAS
Lark, The	Dvorák, A.	FBMS 50ASMR
Lass from the Low Countree, The	Niles, J. J.	15AAS
Lass with the Delicate Air, The	Arne, T.	FBMS SR-2
Last Night	Kjerulf, H.	55AS
Last Rose of Summer, The	Irish	SR-1 56S
Lay of the Imprisoned Huntsman, The	Miliken, R. A. Schubert, F.	FBSS-2 NIE-Bs
Lazy Afternoon	Latouche, J.	FBBS-M
Lazy Summer	Belyea, W. H.	SS-5
Le Charme	Chausson, E.	SBBS
Leaning on a Lamp-Post	Gay, N.	FBBS-B
Legend, A	Tchaikovsky, P.	50ASMR
Let Me Linger near Thee	Rosa, S.	ES-1 FBMS-2 NIE-M
Let Us Break Bread Together	Myers, G., arr.	FBBS
Let Us Dance, Let Us Sing	Purcell, H.	FBSS
Let's Make Music	Sleeth, N.	WS
Liebhaber in allen Gestalten	Schubert, F.	50SS
Liebst du um Schönheit	Schumann, C.	BS

Song Title	Composer	Anthology
Light One Candle	Sleeth, N.	SunS
Like Any Foolish Moth I Fly	Scarlatti, A.	NIE-C
Linnet's Secret, The	Rowley, A.	SS-1
Little Boy Blue	Nevin, E.	ES-1
Little Buttercup	Sullivan, A.	SBMS
Little China Figure, A	Leoni, F.	FBSS
Little David, Play on Your Harp	Kern, P., arr.	SSS
Little Elegy	Rorem, N.	SS-5
Little Folk Song, A	Schumann, R.	SS-5
Little Irish Girl, The	Lohr, H.	SVR-2
		YS-C
		YS-S
		YS-T
Little road to Kerry, The	Cadman, C. W.	AS-1
Liza Jane	Althouse, J., arr.	FSSS
Loch Lomond	Crist, B.	SR-1
	Deis, C., arr.	FBTS
Lonesome Dove, The from "Down in the Valley"	Weill, K.	20CAS
Long Time Ago	American	BS
Long, Long Ago	Bayly, T. H.	AS-1
		STC
Longing For Spring	Mozart, W. A.	PS-1
Look at Me, My little dear	McLean, H. J., arr.	SS-2
Look for the Silver Lining	Kern, J.	FBBS-S
Look to the Rainbow	Lane, B.	FBBS-S
Love Has Eyes	Bishop, Sir H.	55AS
		ES
		ES-2
		FBSS
		PS-3
		YS-S
		YS-T

Song Title	Composer	Anthology
Love Is a Bauble	Leveridge, R.	PS-3
Love Is a Many-Splendored Thing	Fain, S.	BS
Love Is Here to Stay	Gershwin, G.	FS
Love Leads to Battle	Bononcini, G.	NIE-Bs
Love Quickly is Pall'd	Purcell, H.	FBTS-2
Love's Old, Sweet Song	Molloy, J. L.	56S
Loveliest of Trees	Duke, J.	FBMS
Lovely Song My Heart is Singing, The	Goulding, E.	FBMS-2
Lowest Trees Have Tops, The	Dowland, J.	SS-4
Lullaby	Brahms, J.	NIE-S
		SR-1
	Sleeth, N.	SunS
	Telfer, N.	SS-1
Lullaby (Wiegenlied)	Mozart, W. A.	55AS
		SR-1
Lydia	Fauré, G.	FBTS
Maiden Tell Me	Czech	PS-1
Make Believe	Kern, J.	FBBS-S
Malìa	Tosti, F. P.	ES
Man and a Woman, A	Schmidt, H.	FBBS-T
Man Is for the Woman Made	Purcell, H.	FS
Many a New Day	Rodgers, R.	FBBS-S
March of the Kings (La Marche des Rois)	French	PS-2
Marianina	Fletcher, P., arr.	SS-Int
Marianne s'en va-t-au moulin (Marianne Went to the Mill)	Champagne, C., arr.	SS-1
Mary	Richardson, T.	SR-1
May Song	Beethoven, L.	FBTS
Me and My Girl	Gay, N.	FBBS-T
Michael, Row the Boat Ashore	Rodgers, R.	FS
Miller of Dee, The	Christy, V. A., arr.	ES

Song Title	Composer	Anthology
Miller of Dee, The	Christy, V. A., arr.	ES-1
Miller of Mansfield, The	Arne, T.	FS
Minstrel Boy, The	Irish	BS
Mon doux berger/Sweet Shepherd	MacMillan, E., arr.	SS-3
Monotone (Ein Ton)	Cornelius, P.	55AS
Moon River	Mancini, H.	BS
Morning Greeting (Morgengruss)	Schubert, F.	SR-1
Mother (Gamle Mor)	Grieg, E.	PS-4
Mother, O Sing Me to Rest (Mutter, O Sing mich zur Ruh)	Franz, R.	SVR-2
Mother-Love	Voigt, H.	56S
My Cup Runneth Over	Schmidt, H.	FBBS-B
My Defenses Are Down	Berlin, I.	FBBS-B
My Dog Spot	Curwin, C.	SS-2
My Favorite Things	Rodgers, R.	FBBS-M
My Funny Valentine		FBBS-M
My heart ever faithful (Mein gläubiges Herze)	Bach, J. S.	56S
My Heart Stood Still	Rodgers, R.	FBBS-T
My Lord, What a Mornin'	Burleigh, H. T., arr.	CCS-M
	Johnson, H., arr.	FBTS
My Lord, What a Morning	Althouse, J., arr.	SSS
My Love's an Arbutus	Irish	AS-1
	MacMillan, E., arr.	SS-3
My Lovely Celia	Monro, G.	55AS
		ES-2
		FBTS-2
		FS
		STC
		SVR-1
		YS-T
My Lover is a Fisherman	Strickland, L.	AS-2
My Native Land (Gesang Weylas)	Wolf, H.	55AS

Song Title	Composer	Anthology
My Old Kentucky Home	Foster, S. C.	56S
My Own Space	Kander, J.	BR-MS
My Romance	Rodgers, R.	FBBS-T
Nature Beyond Art	Arne, T.	SBTS
Nel cor più non mi sento	Paisiello, G.	26ISAA
		26ISAA
		FS
Next Market Day, The	Irish	BS
Nightingale and the Rose, The	Rimsky-Korsakoff, N.	55AS
No Embers, nor a Firebrand (Kein Feuer, Keine Kohle)	Henschel, G.	AS-2
No Flower That Blows	Linley, T.	FBSS-2
No One is Alone	Sondheim, S.	BS
Nobody Knows the Trouble I've Seen	Althouse, J., arr.	SSS
	Burleigh, H. T., arr.	FBTS-2
Noche Serena	Latin American	FBTS
Now is the Month of Maying	Morley, T.	55AS
		CCS-M
		SS-2
Now Suffer Me, Fair Maiden (Er laube mir, fein's Mädchen)	Brahms, J., arr.	PS-4
Nymphs and Shepherds	Purcell, H.	CCS-M
O cessate di piagarmi	Scarlatti, A.	26ISAA
		28ISAA
O Mistress Mine	Quilter, R.	ASSV
		ES
		FBBS
		NIE-Br
		SVR-2
O No, John!	English	AS-1
O rest in the Lord	Mendelssohn, F.	56S
		ES-1
		FBMS

Song Title	Composer	Anthology
O Saviour So Meek	Schemelli, G. C.	SS-3
O Saviour, Hear Me!	Gluck, C. W. von	FBSS-2
O Sing the Glories of Our Lord	Ridout, A.	SS-2
Oft Have I Sighed	Campion, T.	NIE-C
Oh Sleep, Why Dost Thou Leave Me?	Handel, G. F.	ASSV
		ES
Oh, Tis the Melody	Bayly, T. H.	PS-2
Oh, What a Beautiful City!	Boatner, E., arr.	FBSS
Oh, What a Beautiful Mornin'	Rodgers, R.	FBBS-T
Oh, When I Was in Love With You	V. Williams, R.	ES
Oklahoma	Rodgers, R.	FBBS-B
Ol' Jim	Edwards, C.	FBTS
Old Dan Tucker	Althouse, J., arr.	FSSS-2
Old Devil Moon	Lane, B.	BR-T
		FBBS-T
Old Folks at Home	Foster, S. C.	STC
Old Smokey	Rodgers, R.	FS
Old Woman and the Peddler, The	Christy, V. A., arr.	ES-1
On A Clear Day	Lane, B.	BR-B
On My Own	Schönberg, C. M.	FBBS-M
On Richmond Hill There Lives a Lass	Hook, J.	FBTS-2
On The Street Where You Live	Lerner, A. J.	BR-T
	Loewe, F.	FBBS-T
On Wings of Song (Auf Flügeln des Gesanges)	Mendelssohn, F.	55AS
		NIE-T
		YS-S
Once in Love with Amy	Loesser, F.	FBBS-T
Once You Lose Your Heart	Gay, N.	FBBS-S
One Day at a Time	Sleeth, N.	WS
Open Thy Lattice, Love	Foster, S. C.	55AS

Level 1 Songs

Song Title	Composer	Anthology
Orpheus with His Lute	Sullivan, A.	NIE-M
	V. Williams, R.	SS-4
Out of My Dreams	Rodgers, R.	FBBS-S
Over the Rainbow	Arlen, H.	BS
Panis Angelicus	Franck, C.	FBTS-2
Part of the Plan	Sleeth, N.	SunS
Passing By	Purcell, E. C.	55AS
		56S
		AS-1
		ES
		ES-1
		PS-1
		STC
		SVR-1
		YS-S
Pastoral, A	Carey, H.	55AS
		ES-2
		YS-S
Pastorale addane, A		STC
Pastorella, spera, spera	Bononcini, M. A.	BS
People	Styne, J.	FBBS-M
People Will Say We're In Love	Rodgers, R.	BR-S
Per Non Penar	d'Astorga, E.	FBSS-2
Petit Jean (Little John)	Champagne, C., arr.	SS-2
Piercing Eyes	Haydn, J.	BS
		FBSS
Piper's Song	Inness, G.	SS-4
Pirate Song, A	Smith, W. R.	SS-3
Plague of Love, The	Arne, T.	NIE-Br
		SBTS
Plaint	Czech	PS-3
Plant a Radish	Schmidt, H.	FBBS-T
Pleading (Bitte)	Franz, R.	YS-S

151

Song Title	Composer	Anthology
Pleading (Bitte)	Franz, R.	YS-T
Policeman's Song, The	Sullivan, A.	SBBS
Poor Boy	Schram, R. E., arr.	FSSS-2
Poor Wayfaring Stranger	Althouse, J., arr.	FSSS-2
Porque toco el pandero	Rodrigo, J.	CCS-M
Praise the Lord	Sleeth, N.	SunS
Pregúntale a Las Estrellas	Latin American	FBMS
Pretty as a Picture	Herbert, V.	FBBS-2
Pretty Creature, The	Wilson, H. L., arr.	ES-1
Pretty Polly Oliver	Old English	AS-1
Pretty Ring Time	Warlock, P.	ASSV
Put On a Happy Face	Adams, L.	BS
Rabbits	Belyea, W. H.	SS-Int
Red, Red, Rose, A	Schumann, R.	FS
Religion Is a Fortune	Johnson, H., arr.	FBTS
Remembrance	Ives, C. E.	FS
Rend'il Sereno Al Cigilo	Handel, G. F.	SVR-2
Request (Bitte)	Franz, R.	AS-2
Requiem	Homer, S.	YS-T
Rio Grande	Dougherty, C., arr.	FBTS
Rise Up, Shepherd, and Follow	Hayes, M., arr.	SSS
Rose Complained, The (es hat die Rosesich beklagt)	Franz, R.	AS-1
Rose Complains, The (Es hat die Rose sich beklagt)		PS-3
Rose, The	Clokey, J. W.	AS-1
	McBroom, A.	BS
Rose-Lipt Maid	Brahms, J., arr.	SS-5
Round of Greeting, A	Sleeth, N.	WS
Rules and Regulations	Wuensch, G.	SS-2
Sailor's Song	Haydn, J.	SVR-1
Santa Lucia	Italian	BS

Song Title	Composer	Anthology
Scarborough Fair	Althouse, J., arr.	FSSS
	Smith, J. S.	FS
Se Florindo è fedele	Scarlatti, A.	ASSV
Se nel ben	Stradella, A.	ES
Sea, The	MacDowell, E.	55AS
		ES-1
		FBBS
Searching for a Gift	Telfer, N.	SS-Int
Sebben, crudele	Caldara, A.	26ISAA
		28ISAA
		CCS-T
Secret Love	Czech	PS-1
Self-Banished, The	Blow, Dr. J.	NIE-Bs
Sento nel core	Scarlatti, A.	26ISAA
		26ISAA
		CIS-2
		FBTS
Serenade	Haydn, J.	SVR-2
		YS-T
Serenade (Liebes Mädchen, hör' mir zu)		PS-2
Shaded with Olive Trees	Greaves, T.	SS-6
Sharing it with me	Sleeth, N.	WS
She Never Told Her Love	Haydn, J.	GAS
She's Like the Swallow	Strommen, C., arr.	FSSS
Shenandoah	Althouse, J., arr.	FSSS-2
	Christy, V. A., arr.	ES-1
Silent Worship	Handel, G. F.	FBTS
Silver'd is the Raven Hair	Sullivan, A.	SBMS
Simple Gifts	American	ASSV
	Holman, D., arr.	SS-3
Simple Little Things	Schmidt, H.	FBBS-M
Sing Noel	Sleeth, N.	SunS

Song Title	Composer	Anthology
Sir Niketty Nox	Marchant, S.	SS-4
Skye Boat Song	Lawson, M., arr.	SS-1
Sleep, Little Angel (Hajej, mujandilku)	Czech	PS-4
So Sweet Is Thy Discourse	Campion, T.	NIE-S
Solitary "Yes", A	Conti, F.	SS-5
Some Day	Ouchterlony, D.	SS-1
Some Folks	Foster, S. C.	FS
		SS-1
Something Wonderful	Rodgers, R.	FBBS-M
Sometimes a Day Goes By	Kander, J.	BS
Sometimes I Feel like a Motherless Child	Frey, H., arr.	SS-5
Song for Bedtime, A	McLean, H. J.	SS-3
Song Is You, The	Kern, J.	FBBS-M
Song of Praise	Somer, H.	SS-2
Song of the Blackbird	Quilter, R.	SBSS
Song of the Carter, The	McLean, H. J., arr.	SS-1
Song of the Drummer, The (La chanson du Tambourineur)	French	PS-2
Song of the Nightingale, The (Wehmut)	Schumann, R.	PS-4
Song of the Palanquin Bearers	Shaw, M.	20CAS
Soon It's Gonna Rain	Schmidt, H.	BR-B
		FBBS-B
Sound of Music, The	Rodgers, R.	FBBS-S
Spesso vibra per suo gioco	Scarlatti, A.	ES
Spring Song, A	Parry, C. H.	SS-6
Star-Spangled Banner, The	Smith, J. S.	FS
Starting Here, Starting Now	Shire, D.	BR-MS
Stranger in Paradise	Wright, R.	FBBS-T
Strike the Viol	Purcell, H.	SVR-1

Song Title	Composer	Anthology
Summer on the Prairie	Anderson, W. H.	SS-1
Sun Whose Rays, The	Sullivan, A.	SBSS
Sunrise of The Ganges (Già il sole dal Gange)	Scarlatti, A.	55AS
Suo-Gan	Rowley, A., arr.	SS-3
Surrey with the Fringe on Top, The	Rodgers, R.	FBBS-B
Sweetest Flower That Blows, The	Hawley, C. B.	SVR-2
		YS-S
Swing Low, Sweet Chariot	American	BS
	Burleigh, H. T., arr.	CCS-B
Sylvelin	Sinding, C.	AS-2
		YS-S
		YS-T
Take Me To The World	Sondheim, S.	BR-T
Te Deum	Handel, G. F.	FBMS-2
		GAS
That's Good	Sleeth, N.	SunS
Then you'll remember me	Balfe, M. W.	56S
There Is Nothin' Like a Dame	Rodgers, R.	FBBS-B
There Stands a Little Man	MacMillan, E., arr.	SS-1
They Call the Wind Maria	Loewe, F.	FBBS-B
Think On Me	Scott, A. A.	SVR-1
This is the Day	Sleeth, N.	SunS
This Nearly Was Mine	Rodgers, R.	FBBS-B
Those Happy Days (O Schönezeit)	Goetze, C.	SR-1
Thou Art A Tender Blossom (Du bist wie eine Blume)	Schumann, R.	PS-4
Thou Art Near (Bist du bei mir)	Bach, J. S.	55AS
Thou'rt Like a Lovely Flower	Schumann, R.	NIE-T
Three	Bowles, P.	SS-3
Through the Eyes of Love	Hamlisch, M.	FS
Thy Beaming Eyes	MacDowell, E.	YS-C
		YS-S

Song Title	Composer	Anthology
Thy Beaming Eyes	MacDowell, E.	YS-T
Till There Was You	Willson, M.	FBBS-S
Tis the Last Rose of Summer	Flotow, F.	CCS-S
To Anthea	Hatton, J. L.	NIE-Br
To Be Near Thee (Star vicino)	Rosa, S.	PS-3
To brune øjne	Grieg, E.	ES
To Friendship (An die Freundschaft)	Haydn, J.	PS-2
To Mary	White, M. V.	NIE-T
To Part, Ah Grief Unending (Ach Gott, wie weh tut Scheiden)	Brahms, J., arr.	PS-4
To the Lute	Schubert, F.	SS-3
To the Nightingale		SS-5
To the Sky	Strommen, C., arr.	FSSS
To the Sunshine	Schumann, R.	SS-6
To Thy Fair Charm	Colasse, P.	PS-1
Tobacco	Hume, T.	NIE-Bs
Tra La La	Granados, E.	SS-5
Tragic Story, A	Mozart, W. A.	ES-1
Try Again	Sleeth, N.	WS
Try to Remember	Schmidt, H.	FBBS-B
Turn Thee To Me	Dvořák, A.	SBTS
Turn Ye to Me	McLean, H. J., arr.	SS-4
	Scottish	BS
Tutu Maramba	Christy, V. A., arr.	ES-1
Twas in the Moon of Wintertime (Jesous Ahatouhia)	Willan, H., arr.	SS-1
Two Grenadiers, The (Die beiden Grenadiere)	Schumann, R.	AS-2
Two Roads	Sleeth, N.	WS
Under the Green Wood Tree	Arne, T.	STC
Under the Greenwood Tree		NIE-T
Under The Tree	Schmidt, H.	BR-MS

Level 1 Songs

Song Title	Composer	Anthology
Valentine Wish, A	Sleeth, N.	WS
Verdant-Meadows	Handel, G. F.	NIE-C
Vergin, tutto amor	Durante, F.	CCS-M
Very Soft Shoes	Barer, M.	FBBS-T
Violet, The	Mozart, W. A.	NIE-M
		SR-2
Violet, The (Das Veilchen)		56S
		SVR-2
Vive la Canadienne! (My Canadian Girl)	McLean, H. J., arr.	SS-1
Vouchsafe, O Lord	Handel, G. F.	PS-4
Waldeinsamkeit	Reger, M.	FBSS
Walk Together, Children	Christy, V. A., arr.	FS
Walking the Woods	Warlock, P.	NIE-Br
Watchman's Song	Hefferman, I.	PS-2
Water is Wide, The	British	BS
Water Parted from the Sea	Arne, T.	FBSS
Wayfaring Stranger	Niles, J. J.	FBTS
We Kiss in a Shadow	Rodgers, R.	FBBS-T
We're on Our Way	Sleeth, N.	WS
What Are You Doing the Rest of Your Life?	LeGrand, M.	BS
What I Did For Love	Hamlisch, M.	BR-MS
What if a Day	Campion, T.	FS
What Songs Were Sung	Niles, J. J.	FBTS-2
What's the Use of Wond'rin'	Rodgers, R.	FBBS-M
When Daisies Pied	Arne, T.	FBSS-2
		NIE-M
When First My Old	Sullivan, A.	SBTS
When First We Met	Handel, G. F.	YS-B
		YS-T
When First We Met (Non Io dirò col labbro)		SVR-1

Section 3

Song Title	Composer	Anthology
When from My Love	Bartlet, J.	BS
When I Am Dead, My Dearest	Coleridge-Taylor, S.	ES
When I Have Often Heard Young Maids Complaining	Purcell, H.	FBMS-2
When I was a Lad I Served a Term	Sullivan, A.	SBBS
When I was One-and-Twenty	Gibbs, C. A.	CAS
When Laura Smiles	Rosseter, P.	FS
When Love is Kind	Old English	AS-1
		PS-3
		STC
		YS-S
When the Children Are Asleep	Rodgers, R.	FBBS-T
When The Roses Bloom	Reichardt, L.	YS-S
When the Saints Go Marchin' In	Smith, J. S.	FS
When To Her Lute Corinna Sings	Campion, T.	55AS
Where E'er You Walk	Handel, G. F.	56S
		CCS-T
		FBTS-2
		SVR-1
		YS-T
Where I Believed	Caccini, F.	SS-6
Where or When	Rodgers, R.	FBBS-M
Where the Bee Sucks	Arne, T.	NIE-S
Whispering Hope	Hawthorne, A.	56S
Who Ever Thinks or Hopes of Love	Dowland, J.	NIE-M
Who Has Seen the Wind?	Kasemets, U.	SS-1
Who'll Buy My Lavender?	German, E.	YS-S
Why Do I Love You?	Kern, J.	FBBS-S
Widmung	Franz, R.	BS
Wiegenlied	Flies, J. B.	STC
	Mozart, W. A.	STC
Wind, The	Sharman, C.	SS-1
Winter's a Drag Rag, The	Sleeth, N.	WS

Song Title	Composer	Anthology
Witchcraft	Chopin, F.	SS-3
With a Song in My Heart	Rodgers, R.	FBBS-S
Wonderful Day Like Today, A	Bricusse, L.	FBBS-T
Wonderful Guy, A	Rodgers, R.	FBBS-M
Would You Gain the Tender Creature	Handel, G. F.	NIE-T
Wouldn't It Be Loverly?	Loewe, F.	FBBS-S
Wunderbar	Porter, C.	FBBS-B
Ye Verdant Hills	Handel, G. F.	NIE-T
Yesterday	Lennon & McCartney	FS
Yo no se que decir	Mexican	ES
You and I	Sleeth, N.	SunS
You Never Stop Learning		WS
You've Got to Be Carefully Taught	Rodgers, R.	FBBS-T
Young And Foolish	Hague, A.	BR-T
Younger Than Springtime	Rodgers, R.	FBBS-T

Section 3

Level 2 Songs

Song Title	Composer	Anthology
Ach Lieb, ich muss nun scheiden	Strauss, R.	FS
Across the Western Ocean	Dougherty, C., arr.	20CAS
		FBBS
Adelaide	Beethoven, L.	NIE-T
Adieu	Mozart, W. A.	NIE-C
Adieu pour jamais	Loeffler, C. M.	50ASMR
After a Dream (Après un rêve)	Fauré, G.	ES-2
Ah! mio cor	Handel, G. F.	ASSV
		FBMS-2
Ah! quanto è vero	Cesti, M. A.	CIS-2
Ah, Love of Mine (Caro mio ben)	Giordani, G.	55AS
Ah, No Stormy Wind	Russian	PS-4
Ah, Poor Heart (Ah! mio cor from "Alcina")	Handel, G. F.	ES-2
Ahi, troppo è duro	Monteverde, C.	CIS
Air (Care Selve)	Handel, G. F.	PS-3
Air from Comus	Arne, T.	STC
		SVR-1
All Soul's Day (Allerseelen)	Strauss, R.	56S
		ES-2
All the Pretty Little Horses	American	BS
All Your Shades	Lully, J. B.	NIE-Bs
Allerseelen	Strauss, R.	50SS
		ASSV
Alma del core	Caldara, A.	26ISAA
		28ISAA
		CIS-2
Aloha oe	Liliuokalani, Queen	56S
Alone in the Fields (Wäldeinsamkeit)	Brahms, J.	55AS
Alone in the Forest	Strauss, R.	NIE-M
Amarilli	Caccini, G.	PS-3
Amarilli, mia bella		26ISAA
		28ISAA

Song Title	Composer	Anthology
Amarilli, mia bella	Caccini, G.	STC
Amarylis		NIE-T
Amazing Grace	Althouse, J., arr.	FSSS
Amor dormiglione	Strozzi, B.	CIS-3
An die Geliebte	Beethoven, L.	FBTS-2
An die Leier	Schubert, F.	GAS
An die Musik		CCS-M
		FS
		SBMS
		STC
An die Nachtigall	Brahms, J.	SBMS
An Immorality	Hoiby, L.	CAS
And All That Jazz	Kander, J.	BR-MS
And This Is My Beloved	Wright, R.	FBBS-S
Andenken	Beethoven, L.	FBSS-2
Angels through the Night	Kern, P., arr.	FSSS
Après un rêve	Fauré, G.	50ASMR
		55AS
		ASSV
		BS
April Weather	Archer, V.	SS-6
Arrival of the Royal Barge, The	Purcell, H.	SVR-1
Art Is Calling For Me	Herbert, V.	SBSS
As a Sunbeam at Morn	Caldara, A.	NIE-C
As From the Sun A Ray (Come raggio di sole)		PS-4
As I Walked Forth	Foss, H.	SS-6
Asturiana	de Falla, M.	ES
At Last	Brahms, J.	NIE-S
At Sea	Ives, C. E.	ES
Au bord de l'eau	Fauré, G.	SBMS
Auf dem grünen Balcon	Wolf, H.	50SS
		GAS

Level 2 Songs

Song Title	Composer	Anthology
Auf dem Kirchhofe	Brahms, J.	50SS
Auf dem Meere	Franz, R.	FBMS-2
Auf geheimem Waldespfade	Griffes, C. T.	50ASMR
Aufträge	Schumann, R.	GAS
Aurore	Fauré, G.	50ASMR
		GAS
Autumn Evening	Quilter, R.	SBTS
Ave Maria	Abt, F.	FBSS-2
	Saint-Saëns, C.	FBTS-2
	Schubert, F.	56S
		AS-2
		STC
Ave Verum	Mozart, W. A.	FBMS-2
Away Over Yandro	Christy, V. A., arr.	ES-1
Bali Ha'I	Rodgers, R.	BR-MS
		FBBS-M
Barcarolle	Offenbach, J.	56S
Be Thou Faithful Unto Death	Mendelssohn, F.	SBTS
Beatitudes, The	Malotte, A. H.	FBSS
Beau Soir	Debussy, C.	ASSV
		ES
Because	D'Hardelot, G.	SVR-1
Begli occhi, io non mi pento	Perti, J. A.	CIS-3
Bei Dir!	Schubert, F.	GAS
Bel nume	Cimador, G. B.	ES
Bel Piacere	Handel, G. F.	FBSS
Bells of Aberdovey, The	MacMillan, E., arr.	SS-2
Bells of Clermont Town, The	Goodhart, A. M.	FBBS
Bells, The (Les Cloches)	Debussy, C.	PS-4
Beloved Strand (Spiagge Amate)	Gluck, C. W. von	PS-3
Belshazzar	Schumann, R.	NIE-Br
Benedictus	Schubert, F.	ASSV
Bescheidene Liebe	Wolf, H.	50SS

Song Title	Composer	Anthology
Bescheidene Liebe	Wolf, H.	SBSS
Bird and the Rose, The	Horrocks, A. E.	SR-1
Birds in the High Hall-garden	Somervell, A.	NIE-Br
Bist du bei mir	Bach, J. S.	FBMS-2
		STC
Bitten	Beethoven, L.	FS
Black Roses	Sibelius, J.	SVR-1
Black Swan, The from "The Medium"	Menotti, G. C.	20CAS
Blessed Redeemer (Liebster Herr Jesu)	Bach, J. S.	PS-4
Blind Ploughman, The	Clarke, R. C.	FBBS
Blow, Blow, Thou Winter Wind	Arne, T.	ASSV
	Quilter, R.	FBBS
Blow, Ye Winds	Dougherty, C., arr.	FBBS-2
Blue are Her Eyes	Watts, W.	AS-2
Blue Bird	Crist, B.	SR-1
Blue-Bell, The	MacDowell, E.	FBMS-2
Boat Song (Im Kahne)	Grieg, E.	55AS
Bois épais	Lully, J. B.	ASSV
		ES
		FBBS-2
		SVR-2
Bonjour Suzon	Delibes, L.	YS-S
Bonjour, Suzon!		FBTS-2
Bonne Nuit	Massenet, J.	FBSS
Bonnie Earl of Murray, The	Gurney, I.	NIE-Br
Botschaft	Brahms, J.	50SS
		GAS
Bread of Angels (Panis Angelicus)	Franck, C.	ES-1
Bride's Song, The	Schumann, R.	NIE-M
Bright Is the Ring of Words	V. Williams, R.	BS
		FBBS-2

Level 2 Songs

Song Title	Composer	Anthology
Bring Him Home	Schönberg, C. M.	FBBS-T
Brooklet, The	Loder, E. J.	NIE-T
Brother Will, Brother John	Sacco, J.	20CAS
		FBTS
Buckle, The	Bliss, A.	20CAS
Build Thee More Stately Mansions	Andrews, M.	FBBS-2
By Mendip Side	Coates, E.	FBTS
By the Brook	Grieg, E.	50ASMR
Call, The	V. Williams, R.	SBTS
Calm as the Night (Still wie die Nacht)	Bohm, C.	56S
Calm at Sea (Meeresstille)	Schubert, F.	PS-2
Camptown Races	Althouse, J., arr.	FSSS-2
Can't Help Lovin' Dat Man	Kern, J.	BR-S
Canción del niño por nacer	Gonzalez, L. J.	ES
Cantique de Noël	Adam, A.	STC
Captive, The (L'Esclave)	Lalo, É.	ES-2
Care Selve	Handel, G. F.	NIE-S
Carmeña	Wilson, H. L.	FBMS-2
Caro mio ben	Giordani, G.	CIS
		CCS-T
Cease, Oh Maiden	Scarlatti, A.	NIE-Br
Chanson d'Amour	Fauré, G.	ES
Chanson espagnole	Ravel, M.	50ASMR
Che fiero costume	Legrenzi, G.	26ISAA
		28ISAA
		CIS-2
Chi vuol la zingarella	Paisiello, G.	ES
		FBMS
Chi vuole innomorarsi	Scarlatti, A.	CIS-3
Child of The Flowing Tide	Shaw, M.	SBBS
Christkind	Cornelius, P.	SBTS

Song Title	Composer	Anthology
Christmas Carol, A	Rorem, N.	FS
Cicerenella	Italian	PS-4
Cindy	Althouse, J., arr.	FSSS-2
Clair de lune	Debussy, C.	GAS
Climb Ev'ry Mountain	Rodgers, R.	BR-S
		FBBS-S
Climbin' Up the Mountain	Simms, P. F., arr.	SSS
Cloths of Heaven, The	Dunhill, T.	FBTS-2
Cloud-Shadows	Rogers, J. H.	FBMS
Clouds	Charles, E.	FBMS-2
Cock-Eyed Optimist, A	Rodgers, R.	FBBS-M
Col mio sangue comprerei	Stradella, A.	CIS-2
Come Let's be Merry	Old English	YS-B
Come raggio di sol	Caldara, A.	26ISAA
		28ISAA
		CIS-2
Come Sweet Repose	Bach, J. S.	SR-2
Come Unto These Yellow Sands	Purcell, H.	ES-2
Come Ye Blessed	Scott, J. P.	SBBS
Come, Sweet Death (Komm, Süsser Tod)	Bach, J. S.	PS-3
Comedy Tonight--	Sondheim, S.	FBBS-B
Con amores, la mi madre	Obradors, F. J.	BS
Corals	Treharne, B.	50ASMR
Cosi, amor, mi fai languir!	Stradella, A.	CIS-3
Could I (Vorrei)	Tosti, F. P.	SR-2
Crabbed Age and Youth	White, M. V.	FBMS
Cradle Song	Mendelssohn, F.	NIE-C
	Schubert, F.	NIE-M
Cradle Song (Wiegenlied)		PS-3
Cradles, The (Les Berceaux)	Fauré, G.	ES-2
		PS-2

Song Title	Composer	Anthology
Cradlesong of the Poor	Moussorgsky, M. P.	55AS
Create in Me a Clean Heart, O God	Mueller, C. F.	FBBS
Crépuscule	Massenet, J.	FBMS-2
Cross the Wide Missouri	Besig, D., arr.	FSSS
Crucifixion	Payne, J., arr.	FBMS
Crucifixion, The	Barber, S.	15AAS
		FBSS
Crying of Water, The	Campbell-Tipton, L.	FBSS-2
Cuckoo, The	Lehmann, L.	SVR-1
		YS-C
		YS-S
D'Une Prison	Hahn, R.	GAS
Da unten im Tale	Brahms, J.	ES
Daisies, The	Barber, S.	FBTS
Dance, Maiden, Dance (Danza, danza Fanciulla)	Durante, F.	PS-3
Dank sei Dir, Herr	Handel, G. F.	GAS
Danny Boy	Irish	FBMS-2
	Knowles, J., arr.	FSSS
Dans les Ruines d'une Abbaye	Fauré, G.	GAS
Danza, danza, fanciulla gentile	Durante, F.	26ISAA
		28ISAA
		CIS-2
		STC
Das Erste Veilchen	Mendelssohn, F.	FBMS-2
Das Fischermädchen	Schubert, F.	FBTS-2
Das Leben ist ein Traum	Haydn, J.	GAS
Das Verlassene Mägdlein	Wolf, H.	SBSS
Days of Spring, The (Frühlingszeit)	Becker, R.	55AS
Dear Love of Mine (Caro mio ben)	Giordani, G.	ES-2
Dearest and Best (Caro mio ben)	Giordani, Tommaso	SR-1
Dearest Consort	Handel, G. F.	NIE-C
Dearest, believe (Caro mio ben)	Giordani, G.	56S

Song Title	Composer	Anthology
Death and the Maiden	Schubert, F.	NIE-C
Dedication (Widmung)	Franz, R.	56S
		AS-1
		ES-1
		PS-2
		YS-B
Deep in My Heart	Bishop, Sir H.	NIE-M
Deep River	Burleigh, H. T., arr.	FBBS-2
Deh più a me non v'ascondete	Bononcini, G.	CIS-3
Deh, contentatevi	Carissimi, G.	CIS-2
Deh, rendetemi	Provenzale, F.	CIS-2
Dein Angesicht	Schumann, R.	SBTS
Der Blumenstrauss	Mendelssohn, F.	FBMS
Der Gang Zum Liebchen	Brahms, J.	SBTS
Der Jäger		GAS
Der Lindenbaum	Schubert, F.	SBBS
Der Mond	Mendelssohn, F.	FBTS
Der Musikant	Wolf, H.	ES
Der Neugierige	Schubert, F.	FBTS
Der Nussbaum	Schumann, R.	50SS
Der Schmetterling	Schubert, F.	50SS
		GAS
Der Wanderer		SBBS
Dido's Lament	Purcell, H.	ASSV
Dido's Lament from "Dido and Aeneas"		ES-2
Die Bekehrte	Stange, M.	FBMS
Die Forelle	Schubert, F.	SBTS
Die Hirten	Cornelius, P.	SBBS
Die Könige		FBBS-2
Die Lotosblume	Schumann, R.	50SS
		STC
Die Mainacht	Brahms, J.	GAS

Song Title	Composer	Anthology
Die Nacht	Strauss, R.	SBSS
Die Post	Schubert, F.	SBBS
Die Stille	Schumann, R.	ES
		FBMS-2
Die Stille Wasserrose	Fielitz, A. von	FBMS-2
Dissonance, A	Borodine, A.	56S
Do Not Go, My Love	Hageman, R.	15AAS
		56S
		CCS-S
Don Juan's Serenade	Tchaikovsky, P.	NIE-Br
Dove Sei	Handel, G. F.	ES
Dove sei, amato bene? from "Rodelinda"		GAS
Dove Song, The from "The Wings of the Dove"	Moore, D.	CAS
Down in the Forest	Ronald, L.	SBSS
Dream, A	Bartlett, J. C.	YS-T
Dream-Land	V. Williams, R.	SBTS
Dreaming (Träume)	Wagner, R.	55AS
Dreams (Träume)		56S
Drift Down, Drift Down	Ronald, L.	FBSS-2
Drinking	German	NIE-Bs
Droop Not, Young Lover	Handel, G. F.	NIE-Bs
Dryads, Sylvans		NIE-M
Du bist die Ruh'	Schubert, F.	SBMS
Du bist wie eine Blume	Liszt, F.	FBBS-2
	Schumann, R.	50SS
		ASSV
		CCS-B
		FBBS-2
Du bist wie eine Blume (E'en as a Lovely Flower)	Willan, H.	SS-6
Dust of Snow	Carter, E.	SS-5

Song Title	Composer	Anthology
E dove t'aggiri	Cesti, M. A.	CIS-2
E'en As a Lovely Flower	Bridge, F.	NIE-T
Early in the Morning	Rorem, N.	BS
Earth and Other Minor Things, The	Loewe, F.	FBBS-M
Earth and Sky	Brahms, J.	NIE-Bs
Easter Carol	Shaw, M.	CAS
Echo	Hindemith, P.	ES
Edelweiss	Rodgers, R.	FBBS-B
Ein Ton	Cornelius, P.	FBBS-2
El Majo Timido	Granados, E.	FBMS
El tra la la y el punteado		CCS-S
		FBSS
El Trobador	Mexican	FBTS-2
Eldorado	Walthew, R. H.	FBBS-2
Elégie	Massenet, J.	56S
		FBMS-2
Elegy (Elégie)		55AS
		ES-2
En Barque	Pierné, G.	GAS
En prière	Fauré, G.	50ASMR
Encantadora Maria	Latin American	FBBS
Enchantress, The	Hatton, J. L.	NIE-C
Endless Pleasure, Endless Love	Handel, G. F.	NIE-S
English Usage	Thomson, V.	CAS
Erhebung	Schoenberg, A.	50ASMR
Es Muss ein Wunderbares Sein	Liszt, F.	FBMS-2
Ethiopia Saluting the Colours	Wood, C.	NIE-Bs
Evening Fair (Beau Soir)	Debussy, C.	ES-2
Evening Prayer, The	Moussorgsky, M. P.	50ASMR
Evensong	Lehmann, L.	FBMS
Everybody Says Don't	Sondheim, S.	BR-B
Everyone Sang	Wells, H.	CAS

Song Title	Composer	Anthology
Everywhere I Look!	Carew, M.	FBSS
Exquisite Hour (L'huere Exquise)	Hahn, R.	55AS
Exquisite Hour, The (L'Heure exquise)		ES-2
Eye Hath Not Seen	Gaul, A.	ES-1
		SBMS
Ezekiel's Wheel	Kern, P., arr.	SSS
Fair House of Joy	Quilter, R.	SBTS
Faith in Spring (Frühlingsglaube)	Schubert, F.	AS-2
		ES-1
False Phillis	Wilson, H. L., arr.	FBBS
Fanny	Rome, H.	BR-T
Fare You Well	American	SVR-1
Farewell (Adieu!)	Schubert, F.	PS-1
Farewell, A	Strauss, R.	NIE-S
Farmer by the Sea	Lane, R.	ES
Feast of Love (Liebesfeier)	Franz, R.	PS-1
Ferryman, The	Helyer, M.	SS-Int
Fifty Million Years Ago	Schmidt, H.	BR-T
Filli, non t'amo più	Carissimi, G.	CIS-3
Fiocca la neve	Cimara, P.	50ASMR
		SBSS
Fire Down Below	Althouse, J., arr.	FSSS-2
First Meeting, The (Erstes Begegnen)	Grieg, E.	PS-3
First Primrose, The (Mit einer primula veris)		PS-1
Fleur des Blés	Debussy, C.	GAS
Florian's Song (Chanson de Florian)	Godard, B.	AS-1
		ES-2
For Music (Für Music)	Franz, R.	AS-1
		PS-1
		YS-B
		YS-T

Song Title	Composer	Anthology
Forsake Me Not, My Love, I Pray	Rachmaninoff, S.	GAS
Freudvoll und leidvoll from "Egmont"	Beethoven, L.	GAS
From Far, from Eve and Morning	V. Williams, R.	NIE-T
From the North	Sibelius, J.	50ASMR
Frühlingsglaube	Schubert, F.	ES
Frühlingsnacht	Schumann, R.	50SS
Frühlingsträum	Schubert, F.	SBTS
Fussreise	Wolf, H.	50ASMR
Garland, The	Brahms, J.	NIE-Br
Gefror'ne Thränen	Schubert, F.	SBBS
Gentle Shepherd	Pergolesi, G. B.	NIE-S
Gesang Weylas	Wolf, H.	50ASMR
Già il sole dal Gange	Scarlatti, A.	26ISAA
		26ISAA
Girls' Song	Howells, H.	NIE-M
Glory of God in Nature, The (Die Ehre Grottes in der Natur)	Beethoven, L.	55AS
Go 'Way from My Window	Niles, J. J.	FBMS
Go, Lovely Rose	Quilter, R.	FBTS
God is My Shepherd	Dvořák, A.	FBBS-2
Gonna Be Another Hot Day	Schmidt, H.	BR-B
Good Morning (God Morgen)	Grieg, E.	PS-4
Good-bye	Tosti, F. P.	55AS
Good-bye!		56S
Gott im Frühling	Schubert, F.	FBMS-2
Grandma	Chanler, T.	FBSS-2
Grasshopper Green	Taylor, C.	SS-2
Green Dog, The	Kingsley, H.	20CAS
		FBSS
Green Hills O' Somerset, The	Coates, E.	SBTS
Gretchen at the Spinning Wheel	Schubert, F.	NIE-S

Song Title	Composer	Anthology
Gute Nacht	Franz, R.	ASSV
Hark! How Still (Still Sicherheit)		PS-3
Hark! Hark! The Lark	Schubert, F.	AS-2
Hark! What I Tell to Thee	Haydn, J.	NIE-C
Have You Seen But a White Lillie Grow?	Old English	ASSV
He Is Noble, He Is Patient	Schumann, R.	NIE-S
He Wasn't You She Wasn't You	Lane, B.	FS
He's Gone Away	Schram, R. E., arr.	FSSS-2
Hear My Cry, O God	Franck, C.	FBSS
Hear My Prayer, O Lord	Dvořák, A.	SBSS
Heard Ye His Voice	Rubinstein, A.	SBMS
Heart Worships, The	Holst, G.	FBBS-2
Heaven-Rays (Himmelsfunken)	Schubert, F.	PS-4
Heavenly Grass	Bowles, P.	15AAS
		CAS
Hedge-roses (Heidenröslein)	Schubert, F.	AS-1
Heidenröslein		50SS
		ES
Heimkehr	Strauss, R.	50SS
		GAS
His Coming (Er ist gekommen)	Franz, R.	AS-2
Holiday Song	Schuman, W.	CAS
Homeward Bound	Althouse, J., arr.	FSSS
Honey Shun	Schirmer, R.	20CAS
How Art Thou Fall'n	Handel, G. F.	NIE-Br
How Calm Is My Spirit	Mozart, W. A.	NIE-S
How Could I Ever Know	Simon, L.	BS
How Do I Love Thee?	Dello Joio, N.	STC
How Fair This Spot	Rachmaninoff, S.	NIE-S
How Soft, upon the Evening Air	Dunhill, T.	SS-3
Hugh's Song of the Road	V. Williams, R.	CAS

Song Title	Composer	Anthology
Hush, Be Silent	Purcell, H.	SVR-1
I Am a Roamer	Mendelssohn, F.	NIE-Bs
I Attempt From Love's Sickness to Fly	Purcell, H.	ES-2
I Believe In You	Loesser, F.	FBBS-T
I Dreamed That I Was Weeping (Ich hab' im Traum geweinet)	Schumann, R.	ES-2
I Got Plenty O' Nuttin'	Gershwin, G.	BR-B
I Had Myself A True Love	Arlen, H.	BR-S
I Have Dreamed	Rodgers, R.	FBBS-S
I heard a Cry	Fisher, W. A.	AS-2
I Love and I Must	Purcell, H.	FBTS
I Love thee (Ich liebe dich)	Beethoven, L.	56S
		PS-2
	Grieg, E.	SVR-1
		YS-S
		YS-T
I Loved You Once In Silence	Loewe, F.	BR-S
I Said I Will Forget Thee	Brahms, J.	NIE-Bs
I Sought the Lord	Stevenson, F.	SBMS
I Triumph! I Triumph!	Carissimi, G.	NIE-Bs
I Wept, Beloved, As I Dreamed (J'ai pleurè un rêve)	Hüe, G.	ES-2
I'll Never Ask You to Tell	Fox, O. J.	SR-1
I'll Not Complain (Ich grolle nicht)	Schumann, R.	ES-2
I'll Sail Upon The Dog Star	Purcell, H.	SBTS
I'll Sail upon the Dog-Star		NIE-T
I'm Nobody	Persichetti, V.	ES
I'm Wearing Awa' to the Land O' the Leal	Foote, A.	YS-B
		YS-C
		YS-S
		YS-T

Song Title	Composer	Anthology
I've Been Roaming	Horn, C. E.	YS-C
Ich hab' in Deinem Auge	Schumann, C.	ES
Ich Liebe dich	Beethoven, L.	STC
Ich liebe dich so wie du mich		ASSV
Ich trage meine Minne	Strauss, R.	50SS
Ici-Bas!	Fauré, G.	FBMS
		GAS
If All the Seas Were One Sea	McLean, H. J.	SS-6
If Ever I Would Leave You	Loewe, F.	BR-B
If God left only you	Densmore, J. H.	AS-2
If Music Be the Food of Love	Purcell, H.	SVR-1
If Thou Be Near (Bist du bei mir)	Bach, J. S.	PS-2
If Thou Love Me (Se tu m'ami)	Pergolesi, G. B.	55AS
If Thou Thy Heart Will Give Me	Bach, J. S.	SR-1
Il mio bel foco	Marcello, B.	28ISAA
Il Neige	Bemberg, H.	SVR-2
Im Abendroth	Schubert, F.	50SS
Im Herbst	Franz, R.	SBMS
Impatience (Ungeduld)	Schubert, F.	ES-2
In a Strange Land	Taubert, W.	NIE-M
In dem Schatten meiner Locken	Wolf, H.	50SS
In Der Fremde	Schumann, R.	FBTS-2
In einem Kühlen Grunde	German	FBBS-2
In Evening's Glow (Im Abendrot)	Schubert, F.	PS-1
In Summer Fields (Feldeinsamkeit)	Brahms, J.	AS-2
In the Silence of Night	Rachmaninoff, S.	50ASMR
In the Silent Night (V'mo Hchányinótchi táinoi)		SVR-1
In Waldeseinsamkeit	Brahms, J.	50SS
Incline Thine Ear	Charles, E.	FBTS-2
Intermezzo	Schumann, R.	FBBS
		GAS

Song Title	Composer	Anthology
Intorno All' Idol Mio	Cesti, M. A.	FBSS-2
Invocazione de Orfeo	Peri, J.	CIS
Is It Bliss or is It Sorrow?	Brahms, J.	NIE-T
Island, The	Rachmaninoff, S.	50ASMR
		SBBS
It Must Be Me from "Candide"	Bernstein, L.	20CAS
It Must Be Wonderful Indeed (Es muss ein Wunderbares sein)	Liszt, F.	PS-1
It Must Be Wonderful, Indeed (Es muss ein Wunderbares sein)		55AS
It was a Dream	Lassen, E.	55AS
It Was a Lover and His Lass	Coates, E.	FBTS-2
J'ai pleuré en rêve	Hüe, G.	50ASMR
Jailer's Slumber Song, The	Russian	PS-4
Japanese Night Song	Bennett, C.	SVR-2
Jardin d'amour	Keel, J. F., arr.	SS-5
Jeg elsker Dig	Grieg, E.	ES
Jesus Walked This Lonesome Valley	Myers, G., arr.	FBMS
Jesus, Jesus, Rest Your Head	American	YS-B
		YS-C
Jolly Jolly Breeze, The	Eccles, J.	SBMS
Jolly Roger, The	Robertson, R. R.	FBBS
Joshua Fit the Battle of Jericho	Christy, V. A., arr.	ES-1
Joy of Love, The (Plaisir d'amour)	Martini, G.	ES
Joys of Love, The (Plaisir d'amour)		ES-1
Júrame	Grever, M.	56S
Just One Person	Grossman, L.	BR-T
K'e, The	Dougherty, C.	20CAS
		FBSS
Keine Sorg' um den Weg	Raff, J.	FBMS-2
Kind Fortune Smiles	Purcell, H.	SBMS
King Charles	White, M. V.	NIE-Br

Level 2 Songs

Song Title	Composer	Anthology
King of Love My Shepherd Is, The	Gounod, C.	FBBS
King of Song, The	Thiman, E. H.	SS-5
Kingdom by the Sea, A	Somervell, A.	FBTS-2
Kiss, The (Der kuss)	Beethoven, L.	PS-3
Kitty of Colerain	Irish	PS-3
Kitty of Coleraine	Easson, J., arr.	SS-4
Know'st Thou the Land	Beethoven, L.	NIE-M
Kum Ba Yah	Simms, P. F., arr.	SSS
L'Amour de Moi	French	FBBS-2
L'Amour de mois de mai	Lefevre, J.	ES
L'Anneau D'Argent	Chaminade, C.	FBMS
L'Esclave	Lalo, É.	50ASMR
L'esperto nocchiero	Bononcini, G.	CIS-2
L'Heure exquise	Hahn, R.	50ASMR
		FBSS-2
L'Huere exquise		ASSV
La donna è mobile	Verdi, G.	56S
La Paloma Blanca	Latin American	FBBS
La Partida	Alvarez, F.	GAS
La Pastorella	Schubert, F.	FBSS-2
La Seña	Latin American	FBTS
Lachen und Weinen	Schubert, F.	CCS-S
Lasciatemi morire	Monteverde, C.	FS
Lasciatemi morire!		26ISAA
		28ISAA
		ASSV
Lascitemi morire		CIS
Lass with the Delicate Air, The	Arne, M.	56S
		STC
	Arne, T.	ES-2
Last Toast, The	Schumann, R.	NIE-Bs
Lazy Afternoon	Moross, J.	BR-MS

Song Title	Composer	Anthology
Le Miroir	Ferrari, G.	FBBS-2
		GAS
Le Secret	Fauré, G.	FBBS
Le Violette	Scarlatti, A.	26ISAA
		28ISAA
		GAS
Leave Me in Sorrow (Lascia ch'io pianga)	Handel, G. F.	PS-2
Leave Me to Languish (Lascia ch'io pianga) from "Rinaldo"		ES-2
Leave Me, Loathsome Light		FBBS
Leave me, loathsome light! from "Semele"		GAS
Les berceaux	Fauré, G.	SBMS
Les Cloches	Debussy, C.	SBSS
Les Papillons	Chausson, E.	GAS
Les Roses D'Ispahan	Fauré, G.	SBBS
Let Each Gallant Heart	Purcell, H.	SBBS
Let Me Wander Not Unseen	Handel, G. F.	NIE-S
Let My Song Fill Your Heart	Charles, E.	FBSS
Let the Dreadful Engines	Purcell, H.	NIE-Br
Let Us Break Bread Together	Althouse, J., arr.	SSS
Libera me	Fauré, G.	ASSV
Lied	Franck, C.	PS-2
Lied der Mignon	Schubert, F.	FBSS
Like The Shadow	Handel, G. F.	SBBS
Lilacs	Rachmaninoff, S.	56S
		SBMS
Lime Tree, The	Schubert, F.	NIE-Bs
Linden Lea	V. Williams, R.	FBTS-2
Litany	Schubert, F.	NIE-C
Lithuanian Song (Lithauisches Lied)	Chopin, F.	ES-1
Little Closer, Please, A	Bowles, P.	SS-6

Song Title	Composer	Anthology
Little Elegy	Duke, J.	FBSS
Little Irish Girl, The	Lohr, H.	YS-B
Little Red Lark, The	Nyklicek, G.	SVR-2
Londonderry Air	Irish	56S
Lonely House	Weill, K.	BR-S
Lonely Room	Rodgers, R.	BR-B
Lonesome Valley	Christy, V. A., arr.	ES-1
Long Ago	MacDowell, E.	SBTS
Look To The Rainbow	Lane, B.	BR-MS
Lord God of Abraham	Mendelssohn, F.	SBBS
Lord Is My Light, The	Speaks, O.	FBTS
Lord Is My Shepherd, The	Liddle, S.	SBTS
	Tchaikovsky, P.	FBMS
Lord, I Want to Be a Christian	Payne, J., arr.	FBBS
Lost Chord, The	Sullivan, A.	55AS
		56S
		ES-1
Lost In The Stars	Weill, K.	BR-B
Lotus Flower, The (Die Lotusblume)	Schumann, R.	55AS
		AS-1
		ES-1
		PS-1
Love and a Day	Willan, H.	SS-5
Love Has Eyes	Bishop, Sir H.	YS-B
		YS-C
Love is a Bable	Parry, C. H.	SBBS
Love Song	Brahms, J.	NIE-T
Love Song (Minnelied)		AS-2
Love That's True Will Live for Ever	Handel, G. F.	NIE-Bs
Love Triumphant	Brahms, J.	NIE-C
Love's Philosophy	Quilter, R.	SBSS
		SVR-2
Love, I Have Won You	Ronald, L.	SBMS

Song Title	Composer	Anthology
Love, I Hear	Sondheim, S.	BR-T
Loveliest of Trees	Duke, J.	15AAS
Luci vezzose	Gaffi, B.	CIS-3
Lullaby	Godard, B.	56S
	Scott, C.	FBSS
Lullaby from "The Consul"	Menotti, G. C.	CAS
Lullaby, A	Harty, H.	NIE-S
		SBMS
Lungi Dal Caro Bene	Sarti, G.	FBBS
	Secchi, A.	26ISAA
		CIS
Maiden's Wish, The (Mädchen's Wunch)	Chopin, F.	SVR-2
Mariä Wiegenlied	Reger, M.	FBMS-2
Mattinata	Leoncavallo, R.	GAS
		SBBS
Mein Glaubiges Herze	Bach, J. S.	SBSS
Mein schöner Stern!	Schumann, R.	50SS
Meine Liebe ist grün	Brahms, J.	50SS
Meine Lieder		GAS
Memory	Ireland, J.	SBBS
Memory, A	Ganz, R.	50ASMR
Mermaid's Song, The	Haydn, J.	FBSS
Message, The	Brahms, J.	NIE-Br
Mignon's Song	Liszt, F.	NIE-C
Milkmaids	Warlock, P.	SS-6
Mill-Wheel, The (Das Mühlrad)	Germany	PS-2
Minnelied	Mendelssohn, F.	FBSS
Minor Bird, A	Dougherty, C.	20CAS
Mister Banjo	Christy, V. A., arr.	ES-1
Mistress Mine	Walthew, R. H.	FBTS
Mit deinen blauen Augen	Strauss, R.	GAS

Song Title	Composer	Anthology
Mit Einem Gemalten Band	Beethoven, L.	SBTS
Mit Myrthen und Rosen	Schumann, R.	50SS
Mondnacht		50SS
Money, O!	Head, M.	NIE-Bs
Monk and His Cat, The	Barber, S.	15AAS
Moon-Marketing	Weaver, P.	20CAS
Moonlight	Schumann, R.	NIE-T
More Sweet is That Name	Handel, G. F.	SBBS
Morgen	Strauss, R.	50ASMR
		50SS
		YS-B
		YS-C
		YS-S
		YS-T
Morning	Speaks, O.	FBMS
Morning Hymn	Henschel, G.	YS-S
Morning Hymn (Morgen-Hymne)		SVR-2
Much More	Schmidt, H.	BR-S
Music, When Soft Voices Die	Gold, E.	20CAS
Must the Winter Come so Soon?	Barber, S.	CAS
My Crow Pluto	Thomson, V.	20CAS
My Cup Runneth Over	Schmidt, H.	BR-B
My Dear One's Mouth is Like the Rose (Mein Mädel hat einen Rosenmund)	Brahms, J.	PS-2
My Funny Valentine	Rodgers, R.	BR-MS
My Heart at thy sweet voice (Mon coeur s'ouvre à ta voix)	Saint-Saëns, C.	56S
My Heart Is Like a Singing Bird	Parry, C. H.	SBSS
My Johann	Grieg, E.	FBSS
My Lady Walks in Loveliness	Charles, E.	FBTS
My Last Abode	Schubert, F.	NIE-Bs
My Life's Delight	Quilter, R.	SBTS

Song Title	Composer	Anthology
My Love rode by	Calbreath, M. E.	AS-1
My Mother Bids Me Bind My Hair	Haydn, J.	NIE-M
		SR-2
My Mother Bids Me Bind My Hair (Bind' auf dein Haar)		56S
My Mother Binds My Hair (Bind auf dein Haar)		YS-S
My Soul Is Dark	Schumann, R.	NIE-C
Mystery's Song	Purcell, H.	FBMS-2
Nacht und Träume	Schubert, F.	50SS
Nachtviolen		50SS
Nature's Adoration	Beethoven, L.	SBBS
Nay, Though My Heart Should Break	Tchaikovsky, P.	NIE-C
Ne'er Shade so Dear (Ombra mai fu)	Handel, G. F.	PS-2
Nebbie	Respighi, O.	50ASMR
		YS-T
Nel cor più non mi sento	Paisiello, G.	CIS-3
		CCS-S
Neue Liebe, neues Leben	Beethoven, L.	GAS
Next, Winter Comes Slowly	Purcell, H.	FBBS
Night (Die Nacht)	Strauss, R.	PS-4
Night and Dreams (Nacht und Traüme)	Schubert, F.	PS-4
Night Has A Thousand Eyes, The	Metcalf, J. W.	SVR-2
		YS-T
Night in May, A	Brahms, J.	NIE-C
Night is Falling	Haydn, J.	FBSS
Nimmersatte Liebe	Wolf, H.	50SS
		GAS
Nina	Italian	26ISAA
	Pergolesi, G. B.	28ISAA
		ES-2

Song Title	Composer	Anthology
Nina	Pergolesi, G. B.	FS
		SR-2
Nina (Tre Giorni)		CIS
No, no, non si speri!	Carissimi, G.	CIS
Non è ver!	Mattei, T.	GAS
		STC
Non posso disperar	Bononcini, G.	26ISAA
	De Luca, S.	28ISAA
	Luca, S. De	GAS
Non vogl'io se non vederti	Scarlatti, A.	CIS-2
None but the Lonely Heart (Nor wer die Sehnsucht kennt)	Tchaikovsky, P.	ES-1
None by the Lonely Heart (Nur wer die sehnsucht kennt)		AS-2
Novice, The	Schubert, F.	NIE-S
Now Love Has Falseley Played Me (Die liebe hat gelogen)		PS-4
Now Sleeps the Crimson Petal	Quilter, R.	NIE-T
		YS-B
		YS-C
		YS-S
		YS-T
Now the Dancing Sunbeams Play	Haydn, J.	NIE-M
Nuit d'Etoiles	Debussy, C.	GAS
		SVR-2
Nun Wandre, Maria	Wolf, H.	50SS
		GAS
Nur Wer die Sehnsucht Kennt	Tchaikovsky, P.	FBSS-2
Nymphs and Shepherds	Purcell, H.	FBMS-2
		GAS
		NIE-M
		YS-C
		YS-S
O bellissimi capelli	Falconieri, A.	CIS-2

Song Title	Composer	Anthology
O Calm of Night (In stiller Nacht)	Brahms, J.	ES-1
O Can Ye Sew Cushions	Britten, B.	NIE-C
O cessate di piagarmi	Scarlatti, A.	BS
		CIS
		CCS-B
O Come, O Come, My Dearest	Arne, T.	FBTS-2
O Death Now Come (Lasciatemi morire) from "Ariana"	Monteverde, C.	ES-2
O Del Mio Amato Ben	Donaudy, S.	FBTS-2
O del mio dolce ardor	Gluck, C. W. von	26ISAA
		28ISAA
		ASSV
O Divine Redeemer	Gounod, C.	SBSS
O genti tutte	Marcello, B.	ES
O komme, holde Sommernacht	Brahms, J.	50SS
O Lord, Have Mercy (Pietà, Signore)	Stradella, A.	ES-2
O Lovely Peace from "Judas Maccabaeus"	Handel, G. F.	ES-2
O My Deir Hert	Howells, H.	NIE-C
O Peace, Thou Fairest Child of Heaven	Arne, T.	FBSS
O sole mio	di Capua, E.	56S
O'er the Hills	Hopkinson, F.	FBBS-2
O, Bid Your Faithful Ariel Fly	Linley, T.	NIE-S
O, Divine Redeemer (Repentir)	Gounod, C.	ES-2
Obstination	Fontenailles, H.	ASSV
Offrande	Hahn, R.	GAS
Oh Sleep, Why Dost Thou Leave Me?	Handel, G. F.	FBMS
		PS-3
		SR-2
Oh Sleep, Why Dost Thou Leave Me? from "Semele"		ES-2

Song Title	Composer	Anthology
Oh! Had I Jubal's Lyre	Handel, G. F.	SBSS
Ol' Man River	Kern, J.	BR-B
Ombra cara, amorosa	Traetta, T.	CIS-3
Ombra mai fù	Handel, G. F.	ASSV
		BS
Ombra mai fu'		CCS-M
On the Road to Mandalay	Speaks, O.	FBBS
On Wings of Song (Auf Flügeln des Gesanges)	Mendelssohn, F.	ES-1
		YS-B
		YS-C
		YS-T
One Sweetly Solemn Thought	Ambrose, R. S.	56S
One who has yearn'd alone (Nur, wer die Sehnsucht kennt)	Tchaikovsky, P.	56S
Only Home I Know, The	Geld, G.	FBBS-T
Open Our Eyes	Macfarlane, W. C.	FBMS
Orpheus with His Lute	Coates, E.	FBTS
	Schuman, W.	15AAS
		20CAS
		FBSS-2
	Sullivan, A.	ES-2
		SBMS
	V. Williams, R.	SBTS
Os Tormentos de Amor	Brasilian	FBBS-2
Out of My Soul's Great Sadness (Aus meinen grossen schmerzen)	Franz, R.	AS-1
		ES-1
Ouvre Tes Yeux Bleus	Massenet, J.	SBTS
Owl Is Abroad, The	Smith, J. S.	NIE-Bs
Panis Angelicus	Franck, C.	PS-1
Parting	Brahms, J.	NIE-M
Passing By	Purcell, E. C.	YS-B
		YS-C

Song Title	Composer	Anthology
Passing By	Purcell, E. C.	YS-T
Pastoral, A	Carey, H.	YS-C
	Veracini, F. M.	SBSS
Pastorale	Bizet, G.	SBMS
	Stravinsky, I.	50ASMR
Patiently Have I Waited	Saint-Saëns, C.	SBMS
Peace	Schubert, F.	NIE-M
Peace Prayer of St. Francis of Assisi	Christy, V. A., arr.	ES
Peaceful Evening (Beau Soir)	Debussy, C.	55AS
People	Styne, J.	BR-MS
Per la gloria d'adorarvi from "Griselda"	Bononcini, G.	26ISAA
		28ISAA
		GAS
		STC
Per pietà	Stradella, A.	CIS-3
Petit Noël	Louis, E.	FBSS-2
Phillis Has Such Charming Graces	Young, A.	FBTS-2
Pie Jesu	Fauré, G.	ASSV
Pietà, Signore!	Stradella, A.	26ISAA
Pilgrim's Song	Tchaikovsky, P.	FBBS-2
		YS-B
		YS-T
Plaisir D'Amour	Martini, G.	SBBS
		STC
Pleading (Bitte)	Franz, R.	YS-C
Pleasure's Gentle Zephyrs Play	Handel, G. F.	SBMS
Polly Willis	Arne, T.	SBTS
Prairie Lily, The	Adaskin, M.	SS-4
Praise of God, The	Beethoven, L.	NIE-C
Prayer	Guion, D. W.	FBMS
Prayer Perfect, The	Speaks, O.	FBSS-2
Press Thy Cheek Against Mine Own	Jensen, A.	AS-2

Song Title	Composer	Anthology
Presto, presto lo m'innamoro	Mazzaferrata, G. B.	CIS-2
Pretty Creature, The	Wilson, H. L., arr.	FBBS-2
Psyche	Paladilhe, E.	55AS
Pur dicesti, o bocca bella	Lotti, A.	26ISAA
		28ISAA
		CIS
Quella Barbara Catena	Ciampi, F.	FBSS-2
Quella fiamma che m'accende	Marcello, B.	26ISAA
Qui sedes ad dexteram	Vivaldi, A.	ASSV
Rastlose Liebe	Schubert, F.	50SS
Rataplan	Grever, M.	50ASMR
Reign Here a Queen within the Heart	Brahms, J.	NIE-T
Rend'il Sereno Al Cigilo	Handel, G. F.	FBMS-2
Request (Bitte)	Franz, R.	PS-2
Requiem	Homer, S.	YS-B
Resolve, A (Obstination)	de Fontainailles, H.	56S
		SR-1
	Fontenailles, H.	ES-1
Rest, Sweet Nymph	Pilkington, F.	NIE-T
Return to the Mountain Home (Auf der Reise zur Heimat)	Grieg, E.	PS-4
Revenge! Timotheus Cries	Handel, G. F.	NIE-Br
Ridente la Calma	Mozart, W. A.	STC
Road to Home, The	Strickland, L.	AS-1
Roadside Fire, The	V. Williams, R.	FBBS-2
		YS-B
Rolling Down to Rio	German, E.	FBBS-2
		YS-B
		YS-T
Romance	Debussy, C.	ASSV
		FBSS-2
Rose and the Lily, The (Die Rose, die Lilie, die Taube)	Schumann, R.	PS-4

Song Title	Composer	Anthology
Rose Chérie, Aimable Fleur	Grétry, A. E. M.	SBTS
Rose Softly Blooming	Spohr, L.	FBSS
Rovin' Gambler, The	Niles, J. J.	FBBS
Rugiadose, odorose	Scarlatti, A.	CIS
Russian Picnic	Enders, H.	FBTS-2
Sainte Marguerite	Willan, H., arr.	SS-4
Salvation Belongeth Unto The Lord	Greene, M.	SBBS
Sandman, The	German	PS-1
Sapphic Ode (Sapphische Ode)	Brahms, J.	56S
		AS-2
		ES-2
		NIE-C
Sapphische Ode		ASSV
Schneeglöckchen	Schumann, R.	50SS
Se Florinda è fedele	Scarlatti, A.	26ISAA
		28ISAA
Se i miei sospiri	Fétis, F. J.	26ISAA
Se il mio nome saper	García, M.	ES
Se l'aura spira	Frescobaldi, G.	CIS
Se tu m'ami	Parisotti, A.	26ISAA
		CCS-S
	Pergolesi, G. B.	ASSV
		CIS-3
Se tu m'ami, se sospiri		28ISAA
Sea Fever	Andrews, M.	FBBS-2
	Ireland, J.	FBTS-2
Sea Moods	Tyson, M. L.	FBBS
Sea Wrack	Harty, H.	NIE-C
Sea, The	MacDowell, E.	CCS-B
Sea-Shell	Engel, C.	50ASMR
Sebben crudele	Caldara, A.	ASSV
Secrecy (Verborgenheit)	Wolf, H.	ES-2
Secret, The	Schubert, F.	NIE-T

Song Title	Composer	Anthology
Segador	Chávez, C.	CAS
Seligkeit	Schubert, F.	FBSS-2
Selve amiche, ombrose piante	Caldara, A.	CIS-3
Selve, voi che le speranze	Rosa, S.	28ISAA
		CIS
Seminarian, The	Moussorgsky, M. P.	GAS
Separazione	Sgambati, G., arr.	FBMS-2
		FS
		GAS
Serenade	Gounod, C.	NIE-C
Sérénade		ES
		FBMS-2
Serenade (La Serenata)	Tosti, F. P.	SR-2
Serenade (Standchen)	Schubert, F.	ES-2
Serenade (Ständchen)		56S
Serenata Gitana	Sandoval, M.	GAS
She Never Told Her Love	Haydn, J.	55AS
		ES
		ES-1
		SVR-1
		YS-C
		YS-S
She Wasn't You	Lane, B.	BR-T
Shenandoah	Dougherty, C.	ASSV
	Dougherty, C., arr.	FBBS
Shepherd! Thy Demeanour Vary	Brown, T.	SBSS
		STC
Should He Upbraid	Bishop, Sir H.	NIE-S
Show Me	Loewe, F.	BR-MS
Si mes vers avaient des ailes	Hahn, R.	ES
Si Mes Vers Avaient Des Ailes!		FBSS
Si, tra i ceppi	Handel, G. F.	SBBS
Si, tra i ceppi from "Bernice"		GAS

Song Title	Composer	Anthology
Sigh No More, Ladies	Stevens, R. J.	FS
		NIE-T
Sight in Camp, A	Symons, D. T.	CAS
Silent Noon	V. Williams, R.	50ASMR
		CCS-M
		FBMS
		SVR-2
Silver Swan, The	Gibbons, O.	55AS
Simple Gifts	Hayes, M., arr.	FSSS-2
Simple Joys of Maidenhood, The	Loewe, F.	FBBS-S
Sin tu amor	Sandoval, M.	50ASMR
		GAS
Since From My Dear	Purcell, H.	SBBS
Sing, Smile, Slumber (Sérénade)	Gounod, C.	55AS
Slave, The (L'Esclave)	Lalo, É.	55AS
sleep that flits on baby's eyes, The	Carpenter, J. A.	50ASMR
		FBMS-2
Sleep, Gentle Cherub, Sleep Descend	Arne, T.	SBSS
Sleeping Princess, The	Borodine, A.	50ASMR
Slighted Swain, The	Wilson, H. L., arr.	CCS-B
		FBBS-2
Slow March (Procession triste)	Ives, C. E.	SS-Int
Slumber Song	Gretchaninoff, A.	55AS
		AS-1
	Wagner, R.	NIE-M
Slumber-Song	Gretchaninoff, A.	50ASMR
Smiling Hours, The	Handel, G. F.	SBMS
Snowbells (Schneeglöckchen)	Schumann, R.	PS-1
Snowdrops	Prokofieff, S.	50ASMR
Snowflakes		50ASMR
So In Love	Porter, C.	BR-S
Solveig's Song	Grieg, E.	NIE-S

Song Title	Composer	Anthology
Solvejg's Lied	Grieg, E.	56S
Solvejg's Song		CCS-S
		FBSS-2
Solvejg's Song (Solvejgs Lied)		AS-2
Sombre Woods (Bois épais)	Lully, J. B.	ES-1
Some Enchanted Evening	Rodgers, R.	BR-B
		FBBS-B
Somebody	Schumann, R.	NIE-M
Somewhere	Bernstein, L.	BS
Song of Devotion	Beck, J. N.	CAS
Song of India (Chanson indoue)	Rimsky-Korsakoff, N.	56S
Song of Khivria, The	Moussorgsky, M. P.	GAS
Song of Momus to Mars, The	Boyce, W.	FBBS-2
Song of the Flea, The	Beethoven, L.	NIE-Bs
Song of the Seagull (Chant de la mouette)	McLean, H. J., arr.	SS-Int
Song of the Volga Boatmen	Russian	56S
Songs My Mother Taught Me (Als die alte Mutter)	Dvorák, A.	55AS
		56S
		ES-1
		YS-C
		YS-S
Sonntag	Brahms, J.	FBTS-2
Sonntags am Rhein	Schumann, R.	GAS
Soul of My Heart (Alma del core)	Caldara, A.	PS-4
Sound the Flute!	Dougherty, C.	CAS
Sound the Trumpet	Purcell, H.	ES-2
Speak Once More, Dear (Pur dicesti, o bocca bella)	Lotti, A.	ES-2
Spirate Pur, Spirate	Donaudy, S.	SBTS
Splendour Falls, The	Walthew, R. H.	FBBS
Spring Day	McArthur, E.	STC

Song Title	Composer	Anthology
Spring Is at the Door	Quilter, R.	FBMS-2
Spring Is upon Us	Mendelssohn, F.	SS-6
Spring Morning, A	Carey, H.	SBSS
Spring Song	Schubert, F.	SS-2
Spring's Secret	Brahms, J.	NIE-M
Ständchen		50SS
		GAS
	Schubert, F.	FBTS
	Strauss, R.	50SS
Star vicino	Italian	26ISAA
	Rosa, S.	28ISAA
		CIS-2
Statue at Czarskoe-Selo, The	Cui, C.	FBMS
Stay Well	Weill, K.	BR-S
Steal Away	Burleigh, H. T., arr.	CCS-T
Still as the Night (Still wie die Nacht)	Bohm, C.	55AS
Stille Sicherheit	Franz, R.	FBTS-2
Stopping by Woods on a Snowy Evening	Sargent, P.	CAS
Such a li'l' fellow	Dichmont, W.	AS-1
Suleika's Song	Schumann, R.	NIE-S
Summertime	Gershwin, G.	BR-S
Sun O'er the Ganges, The (Già il sole dal Gange)	Scarlatti, A.	PS-3
Sun Shall Be No More Thy Light, The	Greene, M.	SBSS
Sunday Morning	Brahms, J.	NIE-Br
Sure On This Shining Night	Barber, S.	15AAS
Swan, A	Grieg, E.	YS-C
Swan, A (Ein Schwan)		AS-2
		YS-B
		YS-S
		YS-T

Song Title	Composer	Anthology
Sylvelin	Sinding, C.	56S
		YS-C
Take, O Take Those Lips Away	Beach, Mrs. H. H. A.	SBSS
Take, O, Take Those Lips Away	Thomson, V.	ES
Tally-Ho!	Leoni, F.	FBBS
Tanto sospirerò	Bencini, P. P.	CIS
Te souviens-tu?	Godard, B.	SBMS
Tears of Autumn	Bártok, B.	50ASMR
Tell, O tell her	Rimsky-Korsakoff, N.	50ASMR
That Dirty Old Man	Sondheim, S.	BR-S
That's the Way It Happens	Rodgers, R.	FBBS-T
There is a Lady Sweet and Kind	Dello Joio, N.	STC
There Was a Mighty Monarch	Beethoven, L.	FBBS
These Are They Which Came	Gaul, A.	SBSS
They Call The Wind Maria	Loewe, F.	BR-B
Think on Me	Scott, A. A.	YS-C
This Little Rose	Roy, W.	15AAS
		FBMS
Thou art so like a flower (Du bist wie eine Blume)	Schumann, R.	56S
Thou Knowest Well (Tu to sai)	Torelli, G.	PS-3
Thou Shalt Bring Them In	Handel, G. F.	SBMS
Thou'rt Like unto a Flower (Du bist wie eine Blume)	Rubinstein, A.	SR-1
Thou'rt Lovely as a Flower (Du bist wie eine Blume)	Schumann, R.	AS-1
		ES-1
Thoughts at Eventide	Mozart, W. A.	NIE-Bs
Three Fine Ships	Dunhill, T.	SS-5
Thrice Happy the Monarch	Handel, G. F.	NIE-Br
Thy Fingers Make Early Flowers	Dougherty, C.	20CAS
Thy Lovely Face	Schumann, R.	NIE-Br

Song Title	Composer	Anthology
Tiger, The	Thomson, V.	CAS
Tirana del Caramba	Spanish	ES
To a Brown Girl, Dead	Bonds, M.	FS
To a Wild Rose	MacDowell, E.	FBSS-2
To Be Near Thee (Star vicino)	Rosa, S.	ES-2
To Music	Schubert, F.	NIE-C
To Music (An die Musik)		SR-1
To the Beloved (An die Geliebte)	Beethoven, L.	PS-2
To the Children	Rachmaninoff, S.	GAS
		NIE-M
		SBMS
To the Distant Beloved (An die fern Geliebte)	Beethoven, L.	ES-2
To the Faithless One		NIE-Br
To the Forest	Tchaikovsky, P.	NIE-Bs
To the Moon	Schubert, F.	SS-4
To the Queen of Heaven	Dunhill, T.	CAS
To The Sunshine (An den Sonnenschein)	Schumann, R.	PS-1
To You	Strauss, R.	ES-2
To You (Zueignung)		56S
Toglietemi la Vita Ancor	Scarlatti, A.	FBBS-2
Tomorrow	Strauss, R.	ES-2
Tomorrow (Morgen)		55AS
		PS-4
Total Eclipse	Handel, G. F.	SBTS
Tout Est Si Beau	Rachmaninoff, S.	SVR-2
		YS-T
Traum durch die Dämmerung	Strauss, R.	50SS
Trumpeter, The	Dix, J. A.	YS-B
		YS-T
Tschaikowsky	Weill, K.	BR-T
Tu lo sai	Torelli, G.	26ISAA

Level 2 Songs

Song Title	Composer	Anthology
Tu lo sai	Torelli, G.	26ISAA
		ASSV
		CIS
Turn Then Thine Eyes	Purcell, H.	FBMS
Tus ojillos negros	de Falla, M.	50ASMR
Twas April	Tchaikovsky, P.	NIE-T
Twas in the Lovely Month of May	Schumann, R.	AS-2
(Im wunderschönen Monat Mai)		
Two Grenadiers, The		NIE-Bs
Two Grenadiers, The (Die beiden		56S
Grenadiere)		
Un certo non so che	Vivaldi, A.	CIS-3
		SBMS
Un Doux Lien	Delbruck, A.	FBTS-2
Un Moto Di Gioja	Mozart, W. A.	SBSS
Und willst du deinen Liebsten	Wolf, H.	50SS
sterben sehen		
Under the Rose	Fisher, W. A.	AS-1
Undiscovered Country, The	Berlioz, H.	NIE-M
Ungeduld	Schubert, F.	50SS
		ASSV
		GAS
Unicorn, The	Corigliano, J.	CAS
Vaaren	Grieg, E.	GAS
		SBMS
Vado ben spesso	Bononcini, G.	FS
Vaga luna	Bellini, V.	ES
Vaghissima Sembianza	Donaudy, S.	SBTS
Vain Suit, The	Brahms, J.	NIE-S
Valley, The	Gounod, C.	NIE-Bs
Veille Chanson	Bizet, G.	SBSS
Verborgenheit	Wolf, H.	50SS
		SBMS

Song Title	Composer	Anthology
Verdant Meadows	Handel, G. F.	PS-1
Verdant Meadows (Verdi prati)		ES-1
Vergebliches Ständchen	Brahms, J.	50SS
		SBSS
Vergin, tutt'amor/Solfeggio	Durante, F.	26ISAA
Vergin, tutta amor		CIS
Vergin, tutto amor		28ISAA
		ASSV
Verrathene Liebe	Schumann, R.	FBBS-2
Verschwiegene Liebe	Wolf, H.	50ASMR
Very Commonplace Story, A (Ein sehr gewohnlische Geschichte)	Haydn, J.	ES-1
Very Ordinary Story, A (Eine sehr gewöhnliche Geschichte)		PS-4
Virgin, Fount of Love (Vergin, tutto amor)	Durante, F.	ES-2
Vittoria, mio core!	Carissimi, G.	26ISAA
		28ISAA
		ASSV
		CIS
		STC
Vocalise	Chenoweth, W.	CAS
	Rachmaninoff, S.	GAS
Volksliedchen	Schumann, R.	FBMS
Von ewiger Liebe	Brahms, J.	50SS
Wade in the Water	Hayes, M., arr.	SSS
Waiting	Deis, C.	50ASMR
Wanderer, The	Schubert, F.	NIE-Br
Wanderer, The (Der Wanderer)	Haydn, J.	SVR-1
Wanderers Nachtlied	Schubert, F.	FBTS-2
		FS
Was Ist Sylvia?		FBBS-2
Water is Wide, The	Hayes, M., arr.	FSSS-2

Song Title	Composer	Anthology
We Kiss In A Shadow	Rodgers, R.	BR-T
We Sing to Him	Purcell, H.	SBMS
Weep No More	Handel, G. F.	FBMS-2
Weep No More from "Hercules"		ES-2
Weep You No More	Quilter, R.	CCS-T
		FBTS-2
Weep You No More, Sad Fountains		ES
Welcome Vision, A	Strauss, R.	NIE-Br
Well Thou Knowest	Torelli, G.	ES-2
Were My Songs With Wings Provided (Si mes vers avaient des ailes)	Hahn, R.	56S
		ES-2
What I Did for Love	Hamlisch, M.	FS
What Is A Woman?	Schmidt, H.	BR-MS
What Shall I Do to Show How Much I Love Her?	Purcell, H.	FBTS
When I Bring to You Colour'd Toys	Carpenter, J. A.	CAS
When I Have Sung My Songs	Charles, E.	15AAS
		FBSS
When I was Seventeen	Swedish	AS-2
	Swedish Folk Song	YS-S
When Love is Kind	Old English	YS-C
When on the Surging Wave (Come raggio di sol)	Caldara, A.	ES-2
When the Roses Bloom	Reichardt, L.	YS-C
		YS-T
When the Roses Bloom (Hoffnung)		SVR-1
		YS-B
When Yesterday We Met	Rachmaninoff, S.	NIE-Br
Where Corals Lie	Elgar, E.	NIE-C
		SBMS
Where E'er You Walk	Handel, G. F.	BS

Song Title	Composer	Anthology
Where E'er You Walk	Handel, G. F.	ES-1
		NIE-T
		SR-1
		YS-B
Where the Bee Sucks	Sullivan, A.	NIE-S
Whither	Schubert, F.	NIE-T
Whither Must I Wander?	V. Williams, R.	SBTS
Who Are You Now?	Styne, J.	BR-MS
Who is Sylvia (Was ist Sylvia)	Schubert, F.	AS-1
Who is Sylvia?	Coates, E.	FBTS-2
	Schubert, F.	NIE-T
Who'll Buy My Lavender?	German, E.	YS-C
Why Blame Thee Now?	Schumann, R.	NIE-Br
Why So Pale and Wan	Arne, T.	FBBS
Widmung	Franz, R.	FBBS
		FS
	Schumann, R.	50SS
		STC
Wie Melodien	Brahms, J.	FBMS
Wie Melodien zieht es mir		50SS
Wild Rose, The	Schubert, F.	NIE-M
Willow Song, The	Sullivan, A.	FBMS-2
		NIE-C
Wilt Thou Thy Heart Surrender	Giovannini	PS-3
(Willst du dein Herz mir schenken)		
Wind of the Western Sea	Peel, G.	FBMS
Wind of the Wheat	Phillips, M. F.	FBMS-2
Wind Speaks, The	Grant-Schaefer, G. A.	AS-1
Winter Dedication, A	Strauss, R.	NIE-T
Wish, The	Chopin, F.	SS-4
With a Primrose	Grieg, E.	SS-6
With a Swanlike Beauty Gliding	Mozart, W. A.	NIE-C

Song Title	Composer	Anthology
With A Water Lily (Mit einer Wasser lilie)	Grieg, E.	PS-3
With Cunning Conniving (Che fiero costume)	Legrenzi, G.	ES-2
Without Thee!	Gounod, C.	NIE-S
Wohin?	Schubert, F.	50SS
Woodland Journey, A (Waldfahrt)	Franz, R.	PS-1
Year's At the Spring, The	Beach, Mrs. H. H. A.	YS-S
Yesterday I Loved You	Rodgers, M.	BR-T
You'll Never Walk Alone	Rodgers, R.	BR-S
		FBBS-S
Younger Than Springtime		BR-T
Youth and Love	V. Williams, R.	NIE-Br
Zärtliche Liebe	Beethoven, L.	ES
Zueignung	Strauss, R.	50SS

Section 4

Level 3 Songs

Song Title	Composer	Anthology
Absence	Berlioz, H.	GAS
Amarilli	Caccini, G.	CIS
Arise Ye Subterranean Winds	Purcell, H.	NIE-Bs
		SBBS
At the Cry of the First Bird	Guion, D. W.	20CAS
At the Well	Hageman, R.	50ASMR
Beau Soir	Debussy, C.	56S
By the Grave	Rachmaninoff, S.	NIE-Bs
C'est l'extase langoureuse	Debussy, C.	50ASMR
Cäcilie	Strauss, R.	50ASMR
		50SS
Care Selve	Handel, G. F.	STC
		SVR-2
		YS-S
		YS-T
Charmant Papillon	Campra, A.	FBSS-2
Chère Nuit	Bachelet, A.	GAS
Christmas at the Cloisters	Corigliano, J.	CAS
D'Anne jouant de l'espinette	Ravel, M.	50ASMR
Der Tod, das ist die kühle Nacht	Brahms, J.	50SS
Die Allmacht	Schubert, F.	50SS
Edward	Loewe, C.	NIE-Br
		STC
Erl King, The	Schubert, F.	NIE-Br
Eros	Grieg, E.	GAS
Evening	Ives, C. E.	ES
Extase	Duparc, H.	50ASMR
Extinguish My Eyes	Bernstein, L.	CAS
Gesú Bambino	Yon, P.	FBSS-2
Grace Thy Fair Brow (Rend' il sereno al ciglio)	Handel, G. F.	PS-1
He or She That Hopes to Gain	Berger, J.	ES
He That Keepeth Israel	Schlösser, A.	FBTS

Song Title	Composer	Anthology
Heimliche Aufforderung	Strauss, R.	50SS
Hero, The	Menotti, G. C.	20CAS
How Few the Joys	Rachmaninoff, S.	NIE-C
I Watched the Lady Caroline	Duke, J.	20CAS
Ich atmet' einen linden Duft	Mahler, G.	STC
Il pleure dans mon coeur	Debussy, C.	50ASMR
		STC
In der Frühe	Wolf, H.	50SS
Inn, The	Toye, F.	CAS
Into the Night	Edwards, C.	FBSS
Just-Spring	Duke, J.	STC
L'Invitation au voyage	Duparc, H.	50ASMR
La Zingara	Donizetti, G.	SBSS
Le Soir	Thomas, A.	SBTS
Lebe Wohl!	Wolf, H.	50SS
		GAS
Les Paons	Loeffler, C. M.	50ASMR
Letter Song	Moore, D.	BR-S
Lo! Hear the Gentle Lark	Bishop, Sir H.	STC
Lone and Joyless	Mendelssohn, F.	NIE-S
Loreley, The	Liszt, F.	NIE-S
Mandoline	Debussy, C.	STC
Melmillo	Carey, C.	NIE-M
Mignon	Wolf, H.	50SS
Morning Hymn (Morgen-Hymne)	Henschel, G.	YS-C
Mother	Palmgren, S.	50ASMR
My Lagan Love	Harty, H.	NIE-Bs
Nebbie	Respighi, O.	YS-B
		YS-C
		YS-S
Night is Mournful	Rachmaninoff, S.	NIE-T
Nun Takes the Veil, A	Barber, S.	FBSS-2

Level 3 Songs

Song Title	Composer	Anthology
O Thou Billowy Harvest-Field!	Rachmaninoff, S.	SBTS
Omnipotence	Schubert, F.	NIE-S
Omnipotence (Die Allmacht)		55AS
Parting	Gold, E.	20CAS
Peggy Mitchell	Duke, J.	CAS
Più Vaga e Vezzosetta	Bononcini, G.	SBBS
Psalm XXIII	Creston, P.	20CAS
Ruhe, meine Seele!	Strauss, R.	50SS
Sapphic Ode (Sapphische Ode)	Brahms, J.	YS-C
		YS-S
Serenity	Ives, C. E.	15AAS
Silent Noon	V. Williams, R.	YS-B
		YS-T
Silver	Duke, J.	20CAS
Singer, The	Head, M.	NIE-S
Sleep	Gurney, I.	NIE-T
Solitary One, The	Strauss, R.	NIE-Bs
Song of the Girl at the Window	Szymanowski, K.	50ASMR
Spirit Flower, A	Campbell-Tipton, L.	FBSS-2
Spring	Henschel, G.	NIE-S
Still as the Night (Still wie die Nacht)	Bohm, C.	AS-1
		ES-1
Still wie die Nacht		ASSV
Still wie die Nacht (Still as the Night)		STC
Stille Thränen	Schumann, R.	GAS
Symphony in Yellow	Griffes, C. T.	20CAS
There's Weeping in My Heart (Il pleure dans mon coeur)	Debussy, C.	PS-3
Think On Me	Scott, A. A.	ES-1
To One Who Passed Whistling Through the Night	Gibbs, C. A.	20CAS
To The Birds (A des Oiseaux)	Hüe, G.	SBSS

Song Title	Composer	Anthology
Under the Willow Tree from "Vanessa"	Barber, S.	20CAS
Vagabond, The	V. Williams, R.	SBBS
Villanelle	Dell'Acqua, E.	SBSS
When I Was Seventeen	Swedish	FBSS-2
When My Soul Touches Yours	Bernstein, L.	CAS
When the roses bloom (Hoffnung)	Reichardt, L.	56S
Why Do I Love Thee?	Gibbs, C. A.	NIE-S
Wraith, The	Schubert, F.	NIE-Br
Ye Twice Ten Hundred Deities	Purcell, H.	NIE-Br

Level 3 Songs

Anthologies

15 American Art Songs

Publisher: G. Schirmer
Compiled/Edited by: Gary Arvin
Available in: High and Low Voice

Composer	Song Title
Barber, S.	Crucifixion, The
	Daisies, The
	Monk and His Cat, The
	Sure On This Shining Night
Bowles, P.	Cabin
	Heavenly Grass
Chanler, T.	Lamb, The
Charles, E.	When I Have Sung My Songs
Duke, J.	Loveliest of Trees
Hageman, R.	Do Not Go, My Love
Ives, C. E.	Serenity
Niles, J. J.	Lass from the Low Countree, The
Rich, G.	American Lullaby
Roy, W.	This Little Rose
Schuman, W.	Orpheus with His Lute

20th Century Art Songs

Publisher: G. Schirmer
Compiled/Edited by: N/A
Available in: Medium Voice

Composer	Song Title
Barber, S.	Under the Willow Tree from "Vanessa"
Bernstein, L.	It Must Be Me from "Candide"
Bliss, A.	Buckle, The
Bowles, P.	Cabin
Creston, P.	Psalm XXIII
Dougherty, C.	K'e, The

Melody	Phrase	Rhythm	Text	Accomp.	Harmony	Dynamics	Total	Rank
2	2	2	1	3	2	2	14	2
2	1	1	1	2	1	2	10	1
2	1	2	1	2	2	3	13	2
2	2	2	1	2	2	2	13	2
1	1	2	1	1	2	2	10	1
2	2	3	1	1	2	2	13	2
2	1	1	1	2	1	2	10	1
2	2	1	1	2	1	3	12	2
2	2	1	1	3	2	3	14	2
2	2	1	1	2	2	2	12	2
1	2	3	1	3	3	3	16	3
2	1	1	1	1	1	2	9	1
2	1	1	1	2	1	2	10	1
2	1	1	1	2	2	2	11	2
2	2	2	1	2	2	2	13	2

Melody	Phrase	Rhythm	Text	Accomp.	Harmony	Dynamics	Total	Rank
3	2	1	1	3	2	3	15	3
2	2	2	1	1	1	3	12	2
3	3	1	1	2	1	3	14	2
1	2	1	1	1	2	2	10	1
2	3	1	1	3	2	3	15	3
2	2	2	1	2	2	2	13	2

Dougherty, C.	Minor Bird, A
	Thy Fingers Make Early Flowers
Dougherty, C., arr.	Across the Western Ocean
Duke, J.	I Watched the Lady Caroline
	Silver
Gibbs, C. A.	To One Who Passed Whistling Through the Night
Gold, E.	Music, When Soft Voices Die
	Parting
Griffes, C. T.	Symphony in Yellow
Guion, D. W.	At the Cry of the First Bird
Kingsley, H.	Green Dog, The
Menotti, G. C.	Black Swan, The from "The Medium"
	Hero, The
Roberton, H. S.	All in the April Evening
Sacco, J.	Brother Will, Brother John
Schirmer, R.	Honey Shun
Schuman, W.	Orpheus With His Lute
Shaw, M.	Song of the Palanquin Bearers
Thomson, V.	My Crow Pluto
Weaver, P.	Moon-Marketing
Weill, K.	Lonesome Dove, The from "Down in the Valley"

26 Italian Songs and Arias

Publisher: Alfred Publishing Co.
Compiled/Edited by: John Glenn Paton
Available in: Medium High and Medium Low Voice

Composer	Song Title
Bononcini, G.	Non posso disperar
	Per la gloria d'adorarvi from "Griselda"
Caccini, G.	Amarilli, mia bella
Caldara, A.	Alma del core

Anthologies

Melody	Phrase	Rhythm	Text	Accomp.	Harmony	Dynamics	Total	Rank
1	3	1	1	2	2	2	12	2
2	1	1	1	3	3	3	14	2
1	3	2	1	2	1	2	12	2
2	2	1	1	3	3	3	15	3
2	3	3	1	3	3	3	18	3
2	3	2	1	3	3	1	15	3
2	2	1	1	2	2	3	13	2
3	3	1	1	3	3	3	17	3
2	2	1	1	3	3	3	15	3
3	3	2	1	2	2	2	15	3
2	1	2	1	2	2	2	12	2
2	2	1	1	1	2	2	11	2
2	3	2	1	2	2	3	15	3
1	1	1	1	2	2	2	10	1
2	1	3	1	2	1	2	12	2
3	3	1	1	2	2	1	13	2
2	3	2	1	2	1	2	13	2
2	1	1	1	1	2	2	10	1
2	2	1	1	3	2	3	14	2
2	1	2	1	2	2	1	11	2
2	2	1	1	1	1	2	10	1
2	1	2	2	2	1	2	12	2
2	1	2	2	2	1	2	12	2
2	3	2	2	2	1	2	14	2
1	1	2	2	2	1	2	11	2

Caldara, A.	Come raggio di sol
	Sebben, crudele
Carissimi, G.	Vittoria, mio core!
Durante, F.	Danza, danza, fanciulla gentile
	Vergin, tutt'amor/Solfeggio
Fétis, F. J.	Se i miei sospiri
Giordani, G.	Caro mio ben
Gluck, C. W. von	O del mio dolce ardor
Italian	Nina
	Star vicino
Legrenzi, G.	Che fiero costume
Lotti, A.	Pur dicesti, o bocca bella
Marcello, B.	Quella fiamma che m'accende
Monteverde, C.	Lasciatemi morire!
Paisiello, G.	Nel cor più non mi sento
Parisotti, A.	Se tu m'ami
Scarlatti, A.	Già il sole dal Gange
	Le Violette
	O cessate di piagarmi
	Se Florinda è fedele
	Sento nel core
Torelli, G.	Tu lo sai

28 Italian Songs and Arias

Publisher: Alfred Publishing Co.
Compiled/Edited by: Maurice Hinson
Available in: Medium High and Medium Low Voice

Composer	Song Title
Bononcini, G.	Per la gloria d'adorarvi from "Griselda"
Caccini, G.	Amarilli, mia bella
Caldara, A.	Alma del core
	Come raggio di sol
	Sebben, crudele

Melody	Phrase	Rhythm	Text	Accomp.	Harmony	Dynamics	Total	Rank
2	2	2	2	2	1	2	13	2
2	1	1	2	1	1	1	9	1
2	2	3	2	2	1	2	14	2
2	2	2	2	2	1	2	13	2
2	2	2	2	2	1	2	13	2
2	1	1	2	2	1	3	12	2
2	1	1	2	1	1	2	10	1
3	2	1	2	2	1	2	13	2
2	2	1	2	2	1	2	12	2
1	2	1	2	2	1	2	11	2
2	1	2	2	2	1	2	12	2
2	2	2	2	1	1	3	13	2
3	1	2	2	2	1	2	13	2
1	2	2	2	2	1	2	12	2
1	1	1	2	2	1	1	9	1
3	1	2	2	2	1	3	14	2
2	2	2	2	2	1	1	12	2
2	1	3	2	2	1	1	12	2
1	1	1	2	1	1	2	9	1
1	1	3	2	2	1	1	11	2
2	1	1	2	1	1	2	10	1
2	2	1	2	2	1	3	13	2
2	1	1	2	2	1	2	11	2
2	3	2	2	2	1	2	14	2
1	1	2	2	2	1	2	11	2
2	2	2	2	2	1	2	13	2
2	1	1	2	1	1	1	9	1

Carissimi, G.	Vittoria, mio core!
De Luca, S.	Non posso disperar
Durante, F.	Danza, danza, fanciulla gentile
	Vergin, tutto amor
Giordani, G.	Caro mio ben
Gluck, C. W. von	O del mio dolce ardor
Legrenzi, G.	Che fiero costume
Lotti, A.	Pur dicesti, o bocca bella
Marcello, B.	Il mio bel foco
Monteverde, C.	Lasciatemi morire!
Paisiello, G.	Nel cor più non mi sento
Pergolesi, G. B.	Nina
	Se tu m'ami, se sospiri
Rosa, S.	Selve, voi che le speranze
	Star vicino
Scarlatti, A.	Già il sole dal Gange
	Le Violette
	O cessate di piagarmi
	Se Florinda è fedele
	Sento nel core
Secchi, A.	Lungi dal caro bene
Stradella, A.	Pietà, Signore!
Torelli, G.	Tu lo sai

50 Art Songs from the Modern Repertoire

Publisher: G. Schirmer
Compiled/Edited by: N/A
Available in: Medium High Voice

Composer	Song Title
Bártok, B.	Tears of Autumn
Borodine, A.	Sleeping Princess, The
Carpenter, J. A.	sleep that flits on baby's eyes, The
Cimara, P.	Fiocca la neve

Melody	Phrase	Rhythm	Text	Accomp.	Harmony	Dynamics	Total	Rank
2	2	3	2	2	1	2	14	2
2	1	2	2	2	1	2	12	2
2	2	2	2	2	1	2	13	2
2	2	2	2	2	1	2	13	2
2	1	1	2	1	1	2	10	1
3	2	1	2	2	1	2	13	2
2	1	2	2	2	1	2	12	2
2	2	2	2	1	1	3	13	2
2	1	1	2	2	1	2	11	2
1	2	2	2	2	1	2	12	2
1	1	1	2	2	1	1	9	1
2	2	1	2	1	1	2	11	2
3	1	2	2	2	1	3	14	2
2	1	1	2	2	1	2	11	2
1	2	1	2	2	1	2	11	2
2	2	2	2	2	1	1	12	2
2	1	3	2	2	1	1	12	2
1	1	1	2	1	1	2	9	1
1	1	3	2	2	1	1	11	2
2	1	1	2	1	1	2	10	1
3	1	1	2	1	1	3	12	2
2	2	1	2	2	1	3	13	2
2	2	1	2	2	1	3	13	2
Melody	**Phrase**	**Rhythm**	**Text**	**Accomp.**	**Harmony**	**Dynamics**	**Total**	**Rank**
2	2	1	2	2	3	2	14	2
2	2	1	1	2	1	3	12	2
2	2	1	1	2	1	2	11	2
1	1	1	2	2	1	3	11	2

de Falla, M.	Tus ojillos negros
Debussy, C.	C'est l'extase langoureuse
	Il pleure dans mon coeur
Deis, C.	Waiting
Duparc, H.	Extase
	L'Invitation au voyage
Dvořák, A.	Lark, The
Engel, C.	Sea-Shell
Fauré, G.	Après un rêve
	Aurore
	En prière
Ganz, R.	Memory, A
Gretchaninoff, A.	Slumber-Song
Grever, M.	Rataplan
Grieg, E.	By the Brook
Griffes, C. T.	Auf geheimem Waldespfade
Hageman, R.	At the Well
Hahn, R.	L'Heure exquise
Hüe, G.	J'ai pleuré en rêve
Lalo, É.	L'Esclave
Loeffler, C. M.	Adieu pour jamais
	Les Paons
Moussorgsky, M. P.	Evening Prayer, The
Palmgren, S.	Mother
Prokofieff, S.	Snowdrops
	Snowflakes
Rachmaninoff, S.	In the Silence of Night
	Island, The
Ravel, M.	Chanson espagnole
	D'Anne jouant de l'espinette
Respighi, O.	Nebbie
Rimsky-Korsakoff, N.	Tell, O tell her
Sandoval, M.	Sin tu amor

214

2	1	2	2	2	2	3	14	**2**
3	2	2	2	2	3	3	17	**3**
2	2	1	2	2	3	3	15	**3**
2	3	2	1	2	2	2	14	**2**
2	2	3	2	2	2	3	16	**3**
2	2	3	2	2	1	3	15	**3**
1	1	1	1	2	1	3	10	**1**
1	2	1	1	2	3	1	11	**2**
2	2	1	2	2	2	3	14	**2**
2	2	1	1	2	2	2	12	**2**
1	2	1	2	2	2	2	12	**2**
2	1	1	1	1	2	3	11	**2**
3	1	1	1	2	1	2	11	**2**
2	1	1	2	2	2	3	13	**2**
1	1	1	1	2	2	3	11	**2**
2	1	1	2	2	2	2	12	**2**
3	2	2	1	2	2	3	15	**3**
2	2	1	2	2	1	3	13	**2**
2	2	1	2	1	2	3	13	**2**
2	1	1	2	2	1	3	12	**2**
2	2	1	2	2	2	2	13	**2**
2	3	3	2	3	3	2	18	**3**
2	1	3	1	2	2	2	13	**2**
2	2	3	1	2	2	3	15	**3**
2	1	2	1	2	1	2	11	**2**
2	1	1	1	2	1	3	11	**2**
2	2	1	1	3	2	3	14	**2**
2	1	1	1	2	2	3	12	**2**
1	3	1	2	2	2	3	14	**2**
3	1	2	2	3	3	3	17	**3**
2	2	2	2	1	2	3	14	**2**
2	1	2	1	2	1	3	12	**2**
2	1	2	2	2	1	2	12	**2**

Schoenberg, A.	Erhebung
Sibelius, J.	From the North
Strauss, R.	Cäcilie
	Morgen
Stravinsky, I.	Pastorale
Szymanowski, K.	Song of the Girl at the Window
Tchaikovsky, P.	At the Ball
	Legend, A
Treharne, B.	Corals
V. Williams, R.	Silent Noon
Wolf, H.	Fussreise
	Gesang Weylas
	Verschwiegene Liebe

50 Selected Songs by Schubert, et al.

Publisher: G. Schirmer
Compiled/Edited by: Florence Easton
Available in: High and Low Voice

Composer	Song Title
Brahms, J.	Auf dem Kirchhofe
	Botschaft
	Der Tod, das ist die kühle Nacht
	In Waldeseinsamkeit
	Meine Liebe ist grün
	O komme, holde Sommernacht
	Ständchen
	Vergebliches Ständchen
	Von ewiger Liebe
	Wie Melodien zieht es mir
Schubert, F.	Der Schmetterling
	Die Allmacht
	Heidenröslein
	Im Abendroth

2	1	1	2	2	3	3	14	**2**
2	2	2	2	2	1	1	12	**2**
2	2	2	2	2	2	3	15	**3**
2	2	1	2	2	1	3	13	**2**
2	1	2	1	2	3	3	14	**2**
2	3	1	2	2	3	3	16	**3**
2	1	1	1	2	1	2	10	**1**
2	1	1	2	1	1	2	10	**1**
1	3	1	1	2	2	2	12	**2**
2	2	2	1	2	2	3	14	**2**
2	1	1	2	1	2	3	12	**2**
2	2	1	2	2	1	2	12	**2**
2	1	1	2	2	2	3	13	**2**

Melody	**Phrase**	**Rhythm**	**Text**	**Accomp.**	**Harmony**	**Dynamics**	**Total**	**Rank**
2	2	1	2	2	1	3	13	**2**
2	2	1	2	2	1	2	12	**2**
3	2	2	2	2	2	2	15	**3**
2	3	1	2	2	2	2	14	**2**
2	2	1	2	2	2	2	13	**2**
2	2	1	2	2	2	2	13	**2**
2	1	1	2	1	1	3	11	**2**
2	1	2	2	1	1	3	12	**2**
3	2	1	2	1	1	2	12	**2**
2	1	1	2	2	1	2	11	**2**
2	1	1	1	2	1	3	11	**2**
3	2	2	2	2	2	3	16	**3**
1	2	1	2	2	1	3	12	**2**
2	2	1	2	2	1	3	13	**2**

Schubert, F.	Liebhaber in allen Gestalten
	Nacht und Träume
	Nachtviolen
	Rastlose Liebe
	Ungeduld
	Wohin?
Schumann, R.	Aufträge
	Der Nussbaum
	Die Lotosblume
	Du bist wie eine Blume
	Frühlingsnacht
	Mein schöner Stern!
	Mit Myrthen und Rosen
	Mondnacht
	Schneeglöckchen
	Widmung
Strauss, R.	Allerseelen
	Cäcilie
	Heimkehr
	Heimliche Aufforderung
	Ich trage meine Minne
	Morgen
	Ruhe, meine Seele!
	Ständchen
	Traum durch die Dämmerung
	Zueignung
Wolf, H.	Auf dem grünen Balcon
	Bescheidene Liebe
	In dem Schatten meiner Locken
	In der Frühe
	Lebe Wohl!
	Mignon
	Nimmersatte Liebe

1	1	1	2	1	1	2	9	**1**
2	2	2	2	2	1	1	12	**2**
2	3	1	2	1	1	1	11	**2**
2	2	1	2	2	2	3	14	**2**
2	1	2	2	2	1	2	12	**2**
2	1	3	2	2	1	3	14	**2**
2	1	1	1	2	1	2	10	**1**
2	1	1	2	2	1	2	11	**2**
2	2	1	1	1	1	3	11	**2**
1	2	1	2	2	1	2	11	**2**
2	2	2	2	2	1	2	13	**2**
2	2	1	2	1	2	2	12	**2**
2	2	1	2	1	1	3	12	**2**
2	2	1	2	2	1	2	12	**2**
2	1	2	2	1	1	2	11	**2**
2	2	2	2	2	1	2	13	**2**
2	3	1	1	2	1	3	13	**2**
2	2	2	2	2	2	3	15	**3**
2	2	1	2	2	2	3	14	**2**
2	1	3	2	2	2	3	15	**3**
3	2	1	2	2	1	2	13	**2**
2	2	1	2	2	1	3	13	**2**
3	2	3	2	2	2	2	16	**3**
2	1	1	2	1	1	3	11	**2**
2	1	1	2	2	1	3	12	**2**
2	1	1	2	2	1	3	12	**2**
2	2	1	2	2	2	3	14	**2**
2	1	2	1	1	1	3	11	**2**
2	2	1	2	2	2	3	14	**2**
3	2	1	2	2	2	3	15	**3**
2	2	2	2	2	2	3	15	**3**
3	3	2	2	2	2	3	17	**3**
2	1	1	2	2	2	2	12	**2**

Wolf, H.	Nun Wandre, Maria
	Und willst du deinen Liebsten sterben sehen
	Verborgenheit

55 Art Songs

Publisher: Summy-Birchard Inc.
Compiled/Edited by: Sigmund Spaeth and Carl O. Thompson
Available in: High and Low Voice

Composer	Song Title
Arne, T.	Blow, Blow, Thou Winter Wind
Bach, J. S.	Thou Art Near (Bist du bei mir)
Becker, R.	Days of Spring, The (Frühlingszeit)
Beethoven, L.	Glory of God in Nature, The (Die Ehre Grottes in der Natur)
Bishop, Sir H.	Love Has Eyes
Bohm, C.	Still as the Night (Still wie die Nacht)
Brahms, J.	Alone in the Fields (Wäldeinsamkeit)
Campion, T.	When To Her Lute Corinna Sings
Carey, H.	Pastoral, A
Cornelius, P.	Monotone (Ein Ton)
Debussy, C.	Peaceful Evening (Beau Soir)
Dibdin, C.	Blow High, Blow Low
Dowland, J.	Come Again, Sweet Love
Dvořák, A.	Songs My Mother Taught Me (Als die alte Mutter)
Fauré, G.	Après un rêve
Foster, S. C.	Open Thy Lattice, Love
Franz, R.	Dedication (Widmung)
Gibbons, O.	Silver Swan, The
Giordani, G.	Ah, Love of Mine (Caro mio ben)
Godard, B.	Florian's Song (Chanson de Florian)
Gounod, C.	Sing, Smile, Slumber (Sérénade)
Gretchaninoff, A.	Slumber Song

Anthologies

1	2	1	2	2	2	3	13	**2**
2	1	1	2	2	2	3	13	**2**
2	2	2	2	2	1	3	14	**2**

Melody	Phrase	Rhythm	Text	Accomp.	Harmony	Dynamics	Total	Rank
2	1	1	1	1	1	2	9	**1**
2	1	1	1	1	1	2	9	**1**
2	1	1	1	2	2	2	11	**2**
2	2	3	1	1	1	2	12	**2**
2	1	1	1	1	1	2	9	**1**
2	3	2	1	2	1	3	14	**2**
2	2	1	1	2	2	2	12	**2**
2	1	1	1	1	1	2	9	**1**
2	1	2	1	1	1	2	10	**1**
1	1	1	1	1	1	3	9	**1**
2	2	1	1	3	2	3	14	**2**
2	1	1	1	1	1	2	9	**1**
2	1	1	1	2	1	2	10	**1**
2	2	1	1	2	2	3	13	**2**
2	2	1	1	2	2	3	13	**2**
2	1	2	1	1	1	2	10	**1**
2	1	1	1	1	1	2	9	**1**
2	3	1	1	1	1	2	11	**2**
2	3	1	1	1	1	2	11	**2**
2	1	1	1	2	1	2	10	**1**
3	1	2	1	2	1	2	12	**2**
3	1	1	1	1	1	3	11	**2**

Grieg, E.	Boat Song (Im Kahne)
Hahn, R.	Exquisite Hour (L'huere Exquise)
Haydn, J.	She Never Told Her Love
Hopkinson, F.	Beneath a Weeping Willow's Shade
Horn, C. E.	I've Been Roaming
Kjerulf, H.	Last Night
Lalo, É.	Slave, The (L'Esclave)
Lassen, E.	It was a Dream
Lawes, H.	Bid me To Live
Liszt, F.	It Must Be Wonderful, Indeed (Es muss ein Wunderbares sein)
MacDowell, E.	Sea, The
Martini, G.	Joy of Love, The (Plaisir d'amour)
Massenet, J.	Elegy (Elégie)
Mendelssohn, F.	On Wings of Song (Auf Flügeln des Gesanges)
Monro, G.	My Lovely Celia
Morley, T.	Now is the Month of Maying
Moussorgsky, M. P.	Cradlesong of the Poor
Mozart, W. A.	Lullaby (Wiegenlied)
Paladilhe, E.	Psyche
Pergolesi, G. B.	If Thou Love Me (Se tu m'ami)
Purcell, E. C.	Passing By
Purcell, H.	Come Unto These Yellow Sands
Rimsky-Korsakoff, N.	Nightingale and the Rose, The
Rubinstein, A.	Asra, The (Der Asra)
Scarlatti, A.	Sunrise of The Ganges (Già il sole dal Gange)
Schubert, F.	Omnipotence (Die Allmacht)
Schumann, R.	Lotus Flower, The (Die Lotusblume)
Strauss, R.	Tomorrow (Morgen)
Sullivan, A.	Lost Chord, The
Tchaikovsky, P.	At The Ball
Tosti, F. P.	Good-bye
Wagner, R.	Dreaming (Träume)
Wolf, H.	My Native Land (Gesang Weylas)

2	1	2	1	1	1	3	11	**2**
2	2	1	1	2	1	3	12	**2**
2	1	2	1	2	1	2	11	**2**
2	1	1	1	1	1	3	10	**1**
2	1	1	1	1	1	2	9	**1**
2	1	1	1	2	1	2	10	**1**
2	1	1	1	2	1	3	11	**2**
2	2	3	1	2	1	1	12	**2**
1	1	1	1	1	1	2	8	**1**
2	1	1	1	2	2	2	11	**2**
1	1	1	1	2	1	3	10	**1**
2	1	1	1	2	1	2	10	**1**
2	2	2	1	2	1	3	13	**2**
2	1	1	1	2	1	2	10	**1**
2	1	1	1	1	1	1	8	**1**
1	1	1	1	2	1	2	9	**1**
2	2	1	1	1	1	3	11	**2**
1	1	1	1	1	1	2	8	**1**
3	1	1	1	2	1	2	11	**2**
2	1	1	1	2	1	3	11	**2**
1	1	1	1	2	1	1	8	**1**
2	1	2	1	1	1	2	10	**1**
1	1	1	1	2	1	3	10	**1**
3	1	1	1	1	1	2	10	**1**
1	1	1	1	1	1	2	8	**1**
3	2	2	1	2	2	3	15	**3**
2	2	1	1	1	2	2	11	**2**
2	2	1	1	2	1	3	12	**2**
2	2	1	1	2	1	3	12	**2**
2	1	1	1	2	1	2	10	**1**
2	1	1	1	1	2	3	11	**2**
2	2	3	1	1	2	2	13	**2**
1	2	1	1	2	1	2	10	**1**

56 Songs You Like To Sing

Publisher: G. Schirmer
Compiled/Edited by: N/A
Available in: Medium High Voice

Composer	Song Title
Ambrose, R. S.	One Sweetly Solemn Thought
Arne, M.	Lass with the Delicate Air, The
Bach, J. S.	My heart ever faithful (Mein gläubiges Herze)
Balfe, M. W.	Then you'll remember me
Beethoven, L.	I Love thee (Ich liebe dich)
Bizet, G.	Habanera
Bland, J. A.	Carry me back to old Virginny
Bohm, C.	Calm as the Night (Still wie die Nacht)
Borodine, A.	Dissonance, A
Brahms, J.	Cradle-song (Wiegenlied)
	Sapphic Ode (Sapphische Ode)
de Fontainailles, H.	Resolve, A (Obstination)
Debussy, C.	Beau Soir
di Capua, E.	O sole mio
Dvorák, A.	Songs my mother taught me (Als die alte Mutter)
Foster, S. C.	My Old Kentucky Home
Franz, R.	Dedication (Widmung)
Giordani, G.	Dearest, believe (Caro mio ben)
Godard, B.	Lullaby
Grever, M.	Júrame
Grieg, E.	I love thee (Ich liebe dich)
	Solvejg's Lied
Hageman, R.	Do not go, my love
Hahn, R.	Were My Songs With Wings Provided (Si mes vers avaient des ailes)
Handel, G. F.	Where E'er You Walk

Melody	Phrase	Rhythm	Text	Accomp.	Harmony	Dynamics	Total	Rank
2	2	1	1	2	1	3	12	2
2	3	1	1	1	1	2	11	2
1	2	1	2	1	1	2	10	1
1	2	1	1	2	1	2	10	1
2	2	1	2	1	1	2	11	2
1	2	1	2	1	1	1	9	1
1	2	1	1	1	1	2	9	1
2	2	1	2	2	1	3	13	2
2	1	1	1	2	1	3	11	2
1	2	1	2	1	1	2	10	1
2	2	2	2	2	2	2	14	2
2	1	1	2	2	1	3	12	2
2	3	1	2	2	2	3	15	3
2	2	1	2	1	1	2	11	2
1	2	1	2	2	1	3	12	2
2	1	1	1	2	1	1	9	1
2	1	1	2	1	1	3	11	2
2	2	3	2	1	1	3	14	2
2	2	1	2	2	1	3	13	2
3	2	2	2	1	1	3	14	2
1	1	1	2	1	1	3	10	1
2	2	1	2	2	1	3	13	2
2	2	2	1	2	2	2	13	2
2	2	1	2	2	1	3	13	2
1	1	1	1	2	1	2	9	1

Hawthorne, A.	Whispering Hope
Haydn, J.	My Mother Bids Me Bind My Hair (Bind' auf dein Haar)
Irish	Last Rose of Summer, The
	Londonderry Air
Liliuokalani, Queen	Aloha oe
Massenet, J.	Elégie
Mendelssohn, F.	O rest in the Lord
Molloy, J. L.	Love's Old, Sweet Song
Mozart, W. A.	Violet, The (Das Veilchen)
Offenbach, J.	Barcarolle
Old English	Drink to me only with thine eyes
Purcell, E. C.	Passing By
Rachmaninoff, S.	Lilacs
Reichardt, L.	When the roses bloom (Hoffnung)
Rimsky-Korsakoff, N.	Song of India (Chanson indoue)
Russian	Song of the Volga Boatmen
Saint-Saëns, C.	My Heart at thy sweet voice (Mon coeur s'ouvre à ta voix)
Schubert, F.	Ave Maria
	Serenade (Ständchen)
Schumann, R.	Thou art so like a flower (Du bist wie eine Blume)
	Two Grenadiers, The (Die beiden Grenadiere)
Sinding, C.	Sylvelin
Strauss, R.	All Soul's Day (Allerseelen)
	To You (Zueignung)
Sullivan, A.	Lost Chord, The
Tchaikovsky, P.	One who has yearn'd alone (Nur, wer die Sehnsucht kennt)
Tosti, F. P.	Good-bye!
Verdi, G.	La donna è mobile
Voigt, H.	Mother-Love
Wagner, R.	Dreams (Träume)

226

2	2	1	1	1	1	2	10	**1**
1	2	2	2	1	1	3	12	**2**
1	2	1	1	2	1	2	10	**1**
3	1	1	1	2	1	2	11	**2**
2	1	1	2	1	1	3	11	**2**
2	2	3	2	1	1	3	14	**2**
1	1	1	1	1	1	2	8	**1**
2	1	1	1	2	1	2	10	**1**
1	2	2	2	1	1	1	10	**1**
3	2	1	2	1	1	3	13	**2**
1	1	1	1	1	1	1	7	**1**
1	1	1	1	1	1	3	9	**1**
2	1	1	1	3	1	3	12	**2**
1	3	3	2	2	1	3	15	**3**
2	2	2	2	2	1	3	14	**2**
1	1	3	2	1	1	3	12	**2**
3	2	2	2	2	1	2	14	**2**
1	2	3	2	2	1	3	14	**2**
1	2	1	2	2	2	3	13	**2**
1	3	3	2	2	1	2	14	**2**
2	2	1	2	2	2	2	13	**2**
1	2	2	2	2	1	1	11	**2**
2	3	1	2	1	2	3	14	**2**
1	2	1	2	2	1	3	12	**2**
2	2	1	1	1	1	3	11	**2**
2	2	1	2	2	2	3	14	**2**
2	1	1	1	2	2	3	12	**2**
2	1	1	2	1	1	3	11	**2**
1	2	1	1	1	1	2	9	**1**
2	2	1	2	1	2	2	12	**2**

Yradier, S.	La Paloma

Anthology of Songs for the Solo Voice

Publisher: Prentice-Hall, Inc.
Compiled/Edited by: Kenneth E. Miller
Available in: Medium High and Medium Low Voice

Composer	Song Title
American	Simple Gifts
Arne, T.	Blow, Blow, Thou Winter Wind
Beethoven, L.	Ich liebe dich so wie du mich
Bohm, C.	Still wie die Nacht
Brahms, J.	Sapphische Ode
Caldara, A.	Sebben crudele
Carissimi, G.	Vittoria, mio core!
Debussy, C.	Beau Soir
	Romance
Dougherty, C.	Shenandoah
Durante, F.	Vergin, tutto amor
Fauré, G.	Après un rêve
	Libera me
	Pie Jesu
Fontenailles, H.	Obstination
Franz, R.	Gute Nacht
Gluck, C. W. von	O del mio dolce ardor
Hahn, R.	L'Huere exquise
Handel, G. F.	Ah! mio cor
	Oh Sleep, Why Dost Thou Leave Me?
	Ombra mai fù
Lully, J. B.	Bois épais
Monteverde, C.	Lasciatemi morire!
Old English	Down Among the Dead Men
	Have You Seen But a White Lillie Grow?
Pergolesi, G. B.	Se tu m'ami

			Anthologies					
1	2	1	2	1	1	1	9	**1**

Melody	Phrase	Rhythm	Text	Accomp.	Harmony	Dynamics	Total	Rank
2	1	1	1	1	1	1	8	**1**
2	3	1	1	1	1	2	11	**2**
2	1	1	2	2	1	2	11	**2**
2	3	2	2	2	1	3	15	**3**
2	2	1	2	1	2	2	12	**2**
2	2	1	2	1	1	2	11	**2**
2	2	2	2	1	1	2	12	**2**
2	1	1	1	2	3	3	13	**2**
2	1	1	2	2	2	3	13	**2**
2	2	2	1	2	1	2	12	**2**
2	1	3	2	1	1	3	13	**2**
2	2	1	2	2	2	3	14	**2**
1	1	2	2	2	1	2	11	**2**
2	2	2	2	1	1	3	13	**2**
2	1	1	2	2	1	3	12	**2**
1	1	1	2	2	1	3	11	**2**
3	2	1	2	2	1	3	14	**2**
2	2	1	2	2	1	3	13	**2**
2	1	1	2	2	1	3	12	**2**
2	3	1	1	1	1	1	10	**1**
2	3	2	2	1	1	2	13	**2**
2	3	2	2	1	1	3	14	**2**
2	2	2	2	1	2	3	14	**2**
2	1	1	1	1	1	2	9	**1**
2	1	2	1	1	1	3	11	**2**
2	1	1	2	2	1	3	12	**2**

229

Purcell, H.	Dido's Lament
	I Attempt From Love's Sickness to Fly
Quilter, R.	O Mistress Mine
Scarlatti, A.	Se Florindo è fedele
Schubert, F.	Benedictus
	Ungeduld
Schumann, R.	Du bist wie eine Blume
Strauss, R.	Allerseelen
Torelli, G.	Tu lo sai
Vivaldi, A.	Qui sedes ad dexteram
Warlock, P.	Pretty Ring Time

Art Songs for School and Studio, First Year

Publisher: Oliver Ditson Co.
Compiled/Edited by: Mabelle Glenn and Alfred Spouse
Available in: Medium High and Medium Low Voice

Composer	Song Title
Bayly, T. H.	Long, Long Ago
Bohm, C.	Still as the Night (Still wie die Nacht)
Brahms, J.	Cradle Song (Wiegenlied)
Cadman, C. W.	Little road to Kerry, The
Calbreath, M. E.	My Love rode by
Clokey, J. W.	Rose, The
Dichmont, W.	Such a li'l' fellow
English	O No, John!
Fisher, W. A.	Under the Rose
Franz, R.	Dedication (Widmung)
	For Music (Für Music)
	Out of My Soul's Great Sadness (Aus meinen grossen schmerzen)
	Rose Complained, The (es hat die Rosesich beklagt)
Godard, B.	Florian's Song (Chanson de Florian)

Melody	Phrase	Rhythm	Text	Accomp.	Harmony	Dynamics	Total	Rank
2	1	2	1	2	2	3	13	2
2	1	1	1	2	1	2	10	1
2	1	1	1	1	1	2	9	1
1	1	1	2	1	1	3	10	1
2	1	2	2	2	1	2	12	2
2	1	2	2	2	1	2	12	2
1	2	1	2	2	1	2	11	2
2	3	1	2	2	1	3	14	2
2	1	1	2	1	1	3	11	2
2	2	2	2	1	1	2	12	2
2	1	1	1	1	1	3	10	1

Melody	Phrase	Rhythm	Text	Accomp.	Harmony	Dynamics	Total	Rank
2	1	1	1	2	1	1	9	1
2	3	2	2	2	1	3	15	3
1	1	1	2	2	1	1	9	1
2	1	1	1	1	1	3	10	1
2	1	2	1	2	1	3	12	2
2	1	1	1	1	1	3	10	1
2	1	1	1	2	1	3	11	2
1	1	1	1	2	1	2	9	1
3	2	1	1	1	1	3	12	2
2	1	1	2	1	1	3	11	2
2	1	1	2	1	1	3	11	2
2	1	2	2	1	1	2	11	2
2	1	1	2	1	1	1	9	1
2	1	1	2	2	1	3	12	2

Grant-Schaefer, G. A.	Wind Speaks, The
Gretchaninoff, A.	Slumber Song
Irish	My Love's an Arbutus
Old English	Pretty Polly Oliver
	When Love is Kind
Purcell, E. C.	Passing By
Schubert, F.	Hedge-roses (Heidenröslein)
	Who is Sylvia (Was ist Sylvia)
Schumann, R.	Lotus Flower, The (Die Lotusblume)
	Thou'rt Lovely as a Flower (Du bist wie eine Blume)
Strickland, L.	Road to Home, The

Art Songs for School and Studio, Second Year

Publisher: Oliver Ditson Co.
Compiled/Edited by: Mabelle Glenn and Alfred Spouse
Available in: Medium High and Medium Low Voice

Composer	Song Title
Brahms, J.	In Summer Fields (Feldeinsamkeit)
	Love Song (Minnelied)
	Sapphic Ode (Sapphische Ode)
Densmore, J. H.	If God left only you
Fisher, W. A.	I heard a Cry
Franz, R.	His Coming (Er ist gekommen)
	I wander this Summer morning (Am leuchtenden Sommermorgen)
	Request (Bitte)
Grieg, E.	Solvejg's Song (Solvejgs Lied)
	Swan, A (Ein Schwan)
Henschel, G.	No Embers, nor a Firebrand (Kein Feuer, Keine Kohle)
Jensen, A.	Press Thy Cheek Against Mine Own
Manney, C. F.	Consecration

Anthologies

Melody	Phrase	Rhythm	Text	Accomp.	Harmony	Dynamics	Total	Rank
1	1	2	1	2	1	3	11	2
3	1	1	2	2	1	2	12	2
2	1	1	1	1	1	3	10	1
2	1	1	1	1	1	2	9	1
2	1	1	1	2	1	2	10	1
1	1	1	1	2	1	1	8	1
1	2	1	2	2	1	3	12	2
2	2	2	2	2	1	3	14	2
2	2	1	2	1	1	2	11	2
1	2	1	2	2	1	2	11	2
2	2	2	1	1	2	3	13	2

Melody	Phrase	Rhythm	Text	Accomp.	Harmony	Dynamics	Total	Rank
1	2	1	2	2	2	2	12	2
2	2	1	2	2	1	2	12	2
2	2	1	2	1	2	3	13	2
1	2	1	1	1	2	3	11	2
2	2	1	1	1	2	3	12	2
2	2	2	2	1	2	2	13	2
1	1	1	2	1	1	3	10	1
1	1	1	2	1	1	2	9	1
2	2	1	2	2	1	3	13	2
2	2	1	2	2	1	3	13	2
2	1	1	2	1	1	2	10	1
1	2	1	1	2	1	3	11	2
2	1	1	1	1	1	3	10	1

Schubert, F.	Ave Maria
	Faith in Spring (Frühlingsglaube)
	Hark! Hark! The Lark
Schumann, R.	Twas in the Lovely Month of May (Im wunderschönen Monat Mai)
	Two Grenadiers, The (Die beiden Grenadiere)
Sinding, C.	Sylvelin
Strickland, L.	My Lover is a Fisherman
Swedish	When I was Seventeen
Tchaikovsky, P.	None by the Lonely Heart (Nur wer die sehnsucht kennt)
Watts, W.	Blue are Her Eyes

Basics of Singing Third Edition

Publisher: Schirmer Books
Compiled/Edited by: Jan Schmidt
Available in: High and Low Voice

Composer	Song Title
Adams, L.	Put On a Happy Face
American	All the Pretty Little Horses
	Black is the Color of My True Love's Hair
	Every Night When the Sun Goes In
	Long Time Ago
	Swing Low, Sweet Chariot
Arlen, H.	Over the Rainbow
Bartlet, J.	When from My Love
Bernstein, L.	Somewhere
Bononcini, M. A.	Pastorella, spera, spera
British	Early One Morning
	Water is Wide, The
Dowland, J.	Come Again, Sweet Love
Fain, S.	Love Is a Many-Splendored Thing
Fauré, G.	Après un rêve

234

Anthologies

Melody	Phrase	Rhythm	Text	Accomp.	Harmony	Dynamics	Total	Rank
1	3	3	1	2	1	3	14	2
2	1	1	2	1	1	3	11	2
2	1	1	1	2	2	3	12	2
2	1	1	2	2	2	2	12	2
1	1	2	1	2	1	2	10	1
1	1	1	2	2	1	1	9	1
2	1	1	1	2	1	2	10	1
3	1	3	2	2	1	2	14	2
2	1	1	2	2	1	3	12	2
1	2	1	1	1	2	3	11	2

Melody	Phrase	Rhythm	Text	Accomp.	Harmony	Dynamics	Total	Rank
2	1	1	1	1	1	1	8	1
2	1	1	1	2	1	3	11	2
2	2	1	1	1	1	1	9	1
1	1	1	1	1	1	1	7	1
1	1	1	1	1	1	1	7	1
1	2	2	1	2	1	1	10	1
2	2	1	1	1	1	2	10	1
2	1	1	1	2	1	1	9	1
2	2	1	1	1	1	3	11	2
1	1	1	2	2	1	2	10	1
2	1	1	1	2	1	2	10	1
1	1	1	1	1	1	1	7	1
2	2	1	1	1	1	2	10	1
2	2	1	1	1	1	1	9	1
2	2	1	2	2	2	3	14	2

Ford, N.	In a Simple Way I Love You
Franz, R.	Widmung
Handel, G. F.	Ombra mai fù
	Where E'er You Walk
Haydn, J.	Piercing Eyes
Hopkinson, F.	Beneath a Weeping Willow's Shade
Irish	Down by the Salley Gardens
	Johnny Doolan's Cat
	Juniper Tree, The
	Minstrel Boy, The
	Next Market Day, The
Italian	Santa Lucia
Kander, J.	Sometimes a Day Goes By
Karlin, F.	Come Saturday Morning
Kasha, A.	Candle on the Water
LeGrand, M.	What Are You Doing the Rest of Your Life?
Loewe, F.	Almost Like Being in Love
Mancini, H.	Moon River
McBroom, A.	Rose, The
Obradors, F. J.	Con amores, la mi madre
Rorem, N.	Early in the Morning
Scarlatti, A.	Cara e dolce
	O cessate di piagarmi
Schumann, C.	Liebst du um Schönheit
Scottish	Flow Gently, Sweet Afton
	Turn Ye To Me
Simon, L.	How Could I Ever Know
Sondheim, S.	No One is Alone
V. Williams, R.	Bright Is the Ring of Words
Van Heusen, J.	Call Me Irresponsible

Anthologies

1	1	1	1	1	1	1	7	**1**
1	2	1	2	1	1	1	9	**1**
2	3	2	2	1	1	2	13	**2**
2	1	1	1	2	1	3	11	**2**
2	1	1	1	1	1	2	9	**1**
2	1	1	1	1	1	3	10	**1**
2	1	1	1	1	1	1	8	**1**
1	1	1	1	1	1	1	7	**1**
1	1	1	1	2	1	1	8	**1**
2	1	1	1	1	1	1	8	**1**
2	1	1	1	2	1	1	9	**1**
1	1	1	1	2	1	1	8	**1**
2	1	1	1	2	1	2	10	**1**
1	2	1	1	1	1	1	8	**1**
1	1	1	1	1	1	1	7	**1**
2	1	1	1	1	1	1	8	**1**
2	2	1	1	1	1	2	10	**1**
2	2	1	1	1	1	2	10	**1**
1	1	1	1	1	1	1	7	**1**
2	2	1	1	2	1	3	12	**2**
2	2	1	1	2	1	2	11	**2**
2	1	1	1	1	1	3	10	**1**
1	1	1	2	2	1	3	11	**2**
1	1	1	2	1	1	2	9	**1**
1	1	1	1	2	1	1	8	**1**
2	1	1	1	1	1	1	8	**1**
2	1	1	1	2	1	3	11	**2**
2	1	1	1	2	1	2	10	**1**
2	1	1	1	1	2	3	11	**2**
2	2	1	1	1	1	2	10	**1**

237

Broadway Repertoire, for Bass-Baritone

Publisher: Chappell & Co., Inc.
Compiled/Edited by: Gregory Boals
Available in: Medium Low Voice

Composer	Song Title
Gershwin, G.	I Got Plenty O' Nuttin'
Kern, J.	Ol' Man River
Lane, B.	On A Clear Day
Loewe, F.	I've Grown Accustomed To Her Face
	If Ever I Would Leave You
	They Call The Wind Maria
Rodgers, R.	Lonely Room
	Some Enchanted Evening
Rosenthal, L.	Imagine That
Schmidt, H.	Gonna Be Another Hot Day
	My Cup Runneth Over
	Soon It's Gonna Rain
Sondheim, S.	Everybody Says Don't
Styne, J.	Just In Time
Weill, K.	Lost In The Stars

Broadway Repertoire, for Mezzo-Soprano

Publisher: Chappell & Co., Inc.
Compiled/Edited by: Gregory Boals
Available in: Medium Voice

Composer	Song Title
Hamlisch, M.	What I Did For Love
Kander, J.	And All That Jazz
	My Own Space
Lane, B.	Look To The Rainbow
Loewe, F.	Show Me
Moross, J.	Lazy Afternoon

Melody	Phrase	Rhythm	Text	Accomp.	Harmony	Dynamics	Total	Rank
2	2	1	1	1	2	2	11	2
2	2	1	1	1	1	3	11	2
2	2	1	1	1	1	2	10	1
2	2	1	1	1	1	2	10	1
2	2	1	1	1	1	3	11	2
2	2	1	1	2	1	2	11	2
1	2	1	1	2	1	3	11	2
3	2	1	1	1	1	3	12	2
2	2	1	1	1	1	1	9	1
2	2	2	1	2	1	2	12	2
2	2	1	1	2	1	2	11	2
2	2	1	1	1	1	1	9	1
2	2	1	1	2	1	3	12	2
2	2	1	1	1	1	2	10	1
2	3	1	1	2	1	2	12	2

Melody	Phrase	Rhythm	Text	Accomp.	Harmony	Dynamics	Total	Rank
2	1	1	1	1	1	1	8	1
2	2	1	1	1	2	3	12	2
2	1	1	1	1	1	1	8	1
2	2	1	1	1	1	3	11	2
2	1	2	1	1	1	3	11	2
2	1	1	1	3	1	2	11	2

Rodgers, R.	Bali Ha'I
	My Funny Valentine
Schmidt, H.	Is It Really Me?
	Under The Tree
	What Is A Woman?
Shire, D.	Starting Here, Starting Now
Sondheim, S.	Anyone Can Whistle
Styne, J.	People
	Who Are You Now?

Broadway Repertoire, for Soprano

Publisher: Chappell & Co., Inc.
Compiled/Edited by: Gregory Boals
Available in: High Voice

Composer	Song Title
Arlen, H.	I Had Myself A True Love
Gershwin, G.	Summertime
Hague, A.	It Wonders Me
Kern, J.	Can't Help Lovin' Dat Man
Loewe, F.	I Loved You Once In Silence
Moore, D.	Letter Song
Porter, C.	So In Love
Rodgers, R.	Bewitched
	Climb Ev'ry Mountain
	People Will Say We're In Love
	You'll Never Walk Alone
Schmidt, H.	Much More
Sondheim, S.	That Dirty Old Man
Weill, K.	Lonely House
	Stay Well

Anthologies

Melody	Phrase	Rhythm	Text	Accomp.	Harmony	Dynamics	Total	Rank
2	2	1	1	2	1	2	11	2
2	2	1	1	1	1	3	11	2
2	1	1	1	1	1	1	8	1
2	1	1	1	1	1	1	8	1
2	1	1	1	3	1	2	11	2
2	2	1	1	1	1	2	10	1
2	1	1	1	1	1	2	9	1
2	2	1	1	2	1	3	12	2
2	1	2	1	2	1	3	12	2

Melody	Phrase	Rhythm	Text	Accomp.	Harmony	Dynamics	Total	Rank
3	3	2	1	1	2	2	14	2
1	3	1	1	2	1	2	11	2
3	1	1	1	1	1	2	10	1
3	1	1	1	1	2	3	12	2
2	3	1	1	1	2	2	12	2
3	3	2	1	2	2	2	15	3
2	3	1	1	1	2	2	12	2
1	1	1	1	1	1	1	7	1
2	3	1	1	1	1	3	12	2
2	1	1	1	1	1	2	9	1
3	2	1	1	1	1	3	12	2
3	2	1	1	1	1	2	11	2
2	3	1	1	2	2	1	12	2
2	3	1	1	2	2	3	14	2
3	2	1	1	1	2	3	13	2

Broadway Repertoire, for Tenor

Publisher: Chappell & Co., Inc.
Compiled/Edited by: Gregory Boals
Available in: High Voice

Composer	Song Title
Benton, G.	How Do You Preach?
Grossman, L.	Just One Person
Hague, A.	Young And Foolish
Lane, B.	Old Devil Moon
	She Wasn't You
Lerner, A. J.	On The Street Where You Live
Ornadel, C.	If I Ruled The World
Rodgers, M.	Yesterday I Loved You
Rodgers, R.	I Have Dreamed
	We Kiss In A Shadow
	Younger Than Springtime
Rome, H.	Fanny
Schmidt, H.	Fifty Million Years Ago
Schwartz, S.	Corner Of The Sky
Sondheim, S.	Love, I Hear
	Take Me To The World
Weill, K.	Tschaikowsky

Classic Italian Songs for School and Studio, Vol I

Publisher: Oliver Ditson Co.
Compiled/Edited by: Mabelle Glenn and Bernard U. Taylor
Available in: Medium High and Medium Low Voice

Composer	Song Title
Bencini, P. P.	Tanto sospirerò
Caccini, G.	Amarilli
Carissimi, G.	No, no, non si speri!
	Vittoria, mio core!

Melody	Phrase	Rhythm	Text	Accomp.	Harmony	Dynamics	Total	Rank
2	2	1	1	1	1	1	9	1
2	2	1	1	1	1	3	11	2
2	2	1	1	1	1	2	10	1
2	1	2	1	1	2	1	10	1
3	2	1	1	1	1	3	12	2
2	2	1	1	1	1	2	10	1
2	2	1	1	1	1	2	10	1
2	3	3	1	1	1	3	14	2
2	1	1	1	1	1	1	8	1
2	3	1	1	2	1	2	12	2
2	2	1	1	1	1	3	11	2
2	3	1	1	1	1	3	12	2
2	3	3	1	2	1	2	14	2
2	3	1	1	1	1	1	10	1
2	2	1	1	1	1	3	11	2
2	1	1	1	1	1	3	10	1
3	1	1	1	1	1	3	11	2

Melody	Phrase	Rhythm	Text	Accomp.	Harmony	Dynamics	Total	Rank
1	1	1	2	2	1	3	11	2
2	3	2	2	2	1	3	15	3
2	1	1	2	2	1	2	11	2
2	2	2	2	1	1	2	12	2

Cavalli, F.	Donzelle fuggite
Durante, F.	Vergin, tutta amor
Frescobaldi, G.	Se l'aura spira
Giordani, G.	Caro mio ben
Lotti, A.	Pur dicesti, O bocca bella
Monteverde, C.	Ahi, troppo è duro
	Lascitemi morire
Pergolesi, G. B.	Nina (Tre Giorni)
Peri, J.	Invocazione de Orfeo
Rosa, S.	Selve, voi che le speranze
Scarlatti, A.	O cessate di piagarmi
	Rugiadose, odorose
Secchi, A.	Lungi dal caro bene
Torelli, G.	Tu lo sai

Classic Italian Songs for School and Studio, Vol II

Publisher: Oliver Ditson Co.
Compiled/Edited by: Mabelle Glenn & Bernard U. Taylor
Available in: Medium High and Medium Low Voice

Composer	Song Title
Bononcini, G.	L'esperto nocchiero
Caldara, A.	Alma del core
	Come raggio di sol
Carissimi, G.	Deh, contentatevi
Cesti, M. A.	Ah! quanto è vero
	E dove t'aggiri
Durante, F.	Danza, danza, fanciulla gentile
Falconieri, A.	O bellissimi capelli
Legrenzi, G.	Che fiero costume
Mazzaferrata, G. B.	Presto, presto lo m'innamoro
Provenzale, F.	Deh, rendetemi
Rosa, S.	Star vicino

Anthologies

Melody	Phrase	Rhythm	Text	Accomp.	Harmony	Dynamics	Total	Rank
1	2	1	2	1	1	2	10	1
2	1	3	2	1	1	2	12	2
2	1	1	2	2	1	3	12	2
2	3	1	2	1	1	3	13	2
2	1	2	2	1	1	3	12	2
2	1	2	2	2	2	3	14	2
1	3	2	2	1	2	3	14	2
1	1	2	2	2	1	3	12	2
1	2	2	2	2	1	3	13	2
2	1	1	2	2	1	2	11	2
2	1	1	2	2	1	3	12	2
2	1	3	2	2	1	3	14	2
3	1	1	2	1	1	3	12	2
2	1	1	2	2	1	3	12	2

Melody	Phrase	Rhythm	Text	Accomp.	Harmony	Dynamics	Total	Rank
2	2	3	2	1	1	2	13	2
1	1	2	2	2	1	3	12	2
2	2	1	2	2	1	3	13	2
2	2	1	2	1	2	3	13	2
2	2	1	2	1	1	3	12	2
2	1	2	2	1	1	3	12	2
2	1	2	2	2	1	2	12	2
1	2	1	2	2	1	2	11	2
2	1	2	2	2	1	2	12	2
2	1	3	2	2	1	3	14	2
1	2	1	2	2	1	3	12	2
2	2	1	2	2	1	3	13	2

Scarlatti, A.	Non vogl'io se non vederti
	Sento nel core
Stradella, A.	Col mio sangue comprerei

Classic Italian Songs for School and Studio, Vol III

Publisher: Oliver Ditson Co.
Compiled/Edited by: Mabelle Glenn & Bernard U. Taylor
Available in: Medium High and Medium Low Voice

Composer	Song Title
Bononcini, G.	Deh più a me non v'ascondete
Caldara, A.	Selve amiche, ombrose piante
Carissimi, G.	Filli, non t'amo più
Falconieri, A.	Bella porta di rubini
Gaffi, B.	Luci vezzose
Paisiello, G.	Nel cor più non mi sento
Pergolesi, G. B.	Se tu m'ami
Perti, J. A.	Begli occhi, io non mi pento
Scarlatti, A.	Chi vuole innomorarsi
Stradella, A.	Cosi, amor, mi fai languir!
	Per pietà
Strozzi, B.	Amor dormiglione
Traetta, T.	Ombra cara, amorosa
Vivaldi, A.	Un certo non so che

Classical Contest Solos—Baritone/Bass

Publisher: Hal Leonard Corporation
Compiled/Edited by: N/A
Available in: Medium Low Voice

Composer	Song Title
Burleigh, H. T., arr.	Swing Low, Sweet Chariot
Caldara, A.	Alma del core

Melody	Phrase	Rhythm	Text	Accomp.	Harmony	Dynamics	Total	Rank
1	2	1	2	2	1	2	11	2
2	1	1	2	1	1	2	10	1
2	2	1	2	2	2	3	14	2

Melody	Phrase	Rhythm	Text	Accomp.	Harmony	Dynamics	Total	Rank
2	1	1	2	2	1	3	12	2
1	2	3	2	2	1	3	14	2
2	1	3	2	1	1	2	12	2
1	1	1	2	1	1	3	10	1
1	1	2	2	1	1	3	11	2
2	1	1	2	2	1	2	11	2
2	1	1	2	2	1	3	12	2
2	1	3	2	2	1	3	14	2
2	1	3	2	1	1	3	13	2
2	1	1	2	2	1	3	12	2
2	2	1	2	1	1	3	12	2
2	2	2	2	1	1	3	13	2
2	1	1	2	2	2	3	13	2
2	1	2	2	2	2	3	14	2

Melody	Phrase	Rhythm	Text	Accomp.	Harmony	Dynamics	Total	Rank
2	1	1	1	2	1	2	10	1
1	1	1	2	1	1	2	9	1

Foster, S. C.	Beautiful Dreamer
MacDowell, E.	Sea, The
O'Hara, G.	Give a Man a Horse He Can Ride
Old Welsh	All Through the Night
Rodrigo, J.	Adela
Scarlatti, A.	O cessate di piagarmi
Schumann, R.	Du bist wie eine Blume
Wilson, H. L., arr.	Slighted Swain, The

Classical Contest Solos—Mezzo-Soprano

Publisher: Hal Leonard Corporation
Compiled/Edited by: N/A
Available in: Medium Voice

Composer	Song Title
Burleigh, H. T., arr.	My Lord, What a Mornin'
Durante, F.	Vergin, tutto amor
Handel, G. F.	He shall feed His flock
	Ombra mai fu'
MacDowell, E.	Blue-Bell, The
Morley, T.	Now Is the Month of Maying
Purcell, H.	Nymphs and Shepherds
Rodrigo, J.	Porque toco el pandero
Schubert, F.	An die Musik
V. Williams, R.	Silent Noon

Classical Contest Solos—Soprano

Publisher: Hal Leonard Corporation
Compiled/Edited by: N/A
Available in: High Voice

Composer	Song Title
Burleigh, H. T., arr.	Didn't My Lord Deliver Daniel
Flotow, F.	Tis the Last Rose of Summer

Melody	Phrase	Rhythm	Text	Accomp.	Harmony	Dynamics	Total	Rank
2	2	1	1	1	1	1	9	1
1	1	1	1	2	2	3	11	2
2	1	1	1	2	1	1	9	1
2	1	1	1	2	1	2	10	1
2	1	1	2	2	1	1	10	1
1	1	1	2	2	1	3	11	2
1	1	2	2	2	1	2	11	2
2	1	1	1	2	1	3	11	2

Melody	Phrase	Rhythm	Text	Accomp.	Harmony	Dynamics	Total	Rank
1	1	1	1	2	1	2	9	1
2	1	1	2	1	1	2	10	1
1	2	2	1	1	1	2	10	1
2	2	3	2	1	1	2	13	2
1	1	1	1	2	1	3	10	1
1	1	1	1	1	1	2	8	1
2	1	1	1	2	1	1	9	1
1	1	1	2	1	1	2	9	1
2	1	1	2	2	1	3	12	2
2	2	2	1	2	2	3	14	2

Melody	Phrase	Rhythm	Text	Accomp.	Harmony	Dynamics	Total	Rank
1	2	1	1	1	1	2	9	1
1	2	1	1	2	1	2	10	1

Granados, E.	El tra la la y el punteado
Grieg, E.	Solvejg's Song
Hageman, R.	Do not go, my love
Morley, T.	It Was a Lover and His Lass
Paisiello, G.	Nel cor più non mi sento
Parisotti, A.	Se tu m'ami
Purcell, H.	I Attempt From Love's Sickness to Fly
Schubert, F.	Lachen und Weinen

Classical Contest Solos—Tenor

Publisher: Hal Leonard Corporation
Compiled/Edited by: N/A
Available in: High Voice

Composer	Song Title
Beethoven, L.	An die Geliebte
Burleigh, H. T., arr.	Steal Away
Caldara, A.	Sebben, crudele
Dowland, J.	Come Again, Sweet Love
Giordani, G.	Caro mio ben
Handel, G. F.	Where E'er You Walk
Hughes, H., arr.	Down By the Sally Gardens
Old English	Have You Seen But a White Lillie Grow?
Quilter, R.	Weep You No More
Rodrigo, J.	Adela

Contemporary Art Songs

Publisher: G. Schirmer
Compiled/Edited by: N/A
Available in: Medium Voice

Composer	Song Title
Barber, S.	Must the Winter Come so Soon?
Beck, J. N.	Song of Devotion

Melody	Phrase	Rhythm	Text	Accomp.	Harmony	Dynamics	Total	Rank
2	2	1	2	2	1	2	12	**2**
3	2	1	1	2	1	3	13	**2**
2	2	1	1	2	2	2	12	**2**
1	1	1	1	2	1	1	8	**1**
2	2	1	2	2	1	2	12	**2**
3	1	1	2	2	1	3	13	**2**
2	2	1	1	2	1	1	10	**1**
2	2	1	2	2	1	2	12	**2**

Melody	Phrase	Rhythm	Text	Accomp.	Harmony	Dynamics	Total	Rank
1	1	1	2	2	1	2	10	**1**
1	1	2	1	2	1	3	11	**2**
2	1	1	2	1	1	2	10	**1**
2	1	1	1	2	1	2	10	**1**
2	1	2	2	1	1	2	11	**2**
2	1	1	1	2	1	2	10	**1**
2	1	1	1	2	1	2	10	**1**
2	1	1	1	2	1	2	10	**1**
2	1	1	1	2	1	3	11	**2**
2	1	1	2	2	1	1	10	**1**

Melody	Phrase	Rhythm	Text	Accomp.	Harmony	Dynamics	Total	Rank
2	3	1	1	2	1	2	12	**2**
2	3	1	1	2	2	3	14	**2**

Bernstein, L.	Extinguish My Eyes
	When My Soul Touches Yours
Bowles, P.	Heavenly Grass
Carpenter, J. A.	When I Bring to You Colour'd Toys
Chávez, C.	Segador
Chenoweth, W.	Vocalise
Corigliano, J.	Christmas at the Cloisters
	Unicorn, The
Dougherty, C.	Sound the Flute!
Duke, J.	Peggy Mitchell
Dunhill, T.	To the Queen of Heaven
Gibbs, C. A.	When I was One-and-Twenty
Hoiby, L.	An Immorality
Kingsford, C.	Down Harley Street
Menotti, G. C.	Lullaby from "The Consul"
Moore, D.	Dove Song, The from "The Wings of the Dove"
Sargent, P.	Stopping by Woods on a Snowy Evening
Schuman, W.	Holiday Song
Shaw, M.	Easter Carol
Symons, D. T.	Sight in Camp, A
Thiman, E. H.	I Love All Graceful Things
Thomson, V.	English Usage
	Tiger, The
Toye, F.	Inn, The
V. Williams, R.	Hugh's Song of the Road
Wells, H.	Everyone Sang

2	2	3	1	2	3	3	16	**3**
2	3	2	1	3	3	3	17	**3**
2	3	1	1	1	2	3	13	**2**
2	1	1	1	2	2	3	12	**2**
1	2	2	2	1	2	3	13	**2**
3	1	3	1	2	1	3	14	**2**
3	2	2	1	1	3	3	15	**3**
3	2	1	1	1	3	3	14	**2**
1	1	2	1	2	1	3	11	**2**
2	2	1	1	3	3	3	15	**3**
2	1	1	1	2	1	3	11	**2**
1	1	1	1	1	2	3	10	**1**
2	2	1	1	2	3	3	14	**2**
1	1	1	1	2	1	2	9	**1**
3	1	1	1	1	2	3	12	**2**
2	1	2	1	3	3	2	14	**2**
1	1	1	1	2	3	2	11	**2**
2	1	2	1	1	3	3	13	**2**
2	1	2	1	2	2	3	13	**2**
2	1	2	1	2	3	3	14	**2**
2	1	1	1	2	1	2	10	**1**
2	1	2	1	2	3	3	14	**2**
2	1	1	1	3	3	3	14	**2**
2	2	2	1	3	2	3	15	**3**
2	1	3	1	1	3	3	14	**2**
2	1	1	1	2	3	3	13	**2**

Expressive Singing Song Anthology, Third Edition

Publisher: McGraw-Hill
Compiled/Edited by: Van A. Christy and John Glenn Payton
Available in: High, Medium, and Low Voice

Composer	Song Title
Arne, T.	Blow, Blow, Thou Winter Wind
Beethoven, L.	Zärtliche Liebe
Bellini, V.	Vaga luna
Berger, J.	He or She That Hopes to Gain
Bishop, Sir H.	Love Has Eyes
Bononcini, G.	Bella vittoria
Brahms, J.	Da unten im Tale
Christy, V. A., arr.	Miller of Dee, The
	Peace Prayer of St. Francis of Assisi
Cimador, G. B.	Bel nume
Coleridge-Taylor, S.	When I Am Dead, My Dearest
de Falla, M.	Asturiana
Debussy, C.	Beau soir
Fauré, G.	Chanson d'Amour
Foster, S. C.	Ah, May the Red Rose Live Always
García, M.	Se il mio nome saper
Gonzalez, L. J.	Canción del niño por nacer
Gounod, C.	Sérénade
Grieg, E.	Jeg elsker Dig
	To brune øjne
Hahn, R.	Si mes vers avaient des ailes
Handel, G. F.	Dove Sei
	Oh Sleep, Why Dost Thou Leave Me?
Haydn, J.	She Never Told Her Love
Hindemith, P.	Echo
Ives, C. E.	At Sea

Melody	Phrase	Rhythm	Text	Accomp.	Harmony	Dynamics	Total	Rank
2	1	1	1	1	1	2	9	1
2	1	1	2	2	1	2	11	2
2	1	1	2	2	1	2	11	2
2	2	2	1	2	3	3	15	3
2	1	1	1	2	1	2	10	1
1	1	1	2	2	1	1	9	1
2	1	1	2	1	2	2	11	2
1	1	1	1	2	1	2	9	1
3	2	1	1	2	2	3	14	2
1	1	3	2	2	1	2	12	2
2	1	1	1	2	1	2	10	1
1	3	1	2	2	1	3	13	2
2	1	1	2	2	3	3	14	2
2	1	1	2	2	1	3	12	2
2	1	1	1	2	1	1	9	1
2	1	3	2	2	1	2	13	2
3	1	1	2	2	1	1	11	2
2	2	1	2	2	1	2	12	2
2	1	1	2	2	1	3	12	2
2	1	1	2	1	1	1	9	1
2	2	1	2	2	1	3	13	2
2	1	2	2	1	1	2	11	2
2	3	1	1	1	1	1	10	1
2	1	2	1	2	1	2	11	2
2	1	2	1	2	2	2	12	2
2	2	1	1	2	3	3	14	2

Ives, C. E.	Evening
Lane, R.	Farmer by the Sea
Lefevre, J.	L'Amour de mois de mai
Lefévre, J.	L'Amour au mois de mai
Lully, J. B.	Bois épais
Marcello, B.	O genti tutte
Martini, G.	Joy of Love, The (Plaisir d'amour)
Mendelssohn, F.	Gruss
Mexican	Yo no se que decir
Old English	Have You Seen But a Bright Lily Grow?
Paisiello, G.	Chi vuol la zingarella
Paton, J. G., arr.	Greensleeves
Persichetti, V.	I'm Nobody
Purcell, E. C.	Passing By
Purcell, H.	I Attempt From Love's Sickness to Fly
Quilter, R.	O Mistress Mine
	Weep You No More, Sad Fountains
Scarlatti, A.	Spesso vibra per suo gioco
Schubert, F.	Frühlingsglaube
	Heidenröslein
Schumann, C.	Ich hab' in Deinem Auge
Schumann, R.	Die Stille
Spanish	Tirana del Caramba
Stradella, A.	Se nel ben
Thomson, V.	Take, O, Take Those Lips Away
Tosti, F. P.	Malìa
V. Williams, R.	Oh, When I Was in Love With You
Wolf, H.	Der Musikant

Anthologies

2	2	2	1	2	3	3	15	**3**
1	1	1	1	2	3	2	11	**2**
2	2	1	2	2	1	2	12	**2**
1	1	2	2	1	1	2	10	**1**
2	3	2	2	2	1	1	13	**2**
2	1	3	2	2	1	1	12	**2**
2	3	2	2	2	1	2	14	**2**
2	1	1	2	2	1	1	10	**1**
2	1	1	2	1	1	2	10	**1**
1	1	1	1	2	1	1	8	**1**
2	1	3	2	2	1	3	14	**2**
2	1	1	1	2	1	1	9	**1**
2	1	1	1	2	2	2	11	**2**
1	1	1	1	2	1	3	10	**1**
2	1	1	1	2	1	1	9	**1**
2	1	1	1	1	1	2	9	**1**
2	1	2	1	2	1	3	12	**2**
2	1	1	2	1	1	1	9	**1**
2	1	1	2	1	1	3	11	**2**
1	2	1	2	2	1	3	12	**2**
2	1	2	2	1	1	2	11	**2**
2	1	1	2	1	2	2	11	**2**
2	1	3	2	2	1	1	12	**2**
2	1	1	2	1	1	1	9	**1**
2	2	3	1	2	1	3	14	**2**
1	1	1	2	1	1	2	9	**1**
1	1	3	1	2	1	1	10	**1**
2	1	1	2	2	2	2	12	**2**

257

Expressive Singing Song Anthology, Volume I

Publisher: McGraw-Hill
Compiled/Edited by: Van A. Christy and John Glenn Payton
Available in: High, Medium, and Low Voice

Composer	Song Title
Adams, S.	Holy City, The
Beethoven, L.	I Love Thee (Ich liebe dich)
Bohm, C.	Still as the Night (Still wie die Nacht)
Brahms, J.	Far Down in the Valley (Da unten in Tale)
	O Calm of Night (In stiller Nacht)
Chopin, F.	Lithuanian Song (Lithauisches Lied)
Christy, V. A., arr.	All Through the Night
	Away Over Yandro
	Beautiful Savior
	Begone Dull Care
	Joshua Fit the Battle of Jericho
	Lonesome Valley
	Miller of Dee, The
	Mister Banjo
	Old Woman and the Peddler, The
	Shenandoah
	Tutu Maramba
Dvořák, A.	Songs My Mother Taught Me (Als die alte Mutter)
	Songs My Mother Taught Me (Als die alte Mutter)
Fontenailles, H.	Resolve, A (Obstination)
Franck, C.	Bread of Angels (Panis Angelicus)
Franz, R.	Dedication (Widmung)
	Out of My Soul's Great Sadness (Aus meinen grossen Schmerzen)
Gaul, A.	Eye Hath Not Seen
Grieg, E.	I Love thee (Ich liebe dich)

Melody	Phrase	Rhythm	Text	Accomp.	Harmony	Dynamics	Total	Rank
2	1	1	1	2	1	2	10	1
2	1	1	1	2	1	2	10	1
2	3	2	2	2	1	3	15	3
1	1	1	2	2	1	2	10	1
2	1	2	2	1	1	3	12	2
2	1	1	2	2	1	3	12	2
2	1	1	1	1	1	3	10	1
2	1	2	1	2	1	3	12	2
2	1	1	1	1	1	3	10	1
2	1	2	1	1	1	2	10	1
2	1	2	1	1	1	3	11	2
2	1	2	1	1	1	3	11	2
1	1	1	1	1	1	2	8	1
1	1	3	1	2	1	3	12	2
1	1	2	1	1	1	3	10	1
2	1	2	1	1	1	2	10	1
1	1	1	1	1	1	3	9	1
							0	0
2	1	1	2	2	1	3	12	2
2	1	1	2	2	1	3	12	2
2	1	1	2	2	1	3	12	2
2	1	1	2	1	1	3	11	2
2	1	2	2	1	1	2	11	2
2	2	2	1	1	2	3	13	2
							0	0

Handel, G. F.	Verdant Meadows (Verdi prati)
	Where E'er You Walk
Haydn, J.	She Never Told Her Love
	Very Commonplace Story, A (Ein sehr gewohnlische Geschichte)
Lully, J. B.	Sombre Woods (Bois épais)
MacDowell, E.	Sea, The
Martini, G.	Joys of Love, The (Plaisir d'amour)
Mellish, Col. R.	Drink to Me Only With Thine Eyes
Mendelssohn, F.	O Rest in the Lord
	On Wings of Song (Auf Flügeln des Gesanges)
Mozart, W. A.	Tragic Story, A
Nevin, E.	Little Boy Blue
Purcell, E. C.	Passing By
Schubert, F.	Faith in Spring (Frühlingsglaube)
Schumann, R.	Lotus Flower, The (Die Lotusblume)
	Thou'rt Lovely as a Flower (Du bist wie eine Blume)
Scott, A. A.	Think On Me
Sullivan, A.	Lost Chord, The
Tchaikovsky, P.	Legend, A
	None but the Lonely Heart (Nor wer die Sehnsucht kennt)
Wilson, H. L., arr.	Pretty Creature, The

Expressive Singing Song Anthology, Volume II

Publisher: McGraw-Hill
Compiled/Edited by: Van A. Christy and John Glenn Payton
Available in: High, Medium, and Low Voice

Composer	Song Title
Arne, T.	Lass with the Delicate Air, The
Beethoven, L.	To the Distant Beloved (An die fern Geliebte)
Bishop, Sir H.	Love Has Eyes

Melody	Phrase	Rhythm	Text	Accomp.	Harmony	Dynamics	Total	Rank
2	2	1	2	1	1	3	12	2
2	1	1	1	2	1	3	11	2
2	1	2	2	1	1	2	11	2
2	1	3	1	1	1	2	11	2
2	3	2	2	1	1	3	14	2
1	1	1	1	2	1	3	10	1
2	1	1	2	2	1	2	11	2
1	1	1	1	1	1	3	9	1
2	1	1	1	1	1	3	10	1
2	1	1	1	2	1	3	11	2
1	1	3	1	1	1	1	9	1
1	1	1	1	1	1	2	8	1
1	1	1	1	2	1	3	10	1
2	1	1	2	1	1	3	11	2
2	2	1	2	1	1	3	12	2
1	2	1	2	2	1	2	11	2
2	3	3	1	2	1	3	15	3
2	2	1	1	2	1	3	12	2
2	1	1	1	1	1	3	10	1
2	1	2	2	2	1	3	13	2
2	1	1	1	1	1	3	10	1
2	1	2	1	1	1	3	11	2
2	1	1	2	2	2	3	13	2
2	1	1	1	1	1	2	9	1

Brahms, J.	Sapphic Ode (Sapphische Ode)
Caldara, A.	When on the Surging Wave (Come raggio di sol)
Carey, H.	Pastoral, A
Debussy, C.	Evening Fair (Beau Soir)
Durante, F.	Virgin, Fount of Love (Vergin, tutto amor)
Fauré, G.	After a Dream (Après un rêve)
	Cradles, The (Les Berceaux)
Giordani, G.	Dear Love of Mine (Caro mio ben)
Godard, B.	Florian's Song (Chanson de Florian)
Gounod, C.	O, Divine Redeemer (Repentir)
Hahn, R.	Exquisite Hour, The (L'Heure exquise)
	Were My Songs With Wings Provided (Si mes vers avaient des ailes)
Handel, G. F.	Ah, Poor Heart (Ah! mio cor from "Alcina")
	Leave Me to Languish (Lascia ch'io pianga) from "Rinaldo"
	O Lovely Peace from "Judas Maccabaeus"
	Oh Sleep, Why Dost Thou Leave Me? from "Semele"
	Weep No More from "Hercules"
Hüe, G.	I Wept, Beloved, As I Dreamed (J'ai pleurè un rêve)
Lalo, É.	Captive, The (L'Esclave)
Legrenzi, G.	With Cunning Conniving (Che fiero costume)
Lotti, A.	Speak Once More, Dear (Pur dicesti, o bocca bella)
Massenet, J.	Elegy (Elégie)
Monro, G.	My Lovely Celia
Monteverde, C.	O Death Now Come (Lasciatemi morire) from "Ariana"
Pergolesi, G. B.	Nina
Purcell, H.	Come Unto These Yellow Sands
	Dido's Lament from "Dido and Aeneas"

2	2	1	2	1	2	2	12	**2**
2	2	1	1	2	1	3	12	**2**
2	1	2	1	1	1	2	10	**1**
2	1	1	2	2	3	3	14	**2**
2	1	3	2	1	1	3	13	**2**
2	2	1	2	2	2	3	14	**2**
3	2	1	2	2	1	3	14	**2**
2	3	1	2	1	1	3	13	**2**
2	1	1	2	2	1	3	12	**2**
2	1	1	2	2	1	3	12	**2**
2	2	1	2	2	1	3	13	**2**
2	2	1	2	2	1	3	13	**2**
2	1	1	1	2	1	3	11	**2**
2	1	1	2	1	1	3	11	**2**
2	2	1	1	1	1	3	11	**2**
2	3	1	1	1	1	3	12	**2**
2	1	2	1	2	1	3	12	**2**
2	2	1	2	1	2	3	13	**2**
2	1	1	2	2	1	3	12	**2**
2	1	2	2	2	1	2	12	**2**
2	1	2	2	1	1	3	12	**2**
2	2	2	2	2	1	3	14	**2**
2	1	1	1	1	1	3	10	**1**
1	3	2	2	1	2	3	14	**2**
2	1	2	2	2	1	3	13	**2**
2	1	2	1	1	1	3	11	**2**
2	1	2	1	2	2	3	13	**2**

Purcell, H.	I Attempt From Love's Sickness to Fly
	Sound the Trumpet
Rosa, S.	To Be Near Thee (Star vicino)
Schubert, F.	Impatience (Ungeduld)
	Serenade (Standchen)
Schumann, R.	I Dreamed That I Was Weeping (Ich hab' im Traum geweinet)
	I'll Not Complain (Ich grolle nicht)
Stradella, A.	O Lord, Have Mercy (Pietà, Signore)
Strauss, R.	All Soul's Day (Allerseelen)
	To You
	Tomorrow
Sullivan, A.	Orpheus With His Lute
Torelli, G.	Well Thou Knowest
Wolf. H.	Secrecy (Verborgenheit)

First Book of Baritone/Bass Solos, The

Publisher: G. Schirmer
Compiled/Edited by: Joan Frey Boytim
Available in: Medium Low Voice

Composer	Song Title
Arne, T.	Why So Pale and Wan
Beethoven, L.	There Was a Mighty Monarch
Clarke, R. C.	Blind Ploughman, The
Dibdin, C.	Blow High, Blow Low
Dougherty, C., arr.	Across the Western Ocean
	Shenandoah
Fauré, G.	Le Secret
Franz, R.	Widmung
Goodhart, A. M.	Bells of Clermont Town, The
Gounod, C.	King of Love My Shepherd Is, The
Handel, G. F.	Leave Me, Loathsome Light
Latin American	Encantadora Maria

Melody	Phrase	Rhythm	Text	Accomp.	Harmony	Dynamics	Total	Rank
2	1	1	1	2	1	3	11	2
2	2	2	1	1	1	2	11	2
2	2	1	2	2	1	3	13	2
2	1	2	2	2	1	2	12	2
2	2	1	2	2	2	3	14	2
2	1	1	2	2	1	3	12	2
2	2	1	2	1	1	2	11	2
2	2	1	2	2	1	3	13	2
2	3	1	1	2	1	3	13	2
2	1	1	2	2	1	3	12	2
2	2	1	2	2	1	3	13	2
2	1	1	1	2	1	3	11	2
2	1	1	2	2	1	3	12	2
2	1	1	2	2	3	3	14	2

Melody	Phrase	Rhythm	Text	Accomp.	Harmony	Dynamics	Total	Rank
3	1	1	1	2	1	2	11	2
2	2	1	1	2	1	3	12	2
2	2	1	1	2	2	2	12	2
2	1	1	1	1	1	3	10	1
1	3	2	1	2	1	2	12	2
2	2	3	1	2	1	2	13	2
2	2	1	1	2	2	3	13	2
2	1	1	2	1	1	3	11	2
2	1	3	1	2	1	1	11	2
2	2	1	1	2	1	2	11	2
2	2	3	1	2	1	3	14	2
1	2	1	2	1	1	3	11	2

Latin American	La Paloma Blanca
Leoni, F.	Tally-Ho!
MacDowell, E.	Sea, The
Mendelssohn, F.	Jagdlied
Mueller, C. F.	Create in Me a Clean Heart, O God
Myers, G., arr.	Let Us Break Bread Together
Niles, J. J.	Rovin' Gambler, The
Payne, J., arr.	Lord, I Want to Be a Christian
Purcell, H.	Next, Winter Comes Slowly
Quilter, R.	Blow, Blow, Thou Winter Wind
	O Mistress Mine
Robertson, R. R.	Jolly Roger, The
Sarti, G.	Lungi Dal Caro Bene
Schumann, R.	Hör' Ich das Liedchen Klingen
	Intermezzo
Shield, W.	Friar of Orders Grey, The
Speaks, O.	On the Road to Mandalay
Tyson, M. L.	Sea Moods
Walthew, R. H.	Splendour Falls, The
Wilson, H. L., arr.	False Phillis

First Book of Baritone/Bass Solos, The, Part II

Publisher: G. Schirmer
Compiled/Edited by: Joan Frey Boytim
Available in: Medium Low Voice

Composer	Song Title
Andrews, M.	Build Thee More Stately Mansions
	Sea Fever
Arne, T.	Blow, Blow, Thou Winter Wind
Bach, J. S.	Jesus, Fount of Consolation
Boyce, W.	Song of Momus to Mars, The
Brasilian	Os Tormentos de Amor
Burleigh, H. T., arr.	Deep River

2	1	1	2	2	1	2	11	2
2	2	1	1	2	1	3	12	2
1	1	1	1	2	1	3	10	1
2	2	1	1	1	1	2	10	1
2	2	1	1	1	1	3	11	2
2	1	1	1	2	1	1	9	1
2	2	1	1	2	1	3	12	2
2	1	1	1	2	1	3	11	2
3	3	1	1	2	2	2	14	2
2	2	2	1	2	1	2	12	2
2	1	1	1	1	1	2	9	1
2	2	1	1	2	1	3	12	2
3	1	1	2	2	1	3	13	2
1	1	1	2	2	1	2	10	1
2	1	1	2	2	1	2	11	2
3	2	1	1	1	1	1	10	1
3	1	1	1	1	1	3	11	2
2	2	1	1	2	1	3	12	2
2	2	1	1	2	2	3	13	2
2	2	1	1	1	1	3	11	2

Melody	Phrase	Rhythm	Text	Accomp.	Harmony	Dynamics	Total	Rank
2	1	1	1	1	2	3	11	2
2	2	2	1	1	1	2	11	2
2	1	1	1	1	1	2	9	1
1	2	1	1	1	1	2	9	1
2	1	2	1	1	1	3	11	2
2	2	1	2	2	1	1	11	2
3	2	1	1	1	1	2	11	2

Cornelius, P.	Die Könige
	Ein Ton
Dougherty, C., arr.	Blow, Ye Winds
Dvořák, A.	God is My Shepherd
Ferrari, G.	Le Miroir
French	L'Amour de Moi
German	In einem Kühlen Grunde
German, E.	Rolling Down to Rio
Herbert, V.	Pretty as a Picture
Holst, G.	Heart Worships, The
Hopkinson, F.	O'er the Hills
Kingsford, C.	Down Harley Street
Liszt, F.	Du bist wie eine Blume
Lully, J. B.	Bois épais
Mana-Zucca	First Concert, The
Niles, J. J.	I Wonder As I Wander
O'Hara, G.	Give a Man a Horse He Can Ride
Scarlatti, A.	Toglietemi la Vita Ancor
Schubert, F.	Die Wetterfahne
	Was Ist Sylvia?
Schumann, R.	Du bist wie eine Blume
	Verrathene Liebe
Tchaikovsky, P.	Pilgrim's Song
V. Williams, R.	Bright is the Ring of Words
	Roadside Fire, The
Walthew, R. H.	Eldorado
Wilson, H. L., arr.	Pretty Creature, The
	Slighted Swain, The

Anthologies

1	2	2	2	2	2	2	13	**2**
1	1	1	2	2	1	3	11	**2**
2	2	2	1	2	1	2	12	**2**
2	2	1	2	2	1	3	13	**2**
2	1	1	2	2	1	2	11	**2**
1	2	2	2	1	1	3	12	**2**
2	2	1	2	2	1	1	11	**2**
2	1	3	1	2	1	3	13	**2**
2	1	1	1	1	1	2	9	**1**
2	2	2	1	2	2	2	13	**2**
3	2	1	1	1	1	3	12	**2**
2	1	1	1	2	1	2	10	**1**
2	2	1	2	2	1	2	12	**2**
2	3	2	2	1	1	3	14	**2**
1	1	1	1	2	1	1	8	**1**
2	1	1	1	2	1	2	10	**1**
2	1	1	1	1	1	1	8	**1**
2	1	1	2	1	1	3	11	**2**
1	1	2	2	1	1	2	10	**1**
2	2	2	2	2	1	3	14	**2**
1	2	1	2	2	1	2	11	**2**
2	1	1	2	2	1	2	11	**2**
2	2	1	1	2	1	3	12	**2**
2	1	1	1	1	2	3	11	**2**
2	2	1	1	2	1	3	12	**2**
1	2	3	1	2	2	3	14	**2**
2	1	1	1	2	1	3	11	**2**
2	2	1	1	1	1	3	11	**2**

First Book of Broadway Solos—Baritone/Bass, The

Publisher: Hal Leonard Corporation
Compiled/Edited by: Joan Frey Boytim
Available in: Medium Low Voice

Composer	Song Title
Berlin, I.	Girl That I Marry, The
	My Defenses Are Down
Gay, N.	Leaning on a Lamp-Post
Leigh, M.	Impossible Dream, The
Loewe, F.	Get Me to the Church on Time
	How to Handle a Woman
	I Talk to the Trees
	I've Grown Accustomed to Her Face
	If Ever I Would Leave You
	They Call the Wind Maria
Porter, C.	Wunderbar
Rodgers, R.	Edelweiss
	Oklahoma
	Some Enchanted Evening
	Surrey with the Fringe on Top, The
	There Is Nothin' Like a Dame
	This Nearly Was Mine
Schmidt, H.	Gonna Be Another Hot Day
	My Cup Runneth Over
	Soon It's Gonna Rain
	Try to Remember
Sondheim, S.	Comedy Tonight
Styne, J.	Just in Time

Melody	Phrase	Rhythm	Text	Accomp.	Harmony	Dynamics	Total	Rank
2	2	1	1	1	1	1	9	**1**
2	1	1	1	1	1	1	8	**1**
2	1	1	1	1	1	1	8	**1**
2	1	1	1	1	1	3	10	**1**
2	1	1	1	1	1	2	9	**1**
2	1	1	1	1	1	3	10	**1**
2	1	1	1	1	1	2	9	**1**
2	1	1	1	1	1	2	9	**1**
2	1	1	1	1	1	3	10	**1**
2	1	1	1	1	1	2	9	**1**
2	1	1	1	1	1	2	9	**1**
1	3	1	1	1	1	3	11	**2**
2	1	1	1	1	1	2	9	**1**
2	2	1	1	1	1	3	11	**2**
2	1	1	1	1	1	2	9	**1**
2	1	1	1	1	1	3	10	**1**
2	1	1	1	1	1	2	9	**1**
2	1	1	1	1	1	2	9	**1**
1	1	1	1	2	1	2	9	**1**
2	2	1	1	1	1	1	9	**1**
2	1	1	1	1	1	2	9	**1**
3	1	1	1	1	1	3	11	**2**
2	1	1	1	1	1	1	8	**1**

First Book of Broadway Solos—Mezzo-Soprano, The

Publisher: Hal Leonard Corporation
Compiled/Edited by: Joan Frey Boytim
Available in: Medium High Voice

Composer	Song Title
Bart, L.	As Long as He Needs Me
Kern, J.	Song Is You, The
Latouche, J.	Lazy Afternoon
Loewe, F.	Earth and Other Minor Things, The
	I Loved You Once in Silence
Ornadel, C.	If I Ruled the World
Porter, C.	I Love Paris
Rodgers, R.	Bali Ha'I
	Cock-Eyed Optimist, A
	Falling in Love with Love
	Getting to Know You
	I Enjoy Being a Girl
	In My Own Little Corner
	My Favorite Things
	My Funny Valentine
	Something Wonderful
	What's the Use of Wond'rin'
	Where or When
	Wonderful Guy, A
Schmidt, H.	Is It Really Me?
	Simple Little Things
Schönberg, C. M.	On My Own
Styne, J.	People

Melody	Phrase	Rhythm	Text	Accomp.	Harmony	Dynamics	Total	Rank
1	2	1	1	1	1	2	9	**1**
2	2	1	1	1	1	2	10	**1**
2	2	1	1	1	1	2	10	**1**
2	3	1	1	1	1	2	11	**2**
2	3	1	1	1	1	1	10	**1**
2	1	1	1	1	1	2	9	**1**
2	1	1	1	1	1	2	9	**1**
2	2	1	1	1	2	2	11	**2**
2	2	1	1	2	1	2	11	**2**
2	2	1	1	1	1	2	10	**1**
1	1	1	1	1	1	2	8	**1**
2	1	1	1	1	1	2	9	**1**
1	1	1	1	1	1	1	7	**1**
2	1	1	1	1	1	2	9	**1**
2	2	1	1	1	1	2	10	**1**
2	1	1	1	1	1	2	9	**1**
2	1	1	1	1	1	2	9	**1**
2	2	1	1	1	1	2	10	**1**
2	1	1	1	1	1	2	9	**1**
3	1	1	1	1	1	1	9	**1**
2	1	1	1	1	1	2	9	**1**
2	1	1	1	1	1	2	9	**1**
2	1	1	1	1	1	2	9	**1**

First Book of Broadway Solos—Soprano, The

Publisher: Hal Leonard Corporation
Compiled/Edited by: Joan Frey Boytim
Available in: High Voice

Composer	Song Title
DeSylva, B. G.	Just Imagine
Gay, N.	Once You Lose Your Heart
Kern, J.	All the Things You Are
	Can't Help Lovin' Dat Man
	Look for the Silver Lining
	Make Believe
	Why Do I Love You?
Lane, B.	Look to the Rainbow
Loesser, F.	I'll Know
Loewe, F.	I Could Have Danced All Night
	Simple Joys of Maidenhood, The
	Wouldn't It Be Loverly?
Rodgers, R.	Climb Ev'ry Mountain
	Hello, Young Lovers
	I Have Dreamed
	It's a Grand Night for Singing
	Many a New Day
	Out of My Dreams
	Sound of Music, The
	With a Song in My Heart
	You'll Never Walk Alone
Willson, M.	Goodnight, My Someone
	Till There Was You
Wright, R.	And This Is My Beloved

Melody	Phrase	Rhythm	Text	Accomp.	Harmony	Dynamics	Total	Rank
2	1	1	1	1	1	1	8	**1**
2	1	1	1	1	1	1	8	**1**
3	1	1	1	1	1	2	10	**1**
3	1	1	1	1	1	2	10	**1**
2	1	1	1	1	1	2	9	**1**
2	2	1	1	1	1	2	10	**1**
2	1	1	1	1	1	2	9	**1**
2	2	1	1	1	1	2	10	**1**
2	1	1	1	1	1	2	9	**1**
2	1	1	1	1	1	2	9	**1**
2	3	1	1	1	1	2	11	**2**
2	1	1	1	1	1	1	8	**1**
2	2	1	1	1	1	3	11	**2**
2	1	1	1	1	1	2	9	**1**
3	2	1	1	1	1	2	11	**2**
2	1	1	1	1	1	2	9	**1**
2	1	1	1	1	1	2	9	**1**
2	2	1	1	1	1	2	10	**1**
1	1	1	1	1	1	2	8	**1**
2	2	1	1	1	1	2	10	**1**
3	2	1	1	1	1	3	12	**2**
2	1	1	1	1	1	3	10	**1**
2	1	1	1	1	1	2	9	**1**
3	3	1	1	1	1	3	13	**2**

First Book of Broadway Solos—Tenor, The

Publisher: Hal Leonard Corporation
Compiled/Edited by: Joan Frey Boytim
Available in: High Voice

Composer	Song Title
Barer, M.	Very Soft Shoes
Bricusse, L.	Wonderful Day Like Today, A
Gay, N.	Me and My Girl
Geld, G.	Only Home I Know, The
Lane, B.	Old Devil Moon
Loesser, F.	I Believe In You
	Once in Love with Amy
Loewe, F.	On the Street Where You Live
Rodgers, R.	I Could Write a Book
	I Do Not Know a Day I Did Not Love You
	Kansas City
	My Heart Stood Still
	My Romance
	Oh, What a Beautiful Mornin'
	That's the Way It Happens
	We Kiss in a Shadow
	When the Children Are Asleep
	You've Got to Be Carefully Taught
	Younger Than Springtime
Schmidt, H.	Man and a Woman, A
	Plant a Radish
Schönberg, C. M.	Bring Him Home
Wright, R.	Stranger in Paradise

Melody	Phrase	Rhythm	Text	Accomp.	Harmony	Dynamics	Total	Rank
2	1	1	1	1	1	2	9	**1**
2	1	1	1	1	1	1	8	**1**
2	1	1	1	1	1	1	8	**1**
2	1	1	1	2	1	3	11	**2**
2	1	1	1	1	1	1	8	**1**
2	1	2	1	2	1	3	12	**2**
1	1	1	1	1	1	1	7	**1**
2	1	1	1	1	1	2	9	**1**
1	1	1	1	1	1	2	8	**1**
2	1	1	1	1	1	2	9	**1**
2	1	1	1	2	1	2	10	**1**
2	1	1	1	1	1	2	9	**1**
2	1	1	1	1	1	2	9	**1**
2	1	1	1	1	1	2	9	**1**
2	2	1	1	2	1	3	12	**2**
2	2	1	1	1	1	2	10	**1**
2	1	1	1	1	1	2	9	**1**
2	1	1	1	1	1	1	8	**1**
2	2	1	1	1	1	2	10	**1**
2	1	1	1	1	1	2	9	**1**
2	1	1	1	1	1	2	9	**1**
2	3	3	1	1	1	3	14	**2**
1	2	1	1	1	1	2	9	**1**

First Book of Mezzo-Soprano/Alto Solos, The

Publisher: G. Schirmer
Compiled/Edited by: Joan Frey Boytim
Available in: Medium High Voice

Composer	Song Title
Brahms, J.	Wie Melodien
Chaminade, C.	L'Anneau D'Argent
Chanler, T.	Lamb, The
Cui, C.	Statue at Czarskoe-Selo, The
Duke, J.	Loveliest of Trees
Fauré, G.	Ici-Bas!
Fraser-Simson, H.	Christopher Robin is Saying His Prayers
Gibbs, C. A.	Cherry Tree, The
Granados, E.	El Majo Timido
Guion, D. W.	Prayer
Handel, G. F.	Oh Sleep, Why Dost Thou Leave Me?
Latin American	Pregúntale a Las Estrellas
Lehmann, L.	Evensong
Macfarlane, W. C.	Open Our Eyes
Mendelssohn, F.	Der Blumenstrauss
	O Rest in the Lord
Myers, G., arr.	Jesus Walked This Lonesome Valley
Niles, J. J.	Go 'Way from My Window
	Lass from the Low Countree, The
Paisiello, G.	Chi Vuol la Zingarella
Payne, J., arr.	Crucifixion
Peel, G.	Wind of the Western Sea
Purcell, H.	Turn Then Thine Eyes
Rich, G.	American Lullaby
Rogers, J. H.	Cloud-Shadows
Roy, W.	This Little Rose
Schumann, R.	Volksliedchen

Melody	Phrase	Rhythm	Text	Accomp.	Harmony	Dynamics	Total	Rank
3	2	1	2	2	1	1	12	2
3	2	1	2	2	1	3	14	2
2	1	1	1	2	1	2	10	1
2	3	1	2	2	1	2	13	2
2	1	1	1	2	1	2	10	1
2	2	1	2	2	1	2	12	2
2	1	1	1	1	1	1	8	1
1	1	1	1	2	1	3	10	1
2	1	3	2	2	1	1	12	2
2	2	1	1	1	1	3	11	2
1	3	1	1	2	1	2	11	2
2	1	1	2	1	1	2	10	1
2	3	1	1	2	1	3	13	2
2	2	1	1	1	1	3	11	2
2	2	1	2	2	1	2	12	2
2	1	1	1	1	1	2	9	1
2	2	1	1	2	1	2	11	2
3	2	1	1	2	1	1	11	2
2	2	1	1	1	1	2	10	1
2	1	3	2	1	1	3	13	2
1	2	3	1	2	1	3	13	2
3	2	1	1	2	1	2	12	2
2	2	1	1	2	1	2	11	2
2	1	1	1	2	1	2	10	1
2	2	1	1	2	1	3	12	2
2	2	1	1	2	1	2	11	2
2	1	2	2	1	1	2	11	2

Speaks, O.	Morning
Stange, M.	Die Bekehrte
Tchaikovsky, P.	Lord is My Shepherd, The
V. Williams, R.	Silent Noon
White, M. V.	Crabbed Age and Youth

First Book of Mezzo-Soprano/Alto Solos, The, Part II

Publisher: G. Schirmer
Compiled/Edited by: Joan Frey Boytim
Available in: Medium High Voice

Composer	Song Title
Bach, J. S.	Bist du bei mir
Brahe, M. H.	As I Went A-Roaming
Carpenter, J. A.	Sleep That Flits on Baby's Eyes, The
Charles, E.	Clouds
Crist, B., arr.	C'est Mon Ami
Fielitz, A. von	Die Stille Wasserrose
Franz, R.	Auf dem Meere
Gaul, A.	Come Ye Blessed
Goulding, E.	Lovely Song My Heart is Singing, The
Gounod, C.	Sérénade
Handel, G. F.	Ah! Mio Cor
	Rend'il Sereno Al Cigilo
	Te Deum
	Weep No More
Hopkinson, F.	Beneath a Weeping Willow's Shade
Irish	Danny Boy
Liszt, F.	Es Muss ein Wunderbares Sein
MacDowell, E.	Blue-Bell, The
Massenet, J.	Crépuscule
	Elégie
Mendelssohn, F.	Das Erste Veilchen

3	1	1	1	2	2	3	13	2
2	2	1	2	2	2	3	14	2
2	2	1	1	2	1	3	12	2
2	2	2	1	2	2	3	14	2
2	1	2	1	1	1	3	11	2

Melody	Phrase	Rhythm	Text	Accomp.	Harmony	Dynamics	Total	Rank
2	1	1	2	2	1	2	11	2
2	1	1	1	2	1	2	10	1
2	2	1	1	2	1	2	11	2
2	3	1	1	2	2	2	13	2
2	1	1	2	2	1	1	10	1
2	2	1	2	1	2	3	13	2
3	1	1	2	1	1	2	11	2
2	1	1	1	2	1	2	10	1
2	1	1	1	1	1	1	8	1
2	2	1	2	2	1	2	12	2
2	1	1	2	2	1	2	11	2
2	2	1	2	1	1	3	12	2
1	1	1	2	2	1	2	10	1
2	3	2	1	2	1	2	13	2
2	1	1	1	1	1	2	9	1
3	2	1	1	1	1	3	12	2
2	1	1	2	2	2	2	12	2
1	1	2	1	2	1	3	11	2
2	2	2	2	2	1	3	14	2
2	2	2	2	2	1	3	14	2
2	1	1	2	2	2	3	13	2

Mozart, W. A.	Ave Verum
Niles, J. J.	Carol of the Birds, The
Phillips, M. F.	Wind of the Wheat
Purcell, H.	Mystery's Song
	Nymphs and Shepherds
	When I Have Often Heard Young Maids Complaining
Quilter, R.	Dream Valley
	Spring Is at the Door
Raff, J.	Keine Sorg' um den Weg
Reger, M.	Mariä Wiegenlied
Schubert, F.	Gott im Frühling
Schumann, R.	Die Stille
Sgambati, G., arr.	Separazione
Sullivan, A.	Willow Song, The
Tchaikovsky, P.	Legend, A
Wilson, H. L.	Carmeña

First Book of Soprano Solos, The

Publisher: G. Schirmer
Compiled/Edited by: Joan Frey Boytim
Available in: High Voice

Composer	Song Title
Arne, T.	O Peace, Thou Fairest Child of Heaven
	Water Parted from the Sea
Barber, S.	Crucifixion, The
Bishop, Sir H.	Love Has Eyes
Boatner, E., arr.	Oh, What a Beautiful City!
Carew, M.	Everywhere I Look!
Charles, E.	Let My Song Fill Your Heart
	When I Have Sung My Songs
Dougherty, C.	K'e, The
Duke, J.	Little Elegy

Melody	Phrase	Rhythm	Text	Accomp.	Harmony	Dynamics	Total	Rank
1	3	1	2	1	1	3	12	2
2	1	1	1	1	1	1	8	1
2	1	1	1	2	2	2	11	2
2	1	1	1	2	1	3	11	2
2	2	1	1	2	1	3	12	2
2	1	1	1	1	1	2	9	1
2	1	1	1	2	1	2	10	1
3	1	2	1	2	2	3	14	2
2	1	1	2	2	2	2	12	2
2	1	1	2	1	1	3	11	2
2	1	1	2	2	1	2	11	2
2	1	1	2	1	2	3	12	2
2	2	1	2	2	1	2	12	2
2	1	1	1	2	1	3	11	2
2	1	1	2	1	1	2	10	1
2	3	1	1	2	1	3	13	2

Melody	Phrase	Rhythm	Text	Accomp.	Harmony	Dynamics	Total	Rank
3	3	1	1	2	1	3	14	2
2	2	1	1	1	1	1	9	1
2	2	1	1	3	2	3	14	2
2	1	1	1	1	1	2	9	1
2	1	1	1	2	1	2	10	1
3	1	1	1	2	1	3	12	2
3	2	1	1	1	1	2	11	2
2	2	1	1	2	2	3	13	2
2	2	2	1	2	2	2	13	2
3	2	1	1	2	2	3	14	2

Edwards, C.	Into the Night
Franck, C.	Hear My Cry, O God
Granados, E.	El Majo Discreto
	El Tra La La y el punteado
Grieg, E.	My Johann
Hahn, R.	Si Mes Vers Avaient Des Ailes!
Handel, G. F.	Bel Piacere
Haydn, J.	Mermaid's Song, The
	Night is Falling
	Piercing Eyes
Kingsley, H.	Green Dog, The
Leoni, F.	Little China Figure, A
Malotte, A. H.	Beatitudes, The
Massenet, J.	Bonne Nuit
Mendelssohn, F.	Minnelied
Old English	Have You Seen But a White Lily Grow
Purcell, H.	Let Us Dance, Let Us Sing
Reger, M.	Waldeinsamkeit
Schubert, F.	Lied der Mignon
Scott, C.	Lullaby
Shaw, M.	Heffle Cuckoo Fair
Spohr, L.	Rose Softly Blooming
Thiman, E. H.	I Love All Graceful Things

First Book of Soprano Solos, The, Part II

Publisher: G. Schirmer
Compiled/Edited by: Joan Frey Boytim
Available in: High Voice

Composer	Song Title
Abt, F.	Ave Maria
Arne, T.	When Daisies Pied
Barber, S.	Nun Takes the Veil, A
Beethoven, L.	Andenken

Melody	Phrase	Rhythm	Text	Accomp.	Harmony	Dynamics	Total	Rank
2	3	3	1	2	1	3	15	**3**
2	2	1	1	2	1	3	12	**2**
2	1	1	2	2	1	1	10	**1**
2	1	2	2	2	1	1	11	**2**
3	2	2	1	1	1	3	13	**2**
2	2	1	2	2	1	3	13	**2**
2	2	2	2	1	1	2	12	**2**
2	2	2	1	1	1	2	11	**2**
3	2	1	1	2	1	2	12	**2**
2	1	1	1	1	1	2	9	**1**
2	2	2	1	2	2	1	12	**2**
1	1	1	1	2	1	2	9	**1**
2	3	3	1	1	1	3	14	**2**
2	2	2	1	2	1	2	12	**2**
2	1	1	2	2	1	2	11	**2**
2	2	1	1	1	1	2	10	**1**
2	2	1	1	1	1	2	10	**1**
2	1	1	2	1	1	2	10	**1**
1	2	1	2	2	1	3	12	**2**
2	2	1	1	2	1	3	12	**2**
1	2	1	1	2	1	2	10	**1**
2	3	3	1	1	1	3	14	**2**
2	1	1	1	2	1	2	10	**1**
2	1	1	2	2	1	3	12	**2**
2	1	1	1	2	1	2	10	**1**
2	2	3	1	3	3	3	17	**3**
2	1	1	2	2	1	3	12	**2**

Beethoven, L.	Ich Liebe Dich
Campbell-Tipton, L.	Crying of Water, The
	Spirit Flower, A
Campra, A.	Charmant Papillon
Cesti, M. A.	Intorno All' Idol Mio
Chanler, T.	Grandma
Ciampi, F.	Quella Barbara Catena
d'Astorga, E.	Per Non Penar
Debussy, C.	Romance
Gluck, C. W. von	O Saviour, Hear Me!
Grieg, E.	Solvejg's Song
Hageman, R.	Animal Crackers
Hahn, R.	L'Heure exquise
Handel, G. F.	Come and Trip It
	Here Amid the Shady Woods
Liddle, S.	How Lovely Are Thy Dwellings
Linley, T.	No Flower That Blows
Louis, E.	Petit Noël
MacDowell, E.	To a Wild Rose
Martin, E.	Come to the Fair
Miliken, R. A.	Last Rose of Summer, The
Ronald, L.	Drift Down, Drift Down
Schubert, F.	La Pastorella
	Lachen und Weinen
	Seligkeit
Schuman, W.	Orpheus with His Lute
Speaks, O.	Prayer Perfect, The
Swedish	When I Was Seventeen
Tchaikovsky, P.	Nur Wer die Sehnsucht Kennt
Yon, P.	Gesú Bambino

2	1	1	1	2	1	2	10	**1**
1	2	1	2	2	2	3	13	**2**
3	2	1	2	2	2	3	15	**3**
2	2	2	2	2	2	3	15	**3**
2	3	1	2	2	1	3	14	**2**
2	1	1	1	2	2	2	11	**2**
2	1	1	2	2	1	2	11	**2**
1	1	1	2	2	1	1	9	**1**
2	1	1	2	2	2	3	13	**2**
2	1	1	1	1	1	1	8	**1**
2	2	1	2	2	1	3	13	**2**
2	1	1	1	2	1	1	9	**1**
2	2	1	2	2	1	3	13	**2**
2	1	1	1	1	1	2	9	**1**
2	1	1	1	1	1	1	8	**1**
2	1	1	1	2	1	2	10	**1**
2	1	1	1	1	1	2	9	**1**
1	1	1	2	2	1	3	11	**2**
2	2	1	1	2	1	3	12	**2**
1	1	1	1	1	1	3	9	**1**
1	2	1	1	2	1	2	10	**1**
3	3	1	1	2	1	3	14	**2**
2	2	3	2	2	1	1	13	**2**
2	1	1	2	2	1	1	10	**1**
2	1	1	2	2	1	2	11	**2**
2	3	2	1	2	1	2	13	**2**
2	1	2	1	2	1	2	11	**2**
3	1	3	2	2	1	3	15	**3**
2	1	1	2	2	1	3	12	**2**
3	2	1	2	2	2	3	15	**3**

First Book of Tenor Solos, The

Publisher: G. Schirmer
Compiled/Edited by: Joan Frey Boytim
Available in: High Voice

Composer	Song Title
Barber, S.	Daisies, The
Beethoven, L.	May Song
Charles, E.	My Lady Walks in Loveliness
Coates, E.	By Mendip Side
	Orpheus with His Lute
Deis, C., arr.	Loch Lomond
Dougherty, C., arr.	Rio Grande
Dowland, J.	Come Again, Sweet Love
Edwards, C.	Ol' Jim
Fauré, G.	Lydia
Guion, D. W.	All Day on the Prairie
Handel, G. F.	Silent Worship
Johnson, H., arr.	My Lord, What a Mornin'
	Religion Is a Fortune
Latin American	La Seña
	Noche Serena
Mendelssohn, F.	Der Mond
Niles, J. J.	Black Dress, The
	Black Is the Color of My True Love's Hair
	Wayfaring Stranger
Old Welsh	All through the Night
Purcell, H.	I Attempt from Love's Sickness to Fly
	I Love and I Must
	What Shall I Do to Show How Much I Love Her?
Quilter, R.	Go, Lovely Rose
Sacco, J.	Brother Will, Brother John

Melody	Phrase	Rhythm	Text	Accomp.	Harmony	Dynamics	Total	Rank
2	1	1	1	2	1	3	11	2
1	1	1	1	2	1	2	9	1
2	2	2	1	2	2	2	13	2
2	2	1	1	2	1	2	11	2
2	2	1	1	1	1	3	11	2
2	1	1	1	1	1	3	10	1
1	2	1	1	2	1	2	10	1
1	1	1	1	1	1	3	9	1
2	1	1	1	1	2	2	10	1
1	2	1	1	1	1	2	9	1
1	1	1	1	2	1	1	8	1
1	1	1	1	2	1	2	9	1
1	1	1	1	1	1	1	7	1
1	1	1	1	1	1	2	8	1
1	1	2	1	2	1	3	11	2
2	2	1	1	1	1	2	10	1
2	1	1	1	2	2	3	12	2
2	1	1	1	2	1	1	9	1
2	2	1	1	1	1	2	10	1
2	2	1	1	1	1	1	9	1
2	1	1	1	1	1	3	10	1
2	1	1	1	2	1	2	10	1
2	3	2	1	2	1	2	13	2
2	2	1	1	2	1	2	11	2
1	2	2	1	3	2	3	14	2
2	1	3	1	2	1	2	12	2

Scarlatti, A.	Sento Nel Core
Schlösser, A.	He That Keepeth Israel
Schubert, F.	Der Neugierige
	Ständchen
Schumann, R.	Ein Jüngling Liebt ein Mädchen
Speaks, O.	Lord Is My Light, The
Tchaikovsky, P.	At the Ball
Walthew, R. H.	Mistress Mine
Wesley, S. S.	Jesu, the Very Thought of Thee

First Book of Tenor Solos, The, Part II

Publisher: G. Schirmer
Compiled/Edited by: Joan Frey Boytim
Available in: High Voice

Composer	Song Title
Arne, T.	Fame's an Echo
	O Come, O Come, My Dearest
Bach, J. S.	Forget Me Not
Beethoven, L.	An die Geliebte
Brahms, J.	Sonntag
Burleigh, H. T., arr.	Nobody Knows the Trouble I've Seen
Charles, E.	Incline Thine Ear
Coates, E.	It Was a Lover and His Lass
	Who is Sylvia?
Delbruck, A.	Un Doux Lien
Delibes, L.	Bonjour, Suzon!
Donaudy, S.	O Del Mio Amato Ben
Dunhill, T.	Cloths of Heaven, The
Enders, H.	Russian Picnic
Fauré, G.	Adieu
Franck, C.	Panis Angelicus
Franz, R.	Stille Sicherheit
Handel, G. F.	Where E'er You Walk

2	1	2	1	1	1	2	10	**1**
2	3	3	1	2	1	3	15	**3**
2	2	1	1	2	2	3	13	**2**
2	2	1	1	2	2	3	13	**2**
3	1	1	1	2	1	1	10	**1**
2	3	1	1	1	1	2	11	**2**
2	1	1	1	2	1	2	10	**1**
2	1	3	1	2	1	3	13	**2**
1	1	1	1	1	1	1	7	**1**

Melody	Phrase	Rhythm	Text	Accomp.	Harmony	Dynamics	Total	Rank
2	1	1	1	1	1	1	8	**1**
2	2	2	1	1	1	2	11	**2**
2	2	1	1	1	1	2	10	**1**
1	1	2	2	2	1	2	11	**2**
2	1	1	2	2	1	2	11	**2**
1	1	2	1	1	1	2	9	**1**
2	3	3	1	2	2	1	14	**2**
2	1	1	1	2	1	3	11	**2**
2	2	1	1	1	1	3	11	**2**
2	1	1	2	2	1	2	11	**2**
2	1	2	1	2	1	3	12	**2**
2	2	1	2	2	1	3	13	**2**
2	2	1	1	1	1	3	11	**2**
3	3	2	1	1	1	3	14	**2**
1	1	1	2	1	1	3	10	**1**
1	1	1	2	2	1	2	10	**1**
1	1	2	2	2	1	3	12	**2**
2	1	1	1	2	1	1	9	**1**

Herbert, V.	Every Day is Ladies' Day with Me
Hook, J.	On Richmond Hill There Lives a Lass
Hughes, H., arr.	Down by the Sally Gardens
Ireland, J.	Sea Fever
Mexican	El Trobador
Monro, G.	My Lovely Celia
Neidlinger, W. H.	Birthday of a King, The
Niles, J. J.	What Songs Were Sung
Purcell, H.	Love Quickly is Pall'd
Quilter, R.	Weep You No More
Rubinstein, A.	Du bist wie eine Blume
Saint-Saëns, C.	Ave Maria
Schubert, F.	Das Fischermädchen
	Wanderers Nachtlied
Schumann, R.	In Der Fremde
Somervell, A.	Kingdom by the Sea, A
V. Williams, R.	Linden Lea
Young, A.	Phillis Has Such Charming Graces

Folk Songs for Solo Singers

Publisher: Alfred Publishing Co.
Compiled/Edited by: Jay Althouse
Available in: Medium High and Medium Low Voice

Composer	Song Title
Althouse, J., arr.	Amazing Grace
	Homeward Bound
	Liza Jane
	Scarborough Fair
Besig, D., arr.	Cross the Wide Missouri
Kern, P., arr.	Angels through the Night
	Greensleeves
Knowles, J., arr.	Danny Boy
O'Neill, J., arr.	Farewell, Lad

292

2	1	1	1	2	1	2	10	1
2	1	1	1	2	1	2	10	1
2	1	1	1	2	1	2	10	1
2	3	2	1	2	2	2	14	2
2	1	1	2	2	1	2	11	2
2	1	1	1	1	1	3	10	1
3	1	1	1	2	1	1	10	1
2	2	1	1	1	1	1	9	1
2	1	1	1	2	1	1	9	1
2	1	2	1	2	1	3	12	2
2	1	1	1	2	1	2	10	1
2	2	1	2	2	1	3	13	2
3	1	1	2	2	2	1	12	2
1	1	1	2	2	1	3	11	2
1	2	1	2	2	1	3	12	2
2	2	1	1	2	1	2	11	2
2	1	1	1	2	1	3	11	2
2	2	1	1	2	1	3	12	2

Melody	Phrase	Rhythm	Text	Accomp.	Harmony	Dynamics	Total	Rank
1	2	1	1	2	2	2	11	2
2	2	1	1	1	1	3	11	2
1	1	1	1	1	1	2	8	1
2	2	1	1	1	1	2	10	1
2	3	1	1	2	1	2	12	2
2	1	2	1	2	1	3	12	2
2	2	1	1	1	1	2	10	1
3	2	1	1	2	1	1	11	2
1	1	1	1	1	1	2	8	1

| Strommen, C., arr. | She's Like the Swallow |
| | To the Sky |

Folk Songs for Solo Singers, Volume II

Publisher: Alfred Publishing Co.
Compiled/Edited by: Jay Althouse
Available in: Medium High and Medium Low Voice

Composer	Song Title
Althouse, J., arr.	Camptown Races
	Cindy
	Fire Down Below
	Follow the Drinking Gourd
	Old Dan Tucker
	Poor Wayfaring Stranger
	Shenandoah
Hayes, M., arr.	Simple Gifts
	Water is Wide, The
Schram, R. E., arr.	All My Trials
	All Through the Night
	Go 'Way From My Window
	He's Gone Away
	Poor Boy

Foundations in Singing, Second Edition

Publisher: McGraw-Hill
Compiled/Edited by: Van A. Christy and John Glenn Payton
Available in: High, Medium, and Low Voice

Composer	Song Title
Arne, T.	Miller of Mansfield, The
Beethoven, L.	Bitten
Bock, J.	Far From the Home I Love
Bonds, M.	To a Brown Girl, Dead

Melody	Phrase	Rhythm	Text	Accomp.	Harmony	Dynamics	Total	Rank
2	2	1	1	1	1	2	10	**1**
2	1	1	1	2	1	2	10	**1**

Melody	Phrase	Rhythm	Text	Accomp.	Harmony	Dynamics	Total	Rank
2	1	1	1	3	1	3	12	**2**
2	2	2	1	2	1	3	13	**2**
1	2	1	1	2	1	3	11	**2**
1	1	1	1	2	1	1	8	**1**
1	1	1	1	2	1	3	10	**1**
2	1	1	1	1	1	2	9	**1**
2	1	2	1	1	1	2	10	**1**
2	2	1	1	2	1	2	11	**2**
2	1	2	1	2	1	2	11	**2**
1	2	1	1	1	1	3	10	**1**
2	1	1	1	1	1	3	10	**1**
2	2	1	1	1	1	1	9	**1**
2	2	1	1	2	1	3	12	**2**
2	1	1	1	1	1	3	10	**1**

Melody	Phrase	Rhythm	Text	Accomp.	Harmony	Dynamics	Total	Rank
2	1	1	1	1	1	1	8	**1**
2	2	3	2	1	1	2	13	**2**
2	1	1	1	2	2	1	10	**1**
2	2	3	1	2	1	2	13	**2**

Bononcini, G.	Vado ben spesso
Campion, T.	What if a Day
Chausson, E.	Hebe
Christy, V. A., arr.	Cockles and Mussels
	High Barbaree
	Walk Together, Children
Foster, S. C.	Some Folks
Franz, R.	Widmung
Gershwin, G.	Love Is Here to Stay
Hamlisch, M.	Through the Eyes of Love
	What I Did for Love
Haydn, J.	Bald wehen uns des Frühlings Lüfte
Hilton, J., arr.	Come Follow!
Homer, S.	Country of the Camisards, The
Hughes, H., arr.	Early One Morning
	I Know Where I'm Goin'
Ives, C. E.	Remembrance
Lane, B.	He Wasn't You She Wasn't You
Lennon & McCartney	Yesterday
Lowry, R. R.	At the River
Moffat, A., arr.	Fairy's Lullaby, The
Monro, G.	My Lovely Celia
Monteverde, C.	Lasciatemi morire
Morley, T.	It Was a Lover and His Lass
Paisiello, G.	Nel cor più non mi sento
Paton, J. G., arr.	Aupres de ma Blonde
	El Tecolote
Pergolesi, G. B.	Nina
Porter, C.	Brush Up Your Shakespeare
Purcell, H.	Man Is for the Woman Made
Rodgers, R.	Cock-Eyed Optimist, A
	Do-Re-Mi
	He's Got the Whole World in His Hands

2	2	2	2	2	1	1	12	**2**
1	1	1	1	2	1	1	8	**1**
1	1	1	2	2	1	2	10	**1**
2	1	1	1	1	1	3	10	**1**
1	1	1	1	2	1	3	10	**1**
2	1	1	1	2	1	2	10	**1**
2	1	1	1	2	1	1	9	**1**
2	1	1	2	1	1	3	11	**2**
2	1	1	1	1	1	1	8	**1**
1	1	1	1	2	1	1	8	**1**
2	3	1	1	2	1	1	11	**2**
2	1	1	2	2	1	1	10	**1**
2	1	1	1	1	1	1	8	**1**
1	1	1	1	1	1	2	8	**1**
2	1	1	1	1	1	1	8	**1**
1	1	1	1	1	1	1	7	**1**
1	2	1	1	2	1	2	10	**1**
3	1	1	1	1	1	3	11	**2**
2	1	1	1	1	1	1	8	**1**
1	1	1	1	3	2	1	10	**1**
1	1	1	1	2	1	3	10	**1**
2	1	1	1	1	1	1	8	**1**
1	3	2	2	1	2	1	12	**2**
1	1	1	1	2	1	1	8	**1**
1	1	1	2	2	1	1	9	**1**
2	1	1	2	1	1	1	9	**1**
2	1	1	2	1	1	1	9	**1**
2	1	2	2	1	1	2	11	**2**
2	1	1	1	1	1	1	8	**1**
2	1	1	1	2	1	1	9	**1**
2	2	1	1	1	1	2	10	**1**
1	1	1	1	1	1	1	7	**1**
1	1	1	1	1	1	1	7	**1**

Rodgers, R.	Hinay Ma Tov
	Michael, Row the Boat Ashore
	Old Smokey
Rorem, N.	Christmas Carol, A
Rosseter, P.	When Laura Smiles
Schubert, F.	An die Musik
	Wanderers Nachtlied
Schumann, R.	Red, Red, Rose, A
Sgambati, G., arr.	Separazione
Smith, J. S.	Scarborough Fair
	Star-Spangled Banner, The
	When the Saints Go Marchin' In
Sondheim, S.	Anyone Can Whistle
	Broadway Baby
Stevens, R. J.	Sigh No More, Ladies
Strauss, R.	Ach Lieb, ich muss nun scheiden
Wagner, R.	I Went to Heaven
Waller & Brooks	Ain't Misbehavin'
Ward, S. A.	America the Beautiful
	Auld Lang Syne
Wonder, S.	I Just Called to Say I Love You
Yradier, S.	La Paloma

Great Art Songs of Three Centuries

Publisher: G. Schirmer
Compiled/Edited by: Bernard Taylor
Available in: High and Low Voice

Composer	Song Title
Alvarez, F.	La Partida
Bachelet, A.	Chère Nuit
Beethoven, L.	Freudvoll und leidvoll from "Egmont"
	Neue Liebe, neues Leben
Berlioz, H.	Absence

1	1	1	2	1	1	1	8	1
1	1	1	1	1	1	1	7	1
1	1	1	1	1	1	1	7	1
2	1	2	1	2	2	2	12	2
1	2	1	1	2	1	1	9	1
2	2	1	2	2	1	2	12	2
1	1	1	2	2	1	3	11	2
1	1	?	2	1	1	2	10	1
2	2	1	2	2	1	2	12	2
2	1	1	1	1	1	1	8	1
3	1	1	1	1	1	1	9	1
1	1	1	1	1	1	1	7	1
2	2	1	1	1	1	1	9	1
1	1	1	1	2	1	1	8	1
1	1	3	1	1	1	3	11	2
2	2	1	2	1	2	1	11	2
1	1	1	1	2	1	3	10	1
2	1	1	1	1	1	1	8	1
2	1	1	1	1	1	1	8	1
2	1	1	1	1	1	1	8	1
3	1	1	1	1	1	1	9	1
2	1	2	2	1	1	1	10	1

Melody	Phrase	Rhythm	Text	Accomp.	Harmony	Dynamics	Total	Rank
2	2	3	2	2	1	2	14	2
2	3	1	2	2	2	3	15	3
1	1	3	2	1	1	3	12	2
2	1	2	2	2	1	2	12	2
2	3	3	2	2	2	3	17	3

Bononcini, G.	Per la gloria d'adorarvi from "Griselda"
Brahms, J.	Botschaft
	Der Jäger
	Die Mainacht
	Meine Lieder
	Ständchen
Chausson, E.	Les Papillons
Debussy, C.	Clair de lune
	Fleur des Blés
	Nuit d'Etoiles
Fauré, G.	Aurore
	Dans les Ruines d'une Abbaye
	Ici-bas!
Ferrari, G.	Le Miroir
Grieg, E.	Eros
	Vaaren
Hahn, R.	D'Une Prison
	Offrande
Handel, G. F.	Dank sei Dir, Herr
	Dove sei, amato bene? from "Rodelinda"
	Leave me, loathsome light! from "Semele"
	Si, tra i ceppi from "Bernice"
	Te Deum
Haydn, J.	Das Leben ist ein Traum
	She Never Told Her Love
Leoncavallo, R.	Mattinata
Luca, S. De	Non posso disperar
Mattei, T.	Non è ver!
Moussorgsky, M. P.	Seminarian, The
	Song of Khivria, The
Pierné, G.	En Barque
Purcell, H.	Nymphs and Shepherds
Rachmaninoff, S.	Forsake Me Not, My Love, I Pray

2	1	2	2	1	1	3	12	**2**
2	3	1	2	2	1	2	13	**2**
2	1	1	2	2	1	2	11	**2**
2	2	2	2	2	2	2	14	**2**
2	2	1	2	1	2	3	13	**2**
2	1	1	2	1	1	3	11	**2**
2	1	1	2	2	1	3	12	**2**
2	2	1	2	2	2	3	14	**2**
2	2	2	2	2	2	2	14	**2**
2	1	2	2	2	2	3	14	**2**
2	2	1	2	2	2	2	13	**2**
1	2	1	2	2	1	2	11	**2**
2	2	1	2	2	1	2	12	**2**
2	1	1	2	2	1	2	11	**2**
2	1	3	2	2	2	3	15	**3**
2	2	1	2	2	2	3	14	**2**
2	1	1	2	2	1	3	12	**2**
1	2	1	2	2	1	3	12	**2**
1	2	1	2	2	1	2	11	**2**
2	1	2	2	1	1	2	11	**2**
2	2	3	1	2	1	3	14	**2**
2	3	1	2	1	1	2	12	**2**
1	1	1	2	2	1	2	10	**1**
2	1	3	2	1	1	2	12	**2**
2	1	2	1	1	1	2	10	**1**
2	2	2	2	2	1	3	14	**2**
2	1	3	2	1	1	3	13	**2**
2	1	1	2	2	1	3	12	**2**
2	1	1	1	2	2	3	12	**2**
2	2	2	1	2	2	2	13	**2**
1	2	1	2	2	1	3	12	**2**
2	2	2	1	2	1	3	13	**2**
2	1	1	1	2	2	3	12	**2**

Rachmaninoff, S.	To the Children
	Vocalise
Sandoval, M.	Serenata Gitana
	Sin tu amor
Scarlatti, A.	Le Violette
Schubert, F.	An die Leier
	Bei Dir!
	Der Schmetterling
	Ungeduld
Schumann, R.	Aufträge
	Intermezzo
	Sonntags am Rhein
	Stille Thränen
Sgambati, G., arr.	Separazione
Strauss, R.	Heimkehr
	Mit deinen blauen Augen
Wolf, H.	Auf dem grünen Balcon
	Lebe wohl!
	Nimmersatte Liebe
	Nun wandre, Maria

New Imperial Edition Baritone Songs, The

Publisher: Boosey and Hawkes
Compiled/Edited by: Sydney Northcote
Available in: Medium Low Voice

Composer	Song Title
Arne, T.	Plague of Love, The
Beethoven, L.	To the Faithless One
Brahms, J.	Garland, The
	Message, The
	Sunday Morning
Dowland, J.	Come Again, Sweet Love
Gurney, I.	Bonnie Earl of Murray, The

Melody	Phrase	Rhythm	Text	Accomp.	Harmony	Dynamics	Total	Rank
2	2	2	1	2	2	3	14	2
3	2	1	1	2	2	3	14	2
2	2	1	2	2	1	2	12	2
2	2	2	2	2	1	2	13	2
2	1	3	2	1	1	2	12	2
2	1	1	2	2	1	3	12	2
3	1	1	2	2	1	3	13	2
2	1	1	2	2	1	3	12	2
2	1	2	2	2	1	2	12	2
2	1	1	2	2	1	2	11	2
2	1	1	2	2	1	2	11	2
3	2	1	2	1	1	2	12	2
2	3	3	2	2	1	2	15	3
2	2	1	2	2	1	2	12	2
2	2	1	2	2	2	3	14	2
2	2	1	2	2	2	2	13	2
2	2	1	2	2	2	3	14	2
2	2	2	2	2	2	3	15	3
2	1	1	2	2	2	3	13	2
1	1	2	2	2	2	3	13	2

Melody	Phrase	Rhythm	Text	Accomp.	Harmony	Dynamics	Total	Rank
2	1	1	1	1	1	3	10	1
2	2	1	2	1	2	2	12	2
2	2	2	2	2	2	2	14	2
2	3	1	2	2	1	2	13	2
2	1	1	2	2	1	2	11	2
1	1	1	1	2	1	1	8	1
2	1	2	1	2	1	3	12	2

Handel, G. F.	How Art Thou Fall'n
	Revenge! Timotheus Cries
	Thrice Happy the Monarch
Hatton, J. L.	To Anthea
Loewe, C.	Edward
Purcell, H.	Let the Dreadful Engines
	Ye Twice Ten Hundred Deities
Quilter, R.	O Mistress Mine
Rachmaninoff, S.	When Yesterday We Met
Scarlatti, A.	Cease, Oh Maiden
Schubert, F.	Erl King, The
	Wanderer, The
	Wraith, The
Schumann, R.	Belshazzar
	Thy Lovely Face
	Why Blame Thee Now?
Somervell, A.	Birds in the High Hall-garden
Strauss, R.	Welcome Vision, A
Sullivan, A.	If Doughty Deeds My Lady Please
Tchaikovsky, P.	Don Juan's Serenade
V. Williams, R.	Youth and Love
Warlock, P.	Walking the Woods
White, M. V.	King Charles

New Imperial Edition Bass Songs, The

Publisher: Boosey and Hawkes
Compiled/Edited by: Sydney Northcote
Available in: Low Voice

Composer	Song Title
Arne, T.	Bacchus, God of Mirth and Wine
Beethoven, L.	Song of the Flea, The
Blow, Dr. J.	Self-Banished, The
Bononcini, G.	Love Leads to Battle

Anthologies

Melody	Phrase	Rhythm	Text	Accomp.	Harmony	Dynamics	Total	Rank
2	2	1	1	2	2	2	12	2
3	2	2	1	2	1	2	13	2
3	2	3	1	2	1	2	14	2
1	1	1	1	2	1	3	10	1
3	1	3	2	1	2	3	15	3
3	2	3	1	2	1	2	14	2
3	2	3	1	2	2	3	16	3
2	1	1	1	1	1	2	9	1
2	2	1	2	2	2	3	14	2
1	1	1	2	2	1	3	11	2
3	2	2	2	2	1	3	15	3
3	1	1	2	2	1	3	13	2
3	2	3	2	2	2	3	17	3
3	2	1	2	2	2	2	14	2
2	1	1	2	2	2	2	12	2
2	2	1	2	2	1	2	12	2
2	1	1	1	2	2	3	12	2
2	2	1	2	2	2	3	14	2
2	1	1	1	2	1	2	10	1
3	1	1	1	2	2	3	13	2
2	2	1	1	2	2	3	13	2
2	1	1	1	1	1	1	8	1
2	3	2	1	1	1	3	13	2
3	1	1	1	1	1	2	10	1
2	2	1	2	2	1	2	12	2
2	2	1	1	1	1	2	10	1
2	1	1	2	1	1	2	10	1

Brahms, J.	Earth and Sky
	I Said I Will Forget Thee
Carissimi, G.	I Triumph! I Triumph!
German	Drinking
Gounod, C.	Valley, The
Handel, G. F.	Droop Not, Young Lover
	Love That's True Will Live for Ever
Harty, H.	My Lagan Love
Head, M.	Money, O!
Hume, T.	Tobacco
Lully, J. B.	All Your Shades
Mendelssohn, F.	I Am a Roamer
Mozart, W. A.	Thoughts at Eventide
Old English	Down among the Dead Men
Purcell, H.	Arise Ye Subterranean Winds
	Hear! Ye Gods of Britain
Rachmaninoff, S.	By the Grave
Schubert, F.	Lay of the Imprisoned Huntsman, The
	Lime Tree, The
	My Last Abode
Schumann, R.	Last Toast, The
	Two Grenadiers, The
Smith, J. S.	Owl Is Abroad, The
Strauss, R.	Solitary One, The
Tchaikovsky, P.	To the Forest
Wood, C.	Ethiopia Saluting the Colours

New Imperial Edition Contralto Songs, The

Publisher: Boosey and Hawkes
Compiled/Edited by: Sydney Northcote
Available in: Low Voice

Composer	Song Title
Beethoven, L.	Praise of God, The

Melody	Phrase	Rhythm	Text	Accomp.	Harmony	Dynamics	Total	Rank
2	3	1	2	2	1	2	13	2
2	2	1	2	2	2	2	13	2
1	3	2	2	2	1	2	13	2
3	1	1	1	2	1	2	11	2
2	2	1	2	2	1	3	13	2
3	2	1	1	2	1	3	13	2
2	3	2	2	1	1	2	13	2
2	3	3	1	1	3	3	16	3
2	1	3	1	2	1	2	12	2
2	1	1	1	2	1	2	10	1
2	3	2	2	1	1	1	12	2
3	1	1	1	1	1	3	11	2
2	3	1	2	2	1	2	13	2
2	1	1	1	1	1	2	9	1
3	3	3	1	2	1	2	15	3
3	1	1	1	2	1	1	10	1
2	3	3	1	1	3	3	16	3
1	1	2	2	2	1	1	10	1
2	1	1	2	2	1	3	12	2
3	1	1	2	2	1	3	13	2
3	2	1	2	2	1	3	14	2
1	1	2	2	2	1	3	12	2
3	2	1	1	1	1	2	11	2
3	3	3	2	1	2	3	17	3
2	2	1	1	2	1	3	12	2
2	2	1	1	2	2	2	12	2
2	2	3	1	1	1	3	13	2

Brahms, J.	Love Triumphant
	Night in May, A
	Sapphic Ode (Sapphische Ode)
Britten, B.	O Can Ye Sew Cushions
Caldara, A.	As a Sunbeam at Morn
Campion, T.	Oft Have I Sighed
Elgar, E.	Where Corals Lie
Gluck, C. W. von	Author of All My Joys
Gounod, C.	Serenade
Handel, G. F.	Dearest Consort
	How Changed the Vision
	Verdant-Meadows
Harty, H.	Sea Wrack
Hatton, J. L.	Enchantress, The
Haydn, J.	Hark! What I Tell to Thee
Howells, H.	O My Deir Hert
Liszt, F.	Mignon's Song
Mendelssohn, F.	Cradle Song
Mozart, W. A.	Adieu
	With a Swanlike Beauty Gliding
Rachmaninoff, S.	How Few the Joys
Scarlatti, A.	Dewy Violets
	Like Any Foolish Moth I Fly
Schubert, F.	Death and the Maiden
	Litany
	To Music
Schumann, R.	My Soul Is Dark
Sullivan, A.	Willow Song, The
Tchaikovsky, P.	Nay, Though My Heart Should Break

2	2	1	1	2	2	2	12	2
2	2	2	1	2	2	2	13	2
2	2	1	1	1	2	3	12	2
2	1	1	1	3	1	3	12	2
1	3	1	1	2	1	3	12	2
1	1	2	1	2	1	1	9	1
2	1	1	1	2	1	3	11	2
3	1	1	1	2	1	1	10	1
2	2	1	1	2	1	2	11	2
2	3	2	1	2	1	1	12	2
2	1	1	1	1	1	2	9	1
2	2	1	1	1	1	1	9	1
2	2	1	1	2	2	3	13	2
3	2	2	1	2	1	2	13	2
3	2	1	1	2	1	2	12	2
2	3	1	1	2	1	3	13	2
3	2	1	1	2	2	3	14	2
2	2	1	1	2	1	2	11	2
2	2	1	1	2	1	2	11	2
2	2	1	1	2	1	2	11	2
3	1	3	1	2	3	3	16	3
1	1	3	1	1	1	2	10	1
2	1	1	1	2	1	2	10	1
3	2	2	1	2	1	3	14	2
2	2	1	1	2	1	2	11	2
2	2	1	1	2	1	3	12	2
3	3	2	1	2	1	2	14	2
2	1	1	1	2	1	3	11	2
2	2	1	1	2	1	3	12	2

New Imperial Edition of Mezzo-Soprano Songs, The

Publisher: Boosey and Hawkes
Compiled/Edited by: Sydney Northcote
Available in: Medium High Voice

Composer	Song Title
Arne, T.	When Daisies Pied
Beethoven, L.	Know'st Thou the Land
Berlioz, H.	Undiscovered Country, The
Bishop, Sir H.	Deep in My Heart
Brahms, J.	Blacksmith, The
	Parting
	Spring's Secret
Carey, C.	Melmillo
Dowland, J.	Who Ever Thinks or Hopes of Love
Handel, G. F.	Angels, Ever Bright and Fair
	Dryads, Sylvans
	Here Amid the Shady Woods
Haydn, J.	My Mother Bids Me Bind My Hair
	Now the Dancing Sunbeams Play
Howells, H.	Girls' Song
Mozart, W. A.	Violet, The
Purcell, H.	I Attempt from Love's Sickness to Fly
	Nymphs and Shepherds
Quilter, R.	Dream Valley
Rachmaninoff, S.	To the Children
Rosa, S.	Let Me Linger near Thee
Schubert, F.	Cradle Song
	Peace
	Wild Rose, The
Schumann, R.	Bride's Song, The
	Somebody

Melody	Phrase	Rhythm	Text	Accomp.	Harmony	Dynamics	Total	Rank
2	1	1	1	2	1	2	10	1
2	2	1	1	2	1	3	12	2
2	3	2	1	2	2	2	14	2
2	2	2	1	2	1	3	13	2
1	1	1	1	2	1	2	9	1
1	2	1	1	2	2	2	11	2
1	2	1	1	2	2	2	11	2
1	2	3	1	3	3	3	16	3
2	1	1	1	2	1	2	10	1
1	1	1	1	1	1	3	9	1
3	2	1	1	1	1	3	12	2
2	1	1	1	1	1	1	8	1
1	1	3	1	1	1	3	11	2
2	2	2	1	1	1	2	11	2
2	2	2	1	2	1	2	12	2
2	1	1	1	1	1	3	10	1
2	1	1	1	2	1	2	10	1
2	2	1	1	2	1	3	12	2
2	1	1	1	2	1	2	10	1
2	2	2	1	2	2	3	14	2
2	2	1	1	1	1	1	9	1
2	2	2	1	1	1	3	12	2
2	2	2	1	2	1	3	13	2
1	2	1	1	2	1	3	11	2
3	2	2	1	2	1	2	13	2
2	2	2	1	2	1	2	12	2

Strauss, R.	Alone in the Forest
Sullivan, A.	Orpheus with His Lute
Taubert, W.	In a Strange Land
Wagner, R.	Slumber Song

New Imperial Edition of Soprano Songs, The

Publisher: Boosey and Hawkes
Compiled/Edited by: Sydney Northcote
Available in: High Voice

Composer	Song Title
Arne, T.	Where the Bee Sucks
Bishop, Sir H.	Should He Upbraid
Brahms, J.	At Last
	Lullaby
	Vain Suit, The
Campion, T.	So Sweet Is Thy Discourse
Gibbs, C. A.	Why Do I Love Thee?
Gounod, C.	Without Thee!
Grieg, E.	Solveig's Song
Handel, G. F.	Care Selve
	Endless Pleasure, Endless Love
	Let Me Wander Not Unseen
Harty, H.	Lullaby, A
Head, M.	Singer, The
Henschel, G.	Spring
Ireland, J.	I Have Twelve Oxen
Linley, T.	O, Bid Your Faithful Ariel Fly
Liszt, F.	Loreley, The
Mendelssohn, F.	Lone and Joyless
Mozart, W. A.	How Calm Is My Spirit
Pergolesi, G. B.	Gentle Shepherd
Rachmaninoff, S.	How Fair This Spot
Schubert, F.	Gretchen at the Spinning Wheel

2	3	1	1	2	2	3	14	2
2	1	1	1	2	1	2	10	1
2	2	1	1	2	1	3	12	2
2	2	1	1	2	2	3	13	2

Melody	Phrase	Rhythm	Text	Accomp.	Harmony	Dynamics	Total	Rank
2	1	1	1	1	1	3	10	1
3	2	1	1	2	1	3	13	2
2	1	1	2	2	2	2	12	2
1	1	1	1	2	1	1	8	1
2	1	2	1	1	1	3	11	2
1	1	1	1	2	1	2	9	1
3	1	1	1	3	3	3	15	3
2	2	1	1	1	2	3	12	2
2	2	1	1	2	1	3	12	2
2	3	3	1	1	1	3	14	2
2	2	2	1	2	1	2	12	2
3	2	2	1	2	1	3	14	2
2	1	1	1	3	1	3	12	2
3	2	3	1	3	2	3	17	3
3	2	3	1	2	2	2	15	3
2	1	1	1	1	1	3	10	1
2	2	2	1	2	1	2	12	2
3	3	2	1	2	2	3	16	3
3	2	2	1	2	2	3	15	3
3	1	1	1	2	1	2	11	2
3	1	1	1	2	1	3	12	2
3	1	1	1	2	1	3	12	2
2	2	1	1	2	2	3	13	2

Schubert, F.	Novice, The
	Omnipotence
Schumann, R.	Chestnut, The
	He Is Noble, He Is Patient
	Suleika's Song
Strauss, R.	Farewell, A
Sullivan, A.	Where the Bee Sucks

New Imperial Edition Tenor Songs, The

Publisher: Boosey and Hawkes
Compiled/Edited by: Sydney Northcote
Available in: High Voice

Composer	Song Title
Arne, T.	Under the Greenwood Tree
Beethoven, L.	Adelaide
Brahms, J.	Is It Bliss or is It Sorrow?
	Love Song
	Reign Here a Queen within the Heart
Bridge, F.	E'en As a Lovely Flower
Caccini, G.	Amarylis
Elgar, E.	Is She Not Passing Fair?
Gurney, I.	Sleep
Handel, G. F.	Where E'er You Walk
	Would You Gain the Tender Creature
	Ye Verdant Hills
Loder, E. J.	Brooklet, The
Mendelssohn, F.	On Wings of Song (Auf Flügeln des Gesanges)
Pilkington, F.	Rest, Sweet Nymph
Purcell, H.	I'll Sail upon the Dog-Star
	Knotting Song, The
Quilter, R.	Now Sleeps the Crimson Petal
Rachmaninoff, S.	Night is Mournful
Schubert, F.	Secret, The

2	1	1	1	2	2	3	12	2
3	2	2	1	2	2	3	15	3
2	1	1	1	1	1	2	9	1
3	1	2	1	2	2	2	13	2
2	1	1	1	2	2	2	11	2
2	3	1	1	2	2	3	14	2
3	2	1	1	2	1	3	13	2

Melody	Phrase	Rhythm	Text	Accomp.	Harmony	Dynamics	Total	Rank
2	1	2	1	1	1	2	10	1
2	2	2	1	2	2	3	14	2
2	2	1	1	2	2	2	12	2
2	2	1	2	2	1	2	12	2
2	2	1	1	2	2	2	12	2
2	2	1	1	2	2	3	13	2
2	3	2	1	2	1	1	12	2
2	1	1	1	1	1	3	10	1
3	2	2	1	2	2	3	15	3
2	1	1	1	2	1	3	11	2
2	1	1	1	1	1	2	9	1
1	2	1	1	1	1	1	8	1
2	3	1	1	2	1	3	13	2
1	3	1	1	1	1	2	10	1
1	2	2	1	2	1	3	12	2
2	1	3	1	2	1	3	13	2
2	1	1	1	2	1	1	9	1
2	2	2	1	2	1	3	13	2
2	3	2	1	3	2	2	15	3
2	2	1	1	2	1	3	12	2

Schubert, F.	Whither
	Who Is Sylvia?
Schumann, R.	Moonlight
	Thou'rt Like a Lovely Flower
Stevens, R. J.	Sigh No More, Ladies
Strauss, R.	Winter Dedication, A
Tchaikovsky, P.	Twas April
V. Williams, R.	From Far, from Eve and Morning
Warlock, P.	As Ever I Saw
White, M. V.	To Mary

Pathways of Song Volume 1

Publisher: Warner Bros. Inc.
Compiled/Edited by: Frank LaForge and Will Earhart
Available in: High and Low Voice

Composer	Song Title
Colasse, P.	To Thy Fair Charm
Czech	Dance Song
	Falling Dew, The
	Maiden Tell Me
	Secret Love
Franck, C.	Panis Angelicus
Franz, R.	Feast of Love (Liebesfeier)
	For Music (Für Music)
	Woodland Journey, A (Waldfahrt)
German	Sandman, The
Grieg, E.	First Primrose, The (Mit einer primula veris)
Handel, G. F.	Grace Thy Fair Brow (Rend' il sereno al ciglio)
	Verdant Meadows
Haydn, J.	In the Country (Die Landlust)
Liszt, F.	It Must Be Wonderful Indeed (Es muss ein Wunderbares sein)
Mozart, W. A.	Cradle Song

Melody	Phrase	Rhythm	Text	Accomp.	Harmony	Dynamics	Total	Rank
2	1	3	2	2	1	3	14	2
2	2	2	1	2	1	3	13	2
2	2	1	2	2	1	2	12	2
1	2	1	1	2	1	2	10	1
2	1	3	1	1	1	2	11	2
2	2	1	1	2	2	3	13	2
2	2	1	1	2	2	3	13	2
1	1	2	1	2	3	2	12	2
2	1	1	1	2	1	2	10	1
2	1	1	1	2	1	2	10	1

Melody	Phrase	Rhythm	Text	Accomp.	Harmony	Dynamics	Total	Rank
2	1	1	2	2	1	1	10	1
1	1	2	1	2	1	1	9	1
2	1	2	1	2	1	1	10	1
1	1	2	1	2	1	1	9	1
2	1	1	1	2	1	1	9	1
1	1	3	2	2	1	1	11	2
2	1	2	2	2	1	3	13	2
2	1	1	2	2	1	3	12	2
2	2	1	2	2	1	2	12	2
2	2	1	1	1	1	3	11	2
2	1	1	2	1	1	3	11	2
2	2	3	2	2	1	3	15	3
2	2	3	2	1	1	1	12	2
2	1	2	1	1	1	1	9	1
2	1	1	1	2	1	3	11	2
1	1	1	1	2	1	3	10	1

Mozart, W. A.	Longing For Spring
Purcell, E. C.	Passing By
Schubert, F.	Farewell (Adieu!)
	In Evening's Glow (Im Abendrot)
Schumann, R.	Lotus Flower, The (Die Lotusblume)
	Snowbells (Schneeglöckchen)
	To The Sunshine (An den Sonnenschein)

Pathways of Song Volume 2

Publisher: Warner Bros. Inc.
Compiled/Edited by: Frank LaForge and Will Earhart
Available in: High and Low Voice

Composer	Song Title
Bach, J. S.	If Thou Be Near (Bist du bei mir)
Bayly, T. H.	Oh, Tis the Melody
Beethoven, L.	I Love Thee (Ich liebe dich)
	To the Beloved (An die Geliebte)
Brahms, J.	Below in the Valley (Da unten im Tale)
	Cradle Song (Wiegenlied)
	My Dear One's Mouth is Like the Rose (Mein Mädel hat einen Rosenmund)
Fauré, G.	Cradles, The (Les Berceaux)
Franck, C.	Lied
Franz, R.	Dedication (Widmung)
	Farewell! (Gute Nacht!)
	Request (Bitte)
French	March of the Kings (La Marche des Rois)
	Song of the Drummer, The (La chanson du Tambourineur)
Germany	Mill-Wheel, The (Das Mühlrad)
Handel, G. F.	Leave Me in Sorrow (Lascia ch'io pianga)
	Ne'er Shade so Dear (Ombra mai fu)
Haydn, J.	Serenade (Liebes Mädchen, hör' mir zu)

1	1	1	1	1	1	1	7	1
1	1	1	1	2	1	1	8	1
2	1	1	2	2	1	3	12	2
2	2	3	2	2	1	1	13	2
3	1	1	2	2	1	3	13	2
2	1	2	2	2	1	3	13	2
2	1	1	2	2	1	2	11	2

Melody	Phrase	Rhythm	Text	Accomp.	Harmony	Dynamics	Total	Rank
2	2	1	2	2	1	2	12	2
1	1	1	2	2	1	1	9	1
2	1	1	2	2	1	2	11	2
1	1	2	2	2	1	2	11	2
1	1	1	2	2	1	1	9	1
1	1	1	2	2	1	1	9	1
2	1	2	2	2	1	1	11	2
3	1	1	2	2	1	2	12	2
1	1	1	2	2	1	3	11	2
2	1	1	2	2	1	3	12	2
1	1	1	2	2	1	2	10	1
1	2	1	2	2	1	2	11	2
2	2	1	1	1	1	2	10	1
1	1	2	2	2	1	1	10	1
2	1	1	2	2	1	2	11	2
2	1	1	2	2	1	3	12	2
2	2	3	2	2	1	2	14	2
1	1	1	2	1	1	2	9	1

Haydn, J.	To Friendship (An die Freundschaft)
Hefferman, I.	Watchman's Song
Irish	Eileen Aroon
Lully, J. B.	By the Light of The Moon (Au clair de la lune)
Schubert, F.	Calm at Sea (Meeresstille)

Pathways of Song Volume 3

Publisher: Warner Bros. Inc.
Compiled/Edited by: Frank LaForge and Will Earhart
Available in: High and Low Voice

Composer	**Song Title**
Bach, J. S.	Come, Sweet Death (Komm, Süsser Tod)
Beethoven, L.	Kiss, The (Der kuss)
Bishop, Sir H.	Love Has Eyes
Caccini, G.	Amarilli
Czech	Plaint
Debussy, C.	There's Weeping in My Heart (Il pleure dans mon coeur)
Durante, F.	Dance, Maiden, Dance (Danza, danza Fanciulla)
Franz, R.	Hark! How Still (Still Sicherheit)
	Rose Complains, The (Es hat die Rose sich beklagt)
Giovannini	Wilt Thou Thy Heart Surrender (Willst du dein Herz mir schenken)
Gluck, C. W. von	Beloved Strand (Spiagge Amate)
Grieg, E.	First Meeting, The (Erstes Begegnen)
	With A Water Lily (Mit einer Wasser lilie)
Handel, G. F.	Air (Care Selve)
	Oh Sleep, Why Dost Thou Leave Me?
Irish	Kitty of Colerain
Leveridge, R.	Love Is a Bauble
Old English	Have You Seen But a White Lillie Grow?

2	1	1	2	1	1	1	9	1
1	1	1	1	2	1	2	9	1
1	1	1	1	2	1	1	8	1
1	1	1	2	2	1	1	9	1
2	2	3	2	2	1	1	13	2

Melody	Phrase	Rhythm	Text	Accomp.	Harmony	Dynamics	Total	Rank
2	3	2	1	1	1	3	13	2
2	1	1	2	2	1	2	11	2
2	1	1	1	1	1	2	9	1
2	3	2	1	2	1	3	14	2
1	2	1	1	1	1	2	9	1
3	2	1	1	2	3	3	15	3
2	1	2	1	2	1	3	12	2
1	1	2	1	2	1	3	11	2
2	1	1	1	1	1	1	8	1
2	1	3	1	2	1	3	13	2
2	2	2	1	2	1	2	12	2
3	1	1	1	2	1	3	12	2
2	2	1	1	1	2	3	12	2
2	3	2	1	2	1	2	13	2
2	3	1	1	1	1	3	12	2
2	1	2	1	2	1	2	11	2
2	1	1	1	2	1	2	10	1
1	2	1	1	1	1	2	9	1

Old English	When Love Is Kind
Rosa, S.	To Be Near Thee (Star vicino)
Scarlatti, A.	Sun O'er the Ganges, The (Già il sole dal Gange)
Schubert, F.	Cradle Song (Wiegenlied)
Spanish	I Don't Wish to Marry (No quiero casarme)
Torelli. G.	Thou Knowest Well (Tu to sai)

Pathways of Song Volume 4

Publisher: Warner Bros. Inc.
Compiled/Edited by: Frank LaForge and Will Earhart
Available in: High and Low Voice

Composer	Song Title
Bach, J. S.	Blessed Redeemer (Liebster Herr Jesu)
	Golden Sun Streaming (Die gold'ne Sonne, voll Freud' und Wonne)
Brahms, J., arr.	Now Suffer Me, Fair Maiden (Er laube mir, fein's Mädchen)
	To Part, Ah Grief Unending (Ach Gott, wie weh tut Scheiden)
Caldara, A.	As From the Sun A Ray (Come raggio di sole)
	Soul of My Heart (Alma del core)
Czech	Sleep, Little Angel (Hajej, mujandilku)
Debussy, C.	Bells, The (Les Cloches)
Grieg, E.	Good Morning (God Morgen)
	Mother (Gamle Mor)
	Return to the Mountain Home (Auf der Reise zur Heimat)
Handel, G. F.	Here Amid the Shady Woods
	Vouchsafe, O Lord
Haydn, J.	Equals (Der Gleichsinn)
	Very Ordinary Story, A (Eine sehr gewöhnliche Geschichte)
Italian	Cicerenella

Melody	Phrase	Rhythm	Text	Accomp.	Harmony	Dynamics	Total	Rank
2	1	1	1	2	1	2	10	1
1	2	1	1	1	1	3	10	1
2	1	2	1	1	1	3	11	2
2	2	2	1	1	1	3	12	2
1	1	1	1	2	1	3	10	1
2	1	1	1	2	1	3	11	2

Melody	Phrase	Rhythm	Text	Accomp.	Harmony	Dynamics	Total	Rank
1	2	2	1	1	1	3	11	2
2	2	1	1	1	1	2	10	1
1	1	1	1	2	1	2	9	1
2	1	1	1	2	1	2	10	1
2	2	3	1	2	1	3	14	2
1	1	2	1	2	1	3	11	2
1	2	1	1	1	1	3	10	1
2	3	1	2	2	2	2	14	2
2	1	2	1	2	1	3	12	2
2	1	1	1	1	1	2	9	1
2	1	1	1	2	1	3	11	2
2	1	1	1	1	1	1	8	1
1	1	1	1	2	1	2	9	1
2	1	2	1	1	1	2	10	1
2	1	3	1	1	1	2	11	2
1	1	2	2	2	1	2	11	2

Russian	Ah, No Stormy Wind
	Jailer's Slumber Song, The
Schubert, F.	Heaven-Rays (Himmelsfunken)
	Night and Dreams (Nacht und Traüme)
	Now Love Has Falseley Played Me (Die liebe hat gelogen)
Schumann, R.	Rose and the Lily, The (Die Rose, die Lilie, die Taube)
	Song of the Nightingale, The (Wehmut)
	Thou Art A Tender Blossom (Du bist wie eine Blume)
Strauss, R.	Night (Die Nacht)
	Tomorrow (Morgen)

Second Book of Baritone/Bass Solos, The

Publisher: G. Schirmer
Compiled/Edited by: Joan Frey Boytim
Available in: Medium Low Voice

Composer	Song Title
Beethoven, L.	Nature's Adoration
Bononcini, G.	Più Vaga e Vezzosetta
Chausson, E.	Le Charme
Cornelius, P.	Die Hirten
Dvorák, A.	I will Sing New Songs
Fauré, G.	Les Roses D'Ispahan
Greene, M.	Salvation Belongeth Unto The Lord
Handel, G. F.	Arm, Arm, Ye Brave
	Like The Shadow
	More Sweet is That Name
	Si, tra i ceppi
Ireland, J.	Memory
Leoncavallo, R.	Mattinata
Martini, G.	Plaisir D'Amour

Melody	Phrase	Rhythm	Text	Accomp.	Harmony	Dynamics	Total	Rank
1	2	2	1	2	1	3	12	2
2	1	1	1	2	2	2	11	2
1	2	3	1	2	2	2	13	2
2	2	2	1	2	1	1	11	2
1	1	2	1	1	2	3	11	2
2	1	2	1	1	1	3	11	2
1	1	1	1	1	1	2	8	1
1	2	1	1	2	1	2	10	1
2	1	1	1	2	2	3	12	2
2	2	1	2	2	1	3	13	2

Melody	Phrase	Rhythm	Text	Accomp.	Harmony	Dynamics	Total	Rank
2	2	3	1	1	1	2	12	2
3	2	3	2	1	1	3	15	3
1	1	1	2	1	1	2	9	1
2	1	1	2	2	2	2	12	2
1	1	1	1	1	1	3	9	1
2	2	1	2	2	1	2	12	2
1	2	2	1	2	2	1	11	2
2	2	1	1	1	1	2	10	1
2	2	1	1	2	1	2	11	2
2	2	3	1	2	1	2	13	2
2	3	1	2	1	1	2	12	2
2	2	1	1	2	2	2	12	2
2	2	2	2	2	1	3	14	2
2	1	1	2	2	1	3	12	2

Mendelssohn, F.	Lord God of Abraham
Parry, C. H.	Love is a Bable
Purcell, H.	Arise Ye Subterranean Winds
	Let Each Gallant Heart
	Since From My Dear
Rachmaninoff, S.	Island, The
Schubert, F.	Der Lindenbaum
	Der Wanderer
	Die Post
	Gefror'ne Thränen
Scott, J. P.	Come Ye Blessed
Scott, Lady John	Annie Laurie
Shaw, M.	Child of The Flowing Tide
Sullivan, A.	Policeman's Song, The
	When I was a Lad I Served a Term
V. Williams, R.	Vagabond, The
Wilson, H. L., arr.	Ah! Willow

Second Book of Mezzo-Soprano/Alto Solos, The

Publisher: G. Schirmer
Compiled/Edited by: Joan Frey Boytim
Available in: Medium High Voice

Composer	Song Title
Bizet, G.	Pastorale
Brahms, J.	An die Nachtigall
Eccles, J.	Jolly Jolly Breeze, The
Elgar, E.	Where Corals Lie
Fauré, G.	Au bord de l'eau
	Les berceaux
Franz, R.	Im Herbst
Gaul, A.	Eye Hath Not Seen
Godard, B.	Te souviens-tu?
Gretchaninoff, A.	Hushed The Song of the Nightingale

Anthologies

Melody	Phrase	Rhythm	Text	Accomp.	Harmony	Dynamics	Total	Rank
2	2	1	1	1	2	3	12	**2**
2	1	2	1	2	1	3	12	**2**
3	3	3	1	2	1	3	16	**3**
3	1	1	1	2	1	2	11	**2**
2	3	1	1	2	1	3	13	**2**
2	1	1	1	2	2	3	12	**2**
2	1	1	2	2	1	3	12	**2**
3	1	1	2	2	1	3	13	**2**
2	1	1	2	2	1	3	12	**2**
3	1	1	2	2	1	2	12	**2**
2	2	2	1	2	1	2	12	**2**
2	1	1	1	2	1	2	10	**1**
2	2	1	1	2	2	3	13	**2**
3	1	1	1	2	1	1	10	**1**
2	1	1	1	1	1	2	9	**1**
3	2	2	1	2	2	3	15	**3**
1	1	1	1	2	1	3	10	**1**
3	2	1	1	2	2	2	13	**2**
2	2	1	1	2	2	2	12	**2**
2	2	3	1	2	1	1	12	**2**
2	1	1	1	2	1	3	11	**2**
2	2	1	2	2	2	3	14	**2**
3	2	1	2	2	1	3	14	**2**
3	2	1	2	1	2	3	14	**2**
2	2	2	1	1	2	2	12	**2**
2	1	1	2	1	1	3	11	**2**
2	1	2	1	2	1	1	10	**1**

Grieg, E.	Vaaren
Handel, G. F.	Con Rauco Mormorio
	Pleasure's Gentle Zephyrs Play
	Smiling Hours, The
	Thou Shalt Bring Them In
Harty, H.	Lullaby, A
Purcell, H.	Kind Fortune Smiles
	We Sing to Him
Rachmaninoff, S.	Lilacs
	To The Children
Rogers, J. H.	Great Peace Have They Which Love Thy Law
Ronald, L.	Love, I Have Won You
Rubinstein, A.	Heard Ye His Voice
Saint-Saëns, C.	Patiently Have I Waited
Schubert, F.	An die Musik
	Du bist die Ruh'
Stevenson, F.	I Sought the Lord
Sullivan, A.	Little Buttercup
	Orpheus With His Lute
	Silver'd is the Raven Hair
Vivaldi, A.	Un certo non so che
Wolf, H.	Verborgenheit

Second Book of Soprano Solos, The

Publisher: G. Schirmer
Compiled/Edited by: Joan Frey Boytim
Available in: High Voice

Composer	Song Title
Arne, T.	Sleep, Gentle Cherub, Sleep Descend
Bach, J. S.	Mein Glaubiges Herze
Beach, Mrs. H. H. A.	Take, O Take Those Lips Away
Bizet, G.	Veille Chanson
Brahms, J.	Vergebliches Ständchen

Anthologies

2	2	1	2	2	2	3	14	2
1	2	1	2	2	1	1	10	1
2	2	2	1	2	1	2	12	2
2	2	1	1	2	1	2	11	2
2	3	1	1	2	1	2	12	2
2	1	1	1	3	1	3	12	2
2	2	3	1	1	1	2	12	2
2	2	1	1	2	2	1	11	2
2	1	2	1	2	2	3	13	2
2	2	2	1	2	2	3	14	2
1	2	1	1	2	1	2	10	1
2	3	1	1	2	1	3	13	2
2	2	1	1	2	2	1	11	2
3	2	1	1	2	2	2	13	2
2	2	1	2	2	1	3	13	2
2	2	2	1	2	1	3	13	2
2	3	1	1	1	1	2	11	2
1	2	1	1	1	2	1	9	1
2	1	1	1	2	1	3	11	2
2	1	1	1	1	1	3	10	1
2	1	2	2	2	2	2	13	2
2	2	2	2	2	1	3	14	2

Melody	Phrase	Rhythm	Text	Accomp.	Harmony	Dynamics	Total	Rank
2	2	1	1	2	1	3	12	2
3	1	3	2	2	1	2	14	2
2	3	1	1	2	2	3	14	2
2	2	1	2	1	2	3	13	2
2	1	2	2	2	1	3	13	2

Brown, T.	Shepherd! Thy Demeanour Vary
Carey, H.	Spring Morning, A
Cimara, P.	Fiocca la neve
Debussy, C.	Les Cloches
Dell'Acqua, E.	Villanelle
Donizetti, G.	La Zingara
Dvořák, A.	Hear My Prayer, O Lord
Gaul, A.	These Are They Which Came
Gounod, C.	O Divine Redeemer
Greene, M.	Sun Shall Be No More Thy Light, The
Handel, G. F.	Oh! Had I Jubal's Lyre
Herbert, V.	Art Is Calling For Me
Hüe, G.	To The Birds (A des Oiseaux)
Mozart, W. A.	Un Moto Di Gioja
Parry, C. H.	My Heart Is Like a Singing Bird
Purcell, H.	Hark! The Echoing Air
Quilter, R.	Love's Philosophy
	Song of the Blackbird
Ronald, L.	Down in the Forest
Strauss, R.	Die Nacht
Sullivan, A.	Sun Whose Rays, The
Veracini, F. M.	Pastoral, A
Wolf, H.	Bescheidene Liebe
	Das Verlassene Mägdlein

Second Book of Tenor Solos, The

Publisher: G. Schirmer
Compiled/Edited by: Joan Frey Boytim
Available in: High Voice

Composer	Song Title
Arne, T.	Nature Beyond Art
	Plague of Love, The
	Polly Willis

Melody	Phrase	Rhythm	Text	Accomp.	Harmony	Dynamics	Total	Rank
3	1	2	1	2	1	3	13	2
3	1	2	1	2	1	3	13	2
1	1	1	2	2	1	3	11	2
2	1	1	2	2	2	2	12	2
3	2	3	2	3	2	2	17	3
3	3	2	2	2	2	3	17	3
2	2	1	1	2	1	3	12	2
2	2	2	1	2	2	3	14	2
2	1	1	1	2	1	3	11	2
3	2	1	1	1	2	2	12	2
2	2	3	1	2	1	2	13	2
3	1	1	1	1	1	3	11	2
2	2	2	2	2	2	3	15	3
3	2	2	2	2	1	2	14	2
3	1	1	1	2	1	3	12	2
2	2	1	1	2	1	1	10	1
2	1	1	1	2	1	3	11	2
2	1	1	1	2	1	2	10	1
2	3	1	1	2	2	3	14	2
2	1	1	2	2	2	3	13	2
2	1	1	1	2	1	1	9	1
3	2	1	1	2	1	3	13	2
2	1	2	2	1	1	3	12	2
2	2	1	2	2	2	3	14	2
2	1	1	1	2	1	2	10	1
2	1	1	1	1	1	3	10	1
2	1	2	1	2	1	2	11	2

Beethoven, L.	Mit Einem Gemalten Band
Brahms, J.	Der Gang Zum Liebchen
Coates, E.	Green Hills O' Somerset, The
Cornelius, P.	Christkind
Donaudy, S.	Spirate Pur, Spirate
	Vaghissima Sembianza
Dvořák, A.	Turn Thee To Me
Grétry, A. E. M.	Rose Chérie, Aimable Fleur
Handel, G. F.	Total Eclipse
Liddle, S.	Lord Is My Shepherd, The
MacDowell, E.	Long Ago
Massenet, J.	Ouvre Tes Yeux Bleus
Mendelssohn, F.	Be Thou Faithful Unto Death
Old English	Alleluia!
Purcell, H.	I'll Sail Upon The Dog Star
Quilter, R.	Autumn Evening
	Fair House of Joy
	My Life's Delight
Rachmaninoff, S.	O Thou Billowy Harvest-Field!
Schubert, F.	Die Forelle
	Frühlingsträum
Schumann, R.	Dein Angesicht
Sullivan, A.	Free From His Fetters
	When First My Old
Thomas, A.	Le Soir
V. Williams, R.	Call, The
	Dream-Land
	Orpheus With His Lute
	Whither Must I Wander?

2	2	1	1	2	1	2	11	**2**
2	2	1	2	2	1	2	12	**2**
2	2	1	1	1	1	3	11	**2**
2	2	1	1	2	1	3	12	**2**
2	2	2	2	2	1	3	14	**2**
2	3	1	2	1	1	2	12	**2**
1	2	1	1	1	1	3	10	**1**
3	1	2	2	1	1	3	13	**2**
2	1	1	1	2	2	2	11	**2**
2	2	1	1	2	2	2	12	**2**
2	2	1	1	2	1	3	12	**2**
2	1	1	2	2	1	2	11	**2**
2	3	1	1	2	1	2	12	**2**
1	1	1	1	1	1	2	8	**1**
2	1	3	1	2	1	2	12	**2**
2	1	1	1	1	2	3	11	**2**
2	2	1	1	2	1	3	12	**2**
2	2	2	1	2	1	2	12	**2**
2	3	3	1	2	1	3	15	**3**
2	1	2	2	2	2	2	13	**2**
2	1	2	2	2	2	3	14	**2**
2	1	1	2	2	2	2	12	**2**
1	1	1	1	2	1	2	9	**1**
2	1	1	1	1	1	2	9	**1**
3	1	2	2	3	2	3	16	**3**
2	3	1	1	1	2	3	13	**2**
2	2	1	1	2	2	3	13	**2**
2	2	3	1	2	1	3	14	**2**
2	2	1	1	2	1	3	12	**2**

Singing Road, The, Volume I

Publisher: Carl Fischer
Compiled/Edited by: Arthur E. Ward
Available in: Medium High and Medium Low Voice

Composer	Song Title
Bach, J. S.	If Thou Thy Heart Will Give Me
Brahms, J.	Lullaby
Crist, B.	Blue Bird
	Loch Lomond
de Fontainailles, H.	Resolve, A (Obstination)
Foster, S. C.	Beautiful Dreamer
Fox, O. J.	I'll Never Ask You to Tell
Franz, R.	Dedication (Widmung)
Giordani, Tommaso	Dearest and Best (Caro mio ben)
Goetze, C.	Those Happy Days (O Schönezeit)
Handel, G. F.	Where E'er You Walk
Horn, C. E.	Cherry Ripe
Horrocks, A. E.	Bird and the Rose, The
Kjerulf, H.	Last Night
Mozart, W. A.	Lullaby (Wiegenlied)
Richardson, T.	Mary
Rubinstein, A.	Thou'rt Like unto a Flower (Du bist wie eine Blume)
Schubert, F.	Morning Greeting (Morgengruss)
	To Music (An die Musik)
Schumann, R.	Folk Song (Volksliedchen)
Ward, A. E., arr.	Drink to Me Only with Thine Eyes

Melody	Phrase	Rhythm	Text	Accomp.	Harmony	Dynamics	Total	Rank
2	1	3	1	2	1	2	12	**2**
1	1	1	2	2	1	1	9	**1**
1	1	2	1	2	1	3	11	**2**
2	1	1	1	2	1	2	10	**1**
2	1	1	1	2	1	3	11	**2**
1	1	1	1	2	1	2	9	**1**
1	2	2	1	1	1	3	11	**2**
2	1	1	1	1	1	3	10	**1**
2	2	2	2	1	1	2	12	**2**
1	1	1	1	1	1	2	8	**1**
2	1	2	1	2	1	2	11	**2**
2	1	1	1	2	1	2	10	**1**
2	1	1	1	2	2	3	12	**2**
2	1	1	1	2	1	2	10	**1**
1	1	1	1	1	1	1	7	**1**
2	1	1	1	1	1	3	10	**1**
2	1	1	2	2	1	3	12	**2**
1	1	1	1	2	1	3	10	**1**
2	2	1	1	2	1	3	12	**2**
2	1	2	1	1	1	2	10	**1**
1	1	1	1	2	1	2	9	**1**

Singing Road, The, Volume II

Publisher: Carl Fischer
Compiled/Edited by: Arthur E. Ward
Available in: Medium High and Medium Low Voice

Composer	Song Title
Arne, T.	Lass with the Delicate Air, The
Bach, J. S.	Come Sweet Repose
Handel, G. F.	Oh Sleep, Why Dost Thou Leave Me?
Haydn, J.	My Mother Bids Me Bind My Hair
Mozart, W. A.	Violet, The
Old English	Have You Seen But the White Lillie Grow?
Pergolesi, G. B.	Nina
Tosti, F. P.	Could I (Vorrei)
	Serenade (La Serenata)

Songbook Series 1

Publisher: Frederick Harris Music Co.
Compiled/Edited by: Royal Conservatory of Music
Available in: Medium Voice

Composer	Song Title
Anderson, W. H.	Summer on the Prairie
Champagne, C., arr.	Marianne s'en va-t-au moulin (Marianne Went to the Mill)
Dunhill, T.	Curliest Thing, The
Foster, S. C.	Some Folks
Kasemets, U.	Who Has Seen the Wind?
Lawson, M., arr.	Skye Boat Song
MacMillan, E., arr.	There Stands a Little Man
McLean, H. J., arr.	Song of the Carter, The
	Vive la Canadienne! (My Canadian Girl)
Milhaud, D.	La pomme et l'escargot (The Apple and the Snail)

Melody	Phrase	Rhythm	Text	Accomp.	Harmony	Dynamics	Total	Rank
2	1	2	1	1	1	2	10	**1**
2	2	3	1	1	1	2	12	**2**
2	3	2	1	1	1	1	11	**2**
1	1	3	1	1	1	3	11	**2**
2	1	1	1	1	1	2	9	**1**
1	1	1	1	1	1	3	9	**1**
2	1	2	1	2	1	3	12	**2**
2	2	1	1	1	1	3	11	**2**
2	1	1	1	2	1	3	11	**2**

Melody	Phrase	Rhythm	Text	Accomp.	Harmony	Dynamics	Total	Rank
2	1	1	1	1	1	1	8	**1**
1	1	1	2	2	1	1	9	**1**
1	1	1	1	1	2	2	9	**1**
2	1	1	1	2	1	2	10	**1**
1	1	1	1	1	3	2	10	**1**
1	1	2	1	1	1	1	8	**1**
1	1	1	1	1	1	1	7	**1**
1	1	1	1	1	1	2	8	**1**
1	1	2	2	1	1	2	10	**1**
1	1	1	2	1	2	2	10	**1**

Ouchterlony, D.	Some Day
Rowley, A.	Linnet's Secret, The
Schumann, R.	Blacksmith's Song, A
Sharman, C.	Wind, The
Telfer, N.	Lullaby
Willan, H., arr.	Twas in the Moon of Wintertime (Jesous Ahatouhia)

Songbook Series 2

Publisher: Frederick Harris Music Co.
Compiled/Edited by: Royal Conservatory of Music
Available in: Medium Voice

Composer	Song Title
Burke, J.	Kelligrews Soiree, The
Campion, T.	Jack and Joan
Champagne, C., arr.	Petit Jean (Little John)
Curwin, C.	My Dog Spot
Drynan, M.	Fate of Gilbert Gim, The
MacMillan, E., arr.	Bells of Aberdovey, The
McLean, H. J., arr.	Look at Me, My little dear
Morley, T.	Now is the Month of Maying
Nielsen, C.	Fiddler, The
Parke, D.	In Old Donegal
Ridout, A.	O Sing the Glories of Our Lord
Schubert, F.	Spring Song
Seiber, M., arr.	Handsome Butcher, The
Somer, H.	Song of Praise
Taylor, C.	Grasshopper Green
Whitehead, A.	House to Let
Wuensch, G.	Rules and Regulations

1	1	1	1	1	2	1	8	1
1	1	1	1	1	1	2	8	1
1	1	1	1	1	1	1	7	1
1	1	2	1	1	1	3	10	1
1	1	2	1	1	1	2	9	1
1	1	2	1	1	1	1	8	1

Melody	Phrase	Rhythm	Text	Accomp.	Harmony	Dynamics	Total	Rank
1	2	1	1	1	1	1	8	1
1	1	1	1	1	1	1	7	1
1	1	2	2	1	1	1	9	1
1	1	1	1	1	2	3	10	1
2	1	1	1	2	2	1	10	1
2	2	1	1	1	1	3	11	2
1	1	1	1	1	1	1	7	1
1	1	1	1	1	1	2	8	1
1	1	2	1	2	1	1	9	1
1	1	1	1	1	1	2	8	1
1	1	1	1	1	1	1	7	1
2	2	1	1	2	1	2	11	2
1	1	1	1	2	1	3	10	1
2	1	1	1	2	1	1	9	1
2	1	2	1	2	1	3	12	2
2	1	1	1	1	1	3	10	1
1	1	1	1	1	2	3	10	1

Songbook Series 3

Publisher: Frederick Harris Music Co.
Compiled/Edited by: Royal Conservatory of Music
Available in: Medium Voice

Composer	Song Title
Beaulieu, J.	Boy's Song, A
Bowles, P.	Three
Chopin, F.	Witchcraft
Dunhill, T.	How Soft, upon the Evening Air
Henderson, R. W.	Four Is Wonderful
Holman, D., arr.	Simple Gifts
MacMillan, E., arr.	Golden Slumbers
	Mon doux berger/Sweet Shepherd
	My Love's an Arbutus
McLean, H. J.	Song for Bedtime, A
Ouchterlony, D.	Gloria Deo
Rowley, A., arr.	Suo-Gan
Schemelli, G. C.	O Saviour So Meek
Schubert, F.	To the Lute
Smith, W. R.	Pirate Song, A
Willan, H., arr.	Early One Morning

Songbook Series 4

Publisher: Frederick Harris Music Co.
Compiled/Edited by: Royal Conservatory of Music
Available in: Medium Voice

Composer	Song Title
Adaskin, M.	Prairie Lily, The
Bissell, K., arr.	Harbour Grace
Chopin, F.	Wish, The
Coutts, G.	Highland Lullaby, A
Dowland, J.	Lowest Trees Have Tops, The

Melody	Phrase	Rhythm	Text	Accomp.	Harmony	Dynamics	Total	Rank
2	1	1	1	1	1	3	10	1
1	1	1	1	1	1	1	7	1
1	1	1	1	1	1	1	7	1
2	1	1	1	2	1	3	11	2
1	1	2	1	1	2	2	10	1
1	1	1	1	1	1	2	8	1
1	1	1	1	1	1	2	8	1
1	1	2	2	2	1	1	10	1
2	1	1	1	1	1	2	9	1
1	1	1	1	1	1	2	8	1
1	1	1	1	1	1	2	8	1
1	1	1	1	1	1	3	9	1
1	1	1	1	1	1	1	7	1
1	1	1	1	1	1	1	7	1
2	1	1	1	2	1	1	9	1
2	1	1	1	1	1	2	9	1

Melody	Phrase	Rhythm	Text	Accomp.	Harmony	Dynamics	Total	Rank
1	1	2	1	3	2	3	13	2
2	1	1	1	2	1	2	10	1
2	1	1	1	2	1	3	11	2
1	2	1	1	1	1	3	10	1
1	1	1	1	2	3	1	10	1

Duncan, C.	Beautiful
Easson, J., arr.	Kitty of Coleraine
Handel, G. F.	I Shall Declare I Love Her
Inness, G.	Piper's Song
Marchant, S.	Sir Niketty Nox
McLean, H. J., arr.	Turn Ye to Me
Ouchterlony, D.	Cradle Carol (Berceuse)
Schubert, F.	To the Moon
V. Williams, R.	Orpheus with His Lute
Willan, H., arr.	Sainte Marguerite

Songbook Series 5

Publisher: Frederick Harris Music Co.
Compiled/Edited by: Royal Conservatory of Music
Available in: Medium Voice

Composer	Song Title
Belyea, W. H.	Lazy Summer
Brahms, J., arr.	Rose-Lipt Maid
Bury, W.	I Will Make You Brooches
Carter, E.	Dust of Snow
Conti, F.	Solitary "Yes", A
Dunhill, T.	Three Fine Ships
Frey, H., arr.	Sometimes I Feel like a Motherless Child
Glick, S. I.	Baruch and Hamakom
Granados, E.	Tra La La
Keel, J. F., arr.	Jardin d'amour
Ridout, G.	J'ai cuelli la belle rose (I Have Culled That Lovely Rosebud)
Rorem, N.	Little Elegy
Schemelli, G. C.	Come, Let Us All This Day
Schubert, F.	To the Nightingale
Schumann, R.	Little Folk Song, A
Thiman, E. H.	King of Song, The

Melody	Phrase	Rhythm	Text	Accomp.	Harmony	Dynamics	Total	Rank
2	1	1	1	1	1	3	10	1
2	1	2	1	2	1	2	11	2
2	1	2	1	1	1	1	9	1
1	1	2	1	2	1	2	10	1
1	1	1	1	1	2	1	8	1
2	1	1	1	2	1	2	10	1
2	1	1	2	2	1	1	10	1
2	1	1	1	2	1	3	11	2
2	1	1	1	1	1	2	9	1
1	1	1	2	2	1	3	11	2

Melody	Phrase	Rhythm	Text	Accomp.	Harmony	Dynamics	Total	Rank
1	1	1	1	1	2	1	8	1
1	1	1	1	2	1	2	9	1
2	2	1	1	1	1	2	10	1
1	2	3	1	2	1	2	12	2
2	1	1	1	2	1	2	10	1
2	1	1	1	1	2	3	11	2
2	1	1	1	1	1	2	9	1
1	1	3	2	1	1	1	10	1
2	1	2	1	2	1	1	10	1
2	1	1	2	2	1	3	12	2
1	1	1	2	2	1	1	9	1
2	1	1	1	1	1	1	8	1
2	1	1	1	1	1	1	8	1
1	1	1	1	2	1	1	8	1
2	1	1	1	1	1	2	9	1
2	1	2	1	2	1	2	11	2

| Willan, H. | Love and a Day |
| Willan, H., arr. | La petite hirondelle (Oh, Sweet Little Swallow) |

Songbook Series 6

Publisher: Frederick Harris Music Co.
Compiled/Edited by: Royal Conservatory of Music
Available in: Medium Voice

Composer	Song Title
Archer, V.	April Weather
Bowles, P.	Little Closer, Please, A
Caccini, F.	Where I Believed
Foss, H.	As I Walked Forth
Greaves, T.	Shaded with Olive Trees
Grieg, E.	With a Primrose
Handel, G. F.	Art Thou Troubled?
McLean, H. J.	If All the Seas Were One Sea
Mendelssohn, F.	Spring Is upon Us
Parry, C. H.	Spring Song, A
Purcell, H.	Come unto These Yellow Sands
Ridout, G., arr.	I'll Give My Love an Apple
Schumann, R.	To the Sunshine
Telfer, N.	Blessing, A
Warlock, P.	Milkmaids
Willan, H.	Du bist wie eine Blume (E'en as a Lovely Flower)

Songbook Series Introductory Songbook

Publisher: Frederick Harris Music Co.
Compiled/Edited by: Royal Conservatory of Music
Available in: Medium Voice

Composer	Song Title
Belyea, W. H.	Rabbits

2	1	2	1	3	1	2	12	**2**
1	1	2	2	2	1	1	10	**1**

Melody	Phrase	Rhythm	Text	Accomp.	Harmony	Dynamics	Total	Rank
1	1	3	1	3	1	2	12	**2**
2	1	2	1	1	2	2	11	**2**
1	1	3	1	1	2	1	10	**1**
1	1	1	1	3	1	3	11	**2**
2	1	1	1	2	1	1	9	**1**
2	1	1	1	1	2	3	11	**2**
2	1	2	1	1	1	2	10	**1**
2	1	2	1	2	1	3	12	**2**
2	2	2	1	2	1	3	13	**2**
2	1	1	1	2	1	2	10	**1**
2	1	2	1	1	1	2	10	**1**
2	2	1	1	1	1	1	9	**1**
2	1	1	1	1	1	2	9	**1**
1	3	1	1	1	1	2	10	**1**
2	1	2	1	2	1	3	12	**2**
2	3	2	2	2	1	2	14	**2**

Melody	Phrase	Rhythm	Text	Accomp.	Harmony	Dynamics	Total	Rank
1	1	1	1	2	1	1	8	**1**

Brook, H.	Colours
Crawley, C.	Elephants
	Horses
Fletcher, P., arr.	Marianina
Flies, J. B.	Cradle Song
Helyer, M.	Ferryman, The
Ives, C. E.	Slow March (Procession triste)
Kasemets, U.	Eletelephony
Kurth, B.	Circus Clown, The
McLean, H. J., arr.	Song of the Seagull (Chant de la mouette)
Ohlin, C. P.	I Like Dogs! (J'aime les chiens!)
Reinecke, C. H.	Doll's Cradle Song
Schumann, R.	Children's Bedtime
Smith, L.	Butterflies (Les papillons)
Telfer, N.	Searching for a Gift

Songs Through the Centuries

Publisher: Carl Fischer
Compiled/Edited by: Bernard Taylor
Available in: High and Low Voice

Composer	Song Title
Adam, A.	Cantique de Noël
Arne, M.	Lass with the Delicate Air, The
Arne, T.	Air from Comus
	Under the Green Wood Tree
Bach, J. S.	Bist du bei mir
Bayly, T. H.	Long, Long Ago
Beethoven, L.	Ich Liebe dich
Bishop, Sir H.	Lo! Hear the Gentle Lark
Bohm, C.	Still wie die Nacht (Still as the Night)
Bononcini, G.	Per la gloria d'adorarvi from "Griselda"
Brown, T.	Shepherd! Thy Demeanour Vary
Caccini, G.	Amarilli, mia bella

Melody	Phrase	Rhythm	Text	Accomp.	Harmony	Dynamics	Total	Rank
2	1	1	1	1	1	1	8	1
1	1	1	1	1	1	1	7	1
1	1	1	1	1	1	1	7	1
2	1	1	1	2	1	2	10	1
1	1	1	1	1	1	1	7	1
1	2	1	1	2	1	3	11	2
1	2	2	2	2	1	3	13	2
1	1	1	1	1	1	2	8	1
1	1	1	1	1	1	2	8	1
1	1	3	2	2	1	1	11	2
1	1	1	2	1	1	1	8	1
1	1	1	1	1	1	1	7	1
1	1	1	1	2	1	2	9	1
1	1	1	2	1	1	3	10	1
1	2	1	1	2	1	2	10	1

Melody	Phrase	Rhythm	Text	Accomp.	Harmony	Dynamics	Total	Rank
2	1	1	2	2	1	3	12	2
2	2	2	1	1	1	2	11	2
2	1	3	1	2	1	2	12	2
2	1	2	1	1	1	2	10	1
2	1	1	2	2	1	2	11	2
2	1	1	1	2	1	1	9	1
2	1	1	2	2	1	2	11	2
3	3	2	1	2	1	3	15	3
2	3	2	2	2	1	3	15	3
2	1	2	2	1	1	3	12	2
3	1	2	1	2	1	3	13	2
2	3	2	2	1	1	3	14	2

Carey, H.	Pastorale addane, A
Carissimi, G.	Vittoria, mio core!
Debussy, C.	Il pleure dans mon coeur
	Mandoline
Dello Joio, N.	How Do I Love Thee?
	There is a Lady Sweet and Kind
Duke, J.	Just-Spring
Durante, F.	Danza, danza, fanciulla gentile
Flies, J. B.	Wiegenlied
Foster, S. C.	Come Where My Love Lies Dreaming
	Jeanie With the Light Brown Hair
	Old Folks at Home
Handel, G. F.	Care Selve
Loewe, C.	Edward
Mahler, G.	Ich atmet' einen linden Duft
Martini, G.	Plaisir d'amour
Mattei, T.	Non è ver!
McArthur, E.	Spring Day
Monro, G.	My Lovely Celia
Morley, T.	It Was a Lover and His Lass
Mozart, W. A.	Ridente la Calma
	Wiegenlied
Old English	Drink to Me Only With Thine Eyes
	Have You Seen But the Whyte Lillie Grow?
	When Love Is Kind
Purcell, E. C.	Passing By
Schubert, F.	An die Musik
	Ave Maria
Schumann, R.	Die Lotosblume
	Widmung

Anthologies

2	1	2	1	1	1	2	10	**1**
2	2	2	2	1	1	2	12	**2**
2	2	1	2	2	3	3	15	**3**
2	2	1	2	2	3	3	15	**3**
2	1	2	1	2	3	3	14	**2**
2	1	1	1	2	3	2	12	**2**
3	2	1	1	2	3	3	15	**3**
2	1	2	2	2	1	3	13	**2**
1	1	1	2	1	1	2	9	**1**
1	1	1	1	1	1	2	8	**1**
2	1	1	1	1	1	3	10	**1**
1	1	1	1	1	1	1	7	**1**
2	3	3	2	2	1	3	16	**3**
3	1	3	2	1	2	3	15	**3**
2	2	2	2	2	2	3	15	**3**
2	1	1	2	2	1	3	12	**2**
2	1	1	2	2	1	2	11	**2**
1	3	3	1	2	2	2	14	**2**
2	1	1	1	1	1	3	10	**1**
1	1	1	1	1	1	2	8	**1**
3	1	1	2	2	1	2	12	**2**
1	1	1	2	1	1	2	9	**1**
1	1	1	1	2	1	2	9	**1**
2	1	1	1	1	1	2	9	**1**
2	1	1	1	2	1	2	10	**1**
1	1	1	1	2	1	2	9	**1**
2	2	1	2	2	1	2	12	**2**
1	3	3	2	2	1	2	14	**2**
2	2	1	2	1	1	2	11	**2**
3	2	2	2	2	1	2	14	**2**

Spirituals for Solo Singers

Publisher: Alfred Publishing Co.
Compiled/Edited by: Jay Althouse
Available in: Medium High and Medium Low Voice

Composer	Song Title
Althouse, J., arr.	Amazing Grace
	Let Us Break Bread Together
	My Lord, What a Morning
	Nobody Knows the Trouble I've Seen
Hayes, M., arr.	Rise Up, Shepherd, and Follow
	Wade in the Water
Kern, P., arr.	Ezekiel's Wheel
	Little David, Play on Your Harp
Simms, P. F., arr.	Climbin' Up the Mountain
	Go, Tell it on the Mountain
	Kum Ba Yah

Standard Vocal Repertoire Book One

Publisher: R. D. Row Music Company
Compiled/Edited by: Richard D. Row
Available in: High and Low Voice

Composer	Song Title
American	Fare You Well
Arne, T.	Air from Comus
Bennett, C.	Guitar Player, The
D'Hardelot, G.	Because
Franz, R.	Dedication (Widmung)
Grieg, E.	I Love Thee (Ich liebe dich)
Handel, G. F.	When First We Met (Non Io dirò col labbro)
	Where E'er You Walk
Haydn, J.	Sailor's Song
	She Never Told Her Love

Melody	Phrase	Rhythm	Text	Accomp.	Harmony	Dynamics	Total	Rank
1	2	1	1	2	1	2	10	1
2	2	1	1	2	1	2	11	2
1	1	1	1	1	1	2	8	1
1	2	1	1	1	1	1	8	1
2	1	1	1	1	1	3	10	1
3	1	1	1	1	1	3	11	2
3	2	1	1	2	1	3	13	2
2	1	1	1	1	1	3	10	1
2	2	1	1	2	1	2	11	2
1	1	1	1	1	2	1	8	1
1	2	1	1	2	1	3	11	2

Melody	Phrase	Rhythm	Text	Accomp.	Harmony	Dynamics	Total	Rank
2	3	1	1	2	1	1	11	2
2	1	3	1	2	1	2	12	2
2	2	1	1	1	1	2	10	1
2	3	1	1	2	1	2	12	2
2	1	1	1	1	1	3	10	1
2	1	1	1	2	2	3	12	2
2	1	1	1	1	1	2	9	1
2	1	1	1	2	1	1	9	1
2	2	1	1	1	1	2	10	1
2	1	2	1	2	1	3	12	2

Haydn, J.	Wanderer, The (Der Wanderer)
Irish	Cockles and Mussels
Lehmann, L.	Cuckoo, The
Monro, G.	My Lovely Celia
Purcell, E. C.	Passing By
Purcell, H.	Arrival of the Royal Barge, The
	Hush, Be Silent
	If Music Be the Food of Love
	Strike the Viol
Rachmaninoff, S.	In the Silent Night (V'mo Hchányinótchi táïnoi)
Reichardt, L.	When the Roses Bloom (Hoffnung)
Scott, A. A.	Think On Me
Sibelius, J.	Black Roses

Standard Vocal Repertoire Book Two

Publisher: R. D. Row Music Company
Compiled/Edited by: Richard D. Row
Available in: High Voice

Composer	Song Title
Bemberg, H.	Il Neige
Bennett, C.	Japanese Night Song
Boardman, R., arr	Cindy
Chopin, F.	Maiden's Wish, The (Mädchen's Wunch)
Debussy, C.	Nuit d'Etoiles
Franz, R.	Mother, O Sing Me to Rest (Mutter, O Sing mich zur Ruh)
Handel, G. F.	Care Selve
	Friendship and Song
	Rend'il Sereno Al Cigilo
Hawley, C. B.	Sweetest Flower That Blows, The
Haydn, J.	Serenade
Henschel, G.	Morning Hymn (Morgen-Hymne)
Lohr, H.	Little Irish Girl, The

2	2	1	1	1	2	2	11	**2**
1	1	1	1	2	1	3	10	**1**
3	1	1	1	1	1	3	11	**2**
2	1	1	1	1	1	3	10	**1**
1	1	1	1	2	1	3	10	**1**
2	2	1	1	2	1	2	11	**2**
2	1	1	1	2	1	3	11	**2**
2	2	1	1	2	1	3	12	**2**
2	2	1	1	2	1	1	10	**1**
2	2	1	1	3	2	3	14	**2**
2	1	1	1	2	1	3	11	**2**
2	1	1	1	1	1	2	9	**1**
2	2	1	1	2	1	3	12	**2**

Melody	Phrase	Rhythm	Text	Accomp.	Harmony	Dynamics	Total	Rank
2	2	1	1	2	1	2	11	**2**
1	1	1	1	2	2	3	11	**2**
2	1	1	1	2	1	2	10	**1**
2	1	1	1	2	1	3	11	**2**
2	1	2	2	2	2	3	14	**2**
1	1	1	1	1	1	1	7	**1**
2	3	3	2	2	2	3	17	**3**
1	2	1	1	2	1	2	10	**1**
2	2	1	1	1	1	2	10	**1**
2	1	1	1	1	1	1	8	**1**
1	1	1	1	1	1	1	7	**1**
2	2	1	1	2	2	3	13	**2**
2	1	1	1	2	1	2	10	**1**

Lully, J. B.	Bois épais
Metcalf, J. W.	Night Has A Thousand Eyes, The
Mozart, W. A.	Violet, The (Das Veilchen)
Nyklicek, G.	Little Red Lark, The
Quilter, R.	Love's Philosophy
	O Mistress Mine
Rachmaninoff, S.	Tout Est Si Beau
Sibelius, J.	Black Roses (Svarta rosor)
V. Williams, R.	Silent Noon

Sunday Songbook

Publisher: Hinshaw Music, Inc.
Compiled/Edited by: N/A
Available in: Medium Voice

Composer	Song Title
Sleeth, N.	Children of the Lord
	For These Blessings
	Go Now In Peace
	Holy Book, The
	Light One Candle
	Lullaby
	Part of the Plan
	Praise the Lord
	Sing Noel
	That's Good
	This is the Day
	You and I

Anthologies

Melody	Phrase	Rhythm	Text	Accomp.	Harmony	Dynamics	Total	Rank
2	3	2	1	1	1	3	13	**2**
2	1	1	1	2	1	3	11	**2**
2	1	1	1	1	1	2	9	**1**
2	2	1	1	2	1	2	11	**2**
2	1	1	1	2	1	3	11	**2**
2	1	1	1	1	1	2	9	**1**
3	1	1	2	3	1	2	13	**2**
2	1	1	2	2	1	1	10	**1**
2	2	2	1	2	2	3	14	**2**

Melody	Phrase	Rhythm	Text	Accomp.	Harmony	Dynamics	Total	Rank
1	2	1	1	1	1	1	8	**1**
2	1	1	1	1	1	1	8	**1**
1	1	1	1	1	1	1	7	**1**
1	1	2	1	1	1	1	8	**1**
1	1	1	1	1	1	1	7	**1**
1	1	1	1	1	1	1	7	**1**
1	1	1	1	1	1	1	7	**1**
1	1	1	1	1	1	1	7	**1**
1	1	2	1	1	1	2	9	**1**
1	1	1	1	1	1	1	7	**1**
2	1	1	1	1	1	1	8	**1**
1	1	2	1	1	1	1	8	**1**

Weekday Songbook

Publisher: Hinshaw Music, Inc.
Compiled/Edited by: N/A
Available in: Medium Voice

Composer	Song Title
Sleeth, N.	Here's to America
	Keeping Christmas
	Let's Make Music
	One Day at a Time
	Round of Greeting, A
	Sharing it with me
	Try Again
	Two Roads
	Valentine Wish, A
	We're on Our Way
	Winter's a Drag Rag, The
	You Never Stop Learning

Young Singer, The, Book One, Baritone (Bass)

Publisher: R. D. Row Music Company
Compiled/Edited by: Richard D. Row
Available in: Medium Low Voice

Composer	Song Title
American	Jesus, Jesus, Rest Your Head
Bishop, Sir H.	Love Has Eyes
Dix, J. A.	Trumpeter, The
Foote, A.	I'm Wearing Awa' to the Land O' the Leal
Franz, R.	Dedication (Widmung)
	For Music (Für Music)
German, E.	Rolling Down to Rio
Grieg, E.	Swan, A (Ein Schwan)
Handel, G. F.	When First We Met

Melody	Phrase	Rhythm	Text	Accomp.	Harmony	Dynamics	Total	Rank
1	1	1	1	1	1	1	7	1
1	1	2	1	1	1	1	8	1
2	1	2	1	1	1	1	9	1
1	1	2	1	1	2	1	9	1
1	1	2	1	1	1	1	8	1
1	1	2	1	1	1	1	8	1
1	1	1	1	1	1	1	7	1
1	1	1	1	1	1	1	7	1
1	1	1	1	1	1	1	7	1
1	1	2	1	1	1	1	8	1
1	1	1	1	1	2	1	8	1
1	1	2	1	1	1	1	8	1

Melody	Phrase	Rhythm	Text	Accomp.	Harmony	Dynamics	Total	Rank
2	2	1	1	2	1	2	11	2
2	2	2	1	2	1	2	12	2
2	2	2	1	2	1	3	13	2
2	3	1	1	2	1	3	13	2
1	2	1	2	1	1	3	11	2
2	2	1	2	2	1	2	12	2
2	2	2	1	2	1	3	13	2
2	2	1	2	2	1	3	13	2
1	1	1	1	1	1	2	8	1

Handel, G. F.	Where E'er You Walk
Homer, S.	Requiem
Lohr, H.	Little Irish Girl, The
Mendelssohn, F.	On Wings of Song (Auf Flügeln des Gesanges)
Old English	Come Let's be Merry
Purcell, E. C.	Passing By
Quilter, R.	Now Sleeps the Crimson Petal
Reichardt, L.	When the Roses Bloom (Hoffnung)
Respighi, O.	Nebbie
Strauss, R.	Morgen
Tchaikovsky, P.	Pilgrim's Song
V. Williams, R.	Roadside Fire, The
	Silent Noon

Young Singer, The, Book One, Contralto (Mezzo-Soprano)

Publisher: R. D. Row Music Company
Compiled/Edited by: Richard D. Row
Available in: Medium High Voice

Composer	Song Title
American	Jesus, Jesus, Rest Your Head
Bishop, Sir H.	Love Has Eyes
Brahms, J.	Sapphic Ode (Sapphische Ode)
Carey, H.	Pastoral, A
Dvořák, A.	Songs My Mother Taught Me (Als die alte Mutter)
Foote, A.	I'm Wearing Awa' to the Land o' the Leal
Franz, R.	For Music (Für Music)
	Pleading (Bitte)
German, E.	Who'll Buy My Lavender?
Grieg, E.	Swan, A
Haydn, J.	She Never Told Her Love
Henschel, G.	Morning Hymn (Morgen-Hymne)

Melody	Phrase	Rhythm	Text	Accomp.	Harmony	Dynamics	Total	Rank
2	2	2	1	2	1	2	12	2
2	2	2	1	2	1	2	12	2
2	2	1	1	2	1	2	11	2
2	2	1	2	2	1	2	12	2
2	3	1	1	2	1	2	12	2
1	2	1	1	2	1	3	11	2
2	1	1	1	2	1	3	11	2
2	2	2	2	2	1	2	13	2
2	3	2	2	2	1	3	15	3
2	2	2	2	2	1	3	14	2
2	3	1	1	2	1	3	13	2
2	2	2	1	3	1	3	14	2
2	3	3	1	2	1	3	15	3

Melody	Phrase	Rhythm	Text	Accomp.	Harmony	Dynamics	Total	Rank
2	2	1	1	2	1	2	11	2
2	1	2	1	2	1	2	11	2
2	2	2	2	2	2	3	15	3
2	3	2	1	2	1	3	14	2
2	1	1	2	2	1	3	12	2
2	3	1	1	2	1	3	13	2
1	2	1	2	1	1	2	10	1
1	3	2	2	1	1	2	12	2
2	2	2	1	2	1	3	13	2
2	2	1	2	2	1	3	13	2
2	2	2	1	2	1	2	12	2
2	2	2	2	3	2	3	16	3

Horn, C. E.	I've Been Roaming
Lehmann, L.	Cuckoo, the
Lohr, H.	Little Irish Girl, The
MacDowell, E.	Thy Beaming Eyes
Mendelssohn, F.	On Wings of Song (Auf Flügeln des Gesanges)
Old English	When Love is Kind
Purcell, E. C.	Passing By
Purcell, H.	Nymphs and Shepherds
Quilter, R.	Now Sleeps the Crimson Petal
Reichardt, L.	When the Roses Bloom
Respighi, O.	Nebbie
Scott, A. A.	Think on Me
Sinding, C.	Sylvelin
Strauss, R.	Morgen

Young Singer, The, Book One, Soprano

Publisher: R. D. Row Music Company
Compiled/Edited by: Richard D. Row
Available in: High Voice

Composer	Song Title
American	Jesus, Jesus, Rest Your Head
Beach, Mrs. H. H. A.	Year's At the Spring, The
Bishop, Sir H.	Love Has Eyes
Brahms, J.	Sapphic Ode (Sapphische Ode)
Carey, H.	Pastoral, A
Delibes, L.	Bonjour Suzon
Dvorák, A.	Songs My Mother Taught Me (Als die alte Mutter)
Foote, A.	I'm Wearing Awa' To the Land O' the Leal
Franz, R.	Dedication (Widmung)
	For Music (Für Music)
	Pleading (Bitte)
German, E.	Who'll Buy My Lavender?

2	2	1	1	2	1	2	11	2
2	2	1	1	2	1	3	12	2
2	1	1	1	2	1	2	10	1
2	1	1	1	2	1	2	10	1
2	2	1	2	2	1	2	12	2
2	2	2	1	2	1	2	12	2
1	2	1	1	2	1	3	11	2
2	3	1	1	2	1	3	13	2
2	2	3	1	2	1	3	14	2
2	2	2	2	2	1	2	13	2
2	3	2	2	2	1	3	15	3
2	2	1	1	2	1	2	11	2
1	2	1	2	2	1	2	11	2
2	2	2	2	2	1	3	14	2

Melody	Phrase	Rhythm	Text	Accomp.	Harmony	Dynamics	Total	Rank
2	1	1	1	1	1	2	9	1
2	1	2	1	2	2	3	13	2
2	1	1	1	1	1	2	9	1
2	2	2	2	2	2	3	15	3
2	1	2	1	1	1	2	10	1
2	1	1	2	2	2	3	13	2
2	2	1	1	2	1	3	12	2
2	1	1	1	2	1	3	11	2
2	1	1	1	1	1	3	10	1
2	1	1	1	1	1	3	10	1
2	1	1	2	1	1	2	10	1
2	1	1	1	1	1	3	10	1

Grieg, E.	I Love Thee (Ich liebe dich)
	Swan, A (Ein Schwan)
Handel, G. F.	Care Selve
Hawley, C. B.	Sweetest Flower That Blows, The
Haydn, J.	My Mother Binds My Hair (Bind auf dein Haar)
	She Never Told Her Love
Henschel, G.	Morning Hymn
Horn, C. E.	I've Been Roaming
Lehmann, L.	Cuckoo, The
Lohr, H.	Little Irish Girl, The
MacDowell, E.	Thy Beaming Eyes
Mendelssohn, F.	On Wings of Song (Auf Flügeln des Gesanges)
Old English	When Love is Kind
Purcell, E. C.	Passing By
Purcell, H.	Nymphs and Shepherds
Quilter, R.	Now Sleeps the Crimson Petal
Reichardt, L.	When The Roses Bloom
Respighi, O.	Nebbie
Sinding, C.	Sylvelin
Strauss, R.	Morgen
Swedish Folk Song	When I Was Seventeen

Young Singer, The, Book One, Tenor

Publisher: R. D. Row Music Company
Compiled/Edited by: Richard D. Row
Available in: High Voice

Composer	Song Title
American	Jesus, Jesus, Rest Your Head
Bartlett, J. C.	Dream, A
Bishop, Sir H.	Love Has Eyes
Dix, J. A.	Trumpeter, The
Foote, A.	I'm Wearing Awa' To the Land O' The Leal
Franz, R.	For Music (Für Music)

Anthologies

Melody	Phrase	Rhythm	Text	Accomp.	Harmony	Dynamics	Total	Rank
2	1	1	2	2	1	3	12	**2**
2	2	1	1	2	1	3	12	**2**
2	3	3	2	2	1	3	16	**3**
2	1	1	1	1	1	1	8	**1**
1	1	3	1	1	1	3	11	**2**
2	2	2	1	1	1	3	12	**2**
2	2	1	2	2	2	3	14	**2**
2	1	1	1	1	1	2	9	**1**
3	1	1	1	1	1	3	11	**2**
2	1	1	1	2	1	2	10	**1**
2	1	1	1	1	1	2	9	**1**
2	1	1	1	2	1	2	10	**1**
2	1	1	1	2	1	2	10	**1**
2	1	1	1	1	1	3	10	**1**
2	2	1	1	2	1	3	12	**2**
2	1	3	1	1	1	3	12	**2**
2	1	1	1	1	1	3	10	**1**
2	2	3	2	1	2	3	15	**3**
1	1	1	1	2	1	1	8	**1**
2	2	1	1	2	1	2	11	**2**
3	1	3	1	2	1	2	13	**2**

Melody	**Phrase**	**Rhythm**	**Text**	**Accomp.**	**Harmony**	**Dynamics**	**Total**	**Rank**
2	1	1	1	1	1	2	9	**1**
2	1	1	1	2	2	3	12	**2**
2	1	1	1	1	1	2	9	**1**
2	2	1	1	1	2	3	12	**2**
2	1	1	1	2	1	3	11	**2**
2	1	1	2	1	1	3	11	**2**

Franz, R.	Pleading (Bitte)
German, E.	Rolling Down to Rio
Grieg, E.	I Love Thee (Ich liebe dich)
	Swan, A (Ein Schwan)
Handel, G. F.	Care Selve
	When First We Met
	Where E'er You Walk
Haydn, J.	Serenade
Homer, S.	Requiem
Lohr, H.	Little Irish Girl, The
MacDowell, E.	Thy Beaming Eyes
Mendelssohn, F.	On Wings of Song (Auf Flügeln des Gesanges)
Metcalf, J. W.	Night Has a Thousand Eyes, The
Monro, G.	My Lovely Celia
Purcell, E. C.	Passing By
Quilter, R.	Now Sleeps the Crimson Petal
Rachmaninoff, S.	Tout Est Si Beau
Reichardt, L.	When The Roses Bloom
Respighi, O.	Nebbie
Sinding, C.	Sylvelin
Strauss, R.	Morgen
Tchaikovsky, P.	Pilgrim's Song
V. Williams, R.	Silent Noon

2	1	1	1	1	1	2	9	**1**
2	1	3	1	2	1	3	13	**2**
2	1	1	1	2	1	3	11	**2**
2	2	1	1	2	1	3	12	**2**
2	3	3	2	2	1	3	16	**3**
2	1	1	1	1	1	2	9	**1**
2	1	1	1	2	1	1	9	**1**
1	1	1	1	1	1	1	7	**1**
1	1	1	1	1	1	2	8	**1**
2	1	1	1	2	1	2	10	**1**
2	1	1	1	1	1	2	9	**1**
2	1	1	2	2	1	2	11	**2**
2	1	1	1	2	1	3	11	**2**
2	1	1	1	1	1	3	10	**1**
2	2	2	1	2	1	3	13	**2**
2	2	2	1	2	1	3	13	**2**
3	1	1	2	3	1	2	13	**2**
1	2	3	1	1	1	2	11	**2**
2	2	2	2	1	2	3	14	**2**
1	1	2	1	2	1	2	10	**1**
2	2	1	2	2	1	2	12	**2**
2	2	1	1	2	1	3	12	**2**
2	3	3	1	2	2	3	16	**3**